June 23D

Shadow on the Mountain

Also by Stephen Singular and Joyce Singular

The Spiral Notebook

Also by Stephen Singular

The Wichita Divide
(published in paperback as *A Death in Wichita*)
When Men Become Gods
Unholy Messenger
By Their Works
Catch This
(with Terrell Owens)
Anyone You Want Me to Be
(with John Douglas)
Relentless
The Uncivil War
Joe Lieberman
The Heart of Change
A Season on the Reservation
(with Kareem Abdul-Jabbar)
Presumed Guilty
The Rise and Rise of David Geffen
Power to Burn
Legacy of Deception
Charmed to Death
Sweet Evil
Notre Dame's Greatest Coaches
A Killing in the Family
Talked to Death

Stephen Singular and Joyce Singular

Shadow on the Mountain

Nancy Pfister, Dr. William Styler, and the Murder of Aspen's Golden Girl

St. Martin's Press
New York

www.stmartins.com

Designed by Kathryn Parise

Library of Congress Cataloging-in-Publication Data

Names: Singular, Stephen, author. | Singular, Joyce, author.
Title: Shadow on the mountain : Nancy Pfister, Dr. William Styler, and the murder of Aspen's golden girl / Stephen & Joyce Singular.
Description: New York : St. Martin's Press, [2016]
Identifiers: LCCN 2015042913| ISBN 9781250069412 (hardcover) | ISBN 9781466878174 (e-book)
Subjects: LCSH: Pfister, Nancy. | Murder—Colorado—Aspen—Case studies. | Socialites—Colorado—Aspen—Death—Case studies. | BISAC: TRUE CRIME / Murder / General.
Classification: LCC HV6534.A656 S56 2016 | DDC 364.152/3092—dc23
LC record available at http://lccn.loc.gov/2015042913

Our books may be purchased in bulk for promotional, educational, or business use. Please contact your local bookseller or the Macmillan Corporate and Premium Sales Department at 1-800-221-7945, extension 5442, or by e-mail at MacmillanSpecialMarkets@macmillan.com.

First Edition: March 2016

10 9 8 7 6 5 4 3 2 1

To "Scoop"

Acknowledgments

Several people who were critical in the making of this book wish to remain anonymous, so they will. Two others we can name are Michael Cleverly, who provided a lot of insight into Aspen and Nancy Pfister, and Nancy's friend Teresa Wyatt. Cleverly was particularly good in speaking about the evolution of Aspen since the 1970s and Teresa, among many other things, generously provided us with a number of photos for the book. We want to thank our agent, Mel Berger of WME Entertainment, for connecting us with Charlie Spicer and April Osborn at St. Martin's Press. We enjoy any opportunity to work with Charlie, and April was the hands-on guide through the editorial process for *Shadow on the Mountain.* Her care made this a better book. Finally, we'd like to thank Aspen itself for being a character in our story. There's no place like it.

The truth is rarely pure and never simple.

—Oscar Wilde

Aspen Royalty

1

Within a few hours, an overwrought Kathy Carpenter would tell the police that on this warmish late February evening in 2014 she'd driven up to Nancy Pfister's home above Aspen, Colorado. A trust-funder and world traveler in her mid-fifties, Pfister was often gone for months at a time, exploring a distant continent or visiting friends in Hawaii, Thailand, Nepal, the Caribbean, or India. After seven years of a volatile relationship with Kathy and an on-again, off-again business arrangement, Nancy had come to rely on her, leaving her in charge of the house when away. As a teller at Alpine Bank, Carpenter deposited cash or checks for Nancy and watched Gabe, Pfister's eight-month-old black labradoodle. Some people thought the women were lovers, but others said Nancy was only interested in men.

Set back a hundred yards or so from West Buttermilk Road, the heiress's secluded residence was encircled by snowfall and thick stands of aspen, their limbs bare in the lingering dead of winter. When Kathy reached the driveway, she turned right and followed a long strip of gravel down to the property. In darkness she opened the front door and stepped inside, scanning the main floor and seeing Gabe, who was always excited by her arrival. Wagging his hindquarters and nodding his head, he came toward her and nestled against her leg. Kathy breathed in the powerful stench of the dog's mess, scattered around the house, even though one of the windows was open and letting in chilly air. Why hadn't someone bothered to clean this up?

She moved past Gabe and on past a rarely used billiard table, going upstairs to the master bedroom, with its large walk-in closet filled with clothes, shoes, and Tibetan prayer flags—a space that Nancy called her "special closet." Glancing around, Kathy noticed that the bed was neatly made, the first thing that struck her as odd. Nancy had never made a bed in her life, leaving such details to other people.

Lifting the bedcover, Kathy saw no sheets on the mattress—another oddity—and the mattress itself was slightly askew. Raising her eyes, she spotted a red smear of what looked like blood on the headboard. She instinctively moved toward the closet, ten feet away from the foot of the bed. A few days earlier, she'd slipped a key into the closet door for Nancy, who was coming home after an extended stay in Australia. Attached to the key was an oval tag with "Owner's Closet" written across it; both the key and tag were gone. Kathy looked in her purse for the backup key she kept on a lanyard—she'd had a duplicate made last December when Nancy had insisted she change the lock on the closet door—but she hadn't brought it with her.

She pulled out her cell phone and called her mother, Chris, and then a friend of Nancy's, Patty Stranahan, telling both the same thing: the house felt weird.

Kathy brought Gabe outside with her and loaded him into her Subaru and took West Buttermilk Road down into Aspen to her small apartment on Main Street, housing provided to her by Alpine Bank. This arrangement had become commonplace in town because service people like Kathy couldn't afford to live there without assistance. Aspen and environs had America's most expensive real estate, with the 2014 median listing price for houses or condos standing at roughly $4.5 million. One local residence, the 24,000-square-foot Peak House, rented for $20,000 a day. In 1991, His Royal Highness Prince Bandar bin Sultan bin Abdulaziz, the ex–Saudi Arabian ambassador to the United States, had built a vacation getaway in Aspen's Starwood neighborhood. Sixteen years later, the prince listed it for $135 million, the nation's highest-priced private residence. When Bandar was accused of financing the property through $1 billion in bribes he'd received from a British defense company that sold fighter jets to the Saudis, a judge froze his U.S. assets and he had to make do with his other $20 billion worth of investments. The investigation was ultimately dropped.

Nancy Pfister's relatively modest three-bedroom home was just over 4,000 square feet and had a market value of slightly more than $4 million. She didn't own the house, but she didn't rent or lease it, either. The paper on the property was held by NMP Residence Trust, located within the Aspen law firm of Garfield & Hecht, which for decades had handled the Pfisters' financial affairs. When people spoke of the creation of modern Aspen, they usually brought up Nancy's parents, Art and Betty Pfister. In 1958, Art was a founding partner of the Buttermilk Ski Area, lately made famous by Shaun "The Flying Tomato" White at the Winter X Games, and by the Special Olympics. Art eventually sold his share of the mountain to the Aspen Skiing Company and his other holdings were developed into the Maroon Creek Golf and Tennis Club. In the past few years, both Art and Betty had died, leaving behind the family fortune and three daughters: Suzanne, who lived across the road from Nancy, and Christina, who'd moved to Denver.

Nancy was by far the most adventurous and unconventional. When Aspenites went abroad and told the natives where they were from, they regularly heard, "Do you know Nancy Pfister?" The Colorado blonde hadn't merely visited their countries, but had made an immediate and lasting impression. Her curiosity, her utter spontaneity, her hunger for new experiences, and her sunburst smile were all hard to forget. She had friends in the Far East, in South America, and across Europe. She watched the French Open in Paris with Roman Polanski and flew to Africa with Anjelica Huston. Some called her "Aspen's Ambassador to the World" or "Aspen's Welcome Wagon" or "Aspen's Golden Girl." There were people who called her much less flattering things—but only after they'd gotten to know her and seen the darker parts of her personality.

After retrieving the key from her condo, Kathy headed north out of town and took a left onto West Buttermilk Road, the Subaru winding steeply upward above the Roaring Fork Valley, giving her a spectacular view of Aspen at night. The town was a notch under 8,000 feet in elevation and Nancy's house was a few hundred feet above that. Homes to the right and left of the road reflected the extreme wealth that had settled into Pitkin County during the past half century.

Kathy pulled into the driveway and parked near the house. Leaving Gabe in the car, she went back inside, walked upstairs, tentatively approached the bedroom closet, and reached for her key. She turned the knob and looked into the large space holding Nancy's wardrobe, paintings, and other personal effects. Stretched out on the floor was a mostly white long bundle, which could have easily been taken for sheets or clothing, but the smell was so strong that there was no doubt in Kathy's mind what that bundle was. She bolted out of the room and out of the house.

"Oh, my god! Help me!" she told the 911 operator, her voice barely audible and at the edge of hysteria. "My friend! Oh, my god! My friend!"

Her call had gone into the emergency center that served both the City of Aspen and the Pitkin County Sheriff's Office. Because Nancy's residence was located outside of town, the sheriff's office had jurisdiction.

Before dialing the number on her cell, Kathy had gotten in her car and driven partway down West Buttermilk Road. She told the dispatcher that she'd just left the Pfister home and was on her way to the police station, fearing that a killer might still be inside the house. The dispatcher ordered her to pull over to the shoulder immediately and to park, which she did.

Sobbing, Kathy said that her friend was wrapped in something "full of blood" and that she'd also seen blood in the master bedroom. When she described *where* she'd seen it, the word came out hurriedly and awkwardly: she saw it either on the bed's "headboard" or on the body's "forehead." Either way, after peering into the closet, she surmised that Nancy Pfister was covered up in there and dead.

"What is your friend wrapped in?" the dispatcher asked.

"I-I-I don't know," Carpenter cried. "I don't know!"

As the dispatcher questioned her, Kathy blurted out that Nancy had "really pissed them off," referring to Dr. William Styler III and his wife, Nancy, who until the past few days had been renting Pfister's house.

The dispatcher again told her to stay put in her vehicle and an officer would be there soon.

. . .

Regardless of what Kathy had seen or what words she'd used about the interior of the closet, her report was essentially accurate. Nancy Pfister, the blonde with the jaunty hats and the explosive grin, the globe-trotter who constantly had a drink in her hand, the woman who'd so easily captured men's attention in her youth, including several major movie stars passing through Aspen, was now a disfigured corpse, deep into rigor mortis, beaten so badly that she was all but unrecognizable.

No one would have predicted this end for her, and certainly not in her hometown. She'd had such a confident look in her eye, as if her travels had left her wise to the world and always able to avoid trouble.

"I own the Aspen airport," she liked to brag, when stashing marijuana edibles on board an international flight to countries where the drug could land you in prison, far away from your family's reputation and resources.

Inside her small mountain town, she was "Aspen Royalty" and felt invulnerable, untouchable, yet she'd acted the same way everywhere. She'd gone abroad without a passport, flown small aircraft in Third World countries, had casual sexual encounters with strangers right after meeting them—and nothing had ever gone wrong. If something was about to go sideways, she'd change her plans and catch the next flight home. For nearly six decades, she'd lived as if she were risk-free, not just in terms of legal and illegal substances, but also in human relationships. Wiggling into and out of them countless times, she never seemed to get damaged in the ways that plagued other people. No matter where she went or what happened, she knew that she could always return to Aspen, her safe haven.

"She was magical," said one of her female friends. "When you were around her, you could feel that."

Yet some people in Aspen had long worried that over time the magic had begun to wear off and her allure had begun to diminish; the folks she hung out with now were no longer A-list celebrities, but many notches below that on the social ladder. Her taste for drugs, alcohol, chance encounters with men, and rushing into love affairs with those she barely knew, or a combination of all four, might eventually do her in.

Nancy's death was instantly a hot topic on Aspen's Main Street and throughout the Roaring Fork Valley. This was partly because the town hadn't seen a homicide since 2001 and partly because of the grisly nature of the killing, although law enforcement was being very tight-lipped about exactly how Nancy had been murdered. It was partly because a killer or killers were on the loose, in a community where many didn't bother to lock their doors at night. And partly because of *who* had been killed up on West Buttermilk Road: the daughter of one of Aspen's most respected and historically rooted families, the woman whom some considered the soul or spirit of Aspen, while others looked upon her as a wild child trapped inside the town's excesses of the 1970s and '80s, locked into a long-gone era.

Over Easter weekend of 2013, a female producer for the French television show *Access Privé* (think *Lifestyles of the Rich and Famous*) had come to town to film a segment on Aspen's wealth and celebrities. To gain entrée to the best homes and the most famous people, she needed a tour guide, someone who'd been around for decades and knew the territory. With an assist from a pair of Nancy's friends, the TV program was nudged in her direction and the French producer eventually decided to use Pfister in this role. Nancy took her to the Home Run Ranch, belonging to Goldie Hawn and Kurt Russell; to Owl Creek Farm, owned by the late Hunter Thompson; to Kevin Costner's residence; and up to the red house owned by Jack Nicholson, whom Nancy had once dated. At Jack's place, she'd point out the bedroom she'd shared with the movie star. People close to Nancy said that she'd never quite gotten over their romance and still spoke of him wistfully.

The night before the *Access Privé* shooting, Nancy invited the producer to a party at a home owned by the late printmaker Thomas Benton. One of Nancy's best friends, Bob Braudis, the legendary ex-sheriff of Aspen, was there, along with some other locals. The boozing and pot smoking went on and on, wowing the French TV exec.

"Zis town is so crazy!" she kept saying. "I love zis town."

The next morning, Nancy's eyes were covered by sunglasses as she nursed a serious hangover and moved a bit gingerly, but she emerged from her house on time for the filming. Throughout the day, as she showed *Access Privé* the homes of the stars, she offered up her best girly smile and her patented giggle, and at the end of the televised segment, she rode off into the dusk in a horse-drawn carriage on a perfect winter's eve in the Colorado Rockies, the sunlight fading behind her in the west. With a floppy felt hat—embellished by a red feather—perched on her head and an elegant crimson scarf wrapped around her neck, she sipped a flute of champagne, precisely the way that many would have wanted to remember her. She was so fond of bubbly that some of her pals had called her "Fizz."

She was having fun and wanted everyone to know it. Nancy was like that and so very different from her two dark-haired sisters, people around Aspen always said. Suzanne and Christina were much more conservative and low-key. Suzanne had worked as a real estate broker and Christina was the president of the Silver Queen Collection of furs, cashmere, linens, and bath products, but Nancy...

She'd never really worked anywhere, but told people that she was an architect or an entertainment producer and she touted herself as a Buddhist, with her Eastern philosophy and Tibetan prayer flags. The contrasts with her sisters went deeper than her looks and beliefs. She acted differently from them in unsettling ways, ways that some people had been worried about for a long time, ways that one day could get her into the kind of trouble she couldn't escape with a last-minute plane ticket, and ways that her parents and an earlier generation in Aspen would never have condoned—ways that could even get you killed.

2

At 6:15 p.m., shortly after Kathy Carpenter had made the 911 call, Deputy Ryan Turner arrived at her vehicle and spoke with her on the side of West Buttermilk Road. He thought that she smelled of alcohol, even though she was regularly attending meetings of Alcoholics Anonymous and had gone to see her twelve-step counselor just three days earlier.

"How much have you had to drink?" Turner asked her.

She denied having had anything at all.

He took note of the smell anyway.

An hour later, Pitkin County Peace Officer Brad Gibson came to Nancy Pfister's home, where Undersheriff Ron Ryan, Deputy Grant Jahnke, and Deputy Eric Hansen were already gathered. The men walked upstairs and looked in the master bedroom closet. Hansen shone a flashlight onto the floor and saw a lump wrapped in at least one towel, at least one blanket, and at least one sheet. He thought that it looked like "a small person, a large animal or a pile of laundry."

The towel was bloodstained and one end of the lump was wrapped in two white plastic trash bags. Hansen removed some of the coverings and saw a heavy-duty yellow extension cord wrapped around a woman's neck. The inner white bag was smeared red. Hansen probed the corpse's head and said that the skull appeared to be quite soft. From the shoulders down, the naked body was wrapped in another plastic trash bag, textured in such a way that made it resistant to tearing. The knees were folded up into a fetal position and the remainder of the cord was wrapped around them to make her smaller. The four men looked over the rest of the bedroom and saw no blood on the carpet or anywhere else, except for the same trace on the headboard that Kathy had seen earlier.

Based on his experience as a crime scene investigator and as someone who'd moved dozens of dead bodies, Officer Gibson immediately sensed that they'd be looking for multiple assailants—it would have been extremely difficult for one person to have created the scene in the closet. Because dead weight was so cumbersome and seemed so much heavier than the same weight of a living individual, it often took a handful of people to reposition or relocate a corpse. How could a single individual, even a strong one, have gotten the body off the bed, tied it up with electrical cord, bent it in half, put it into a plastic trash bag, and dragged or carried it into the closet? How could anyone have accomplished all this without getting any blood on the bed or the rug? It was very unlikely, Gibson would later write in his report, for someone to have carried out the "moving, binding, and packaging" of the body alone.

After observing the contents of the closet, Gibson went outside and saw a large pile of plastic ForceFlex trash bags leaning against the garage door, similar to the bags the woman had been wrapped in.

While crime scene investigators processed the Pfister home, another set of authorities took Kathy Carpenter to a hospital, where she was given a double dose of Ativan, a tranquilizer used in the treatment of anxiety disorders. She was later escorted to the Pitkin County District Courthouse in downtown Aspen and at 9:15 p.m. Brad Gibson began speaking with her. She told him the same story about finding the body in the closet that she'd told the 911 dispatcher, but she didn't bring up one detail that she'd mentioned to Deputy Turner a few hours before, as they were talking by the side of the road. When she'd first arrived at the West Buttermilk Road residence around 5:45 on this Wednesday evening, she said that she'd seen two people whom she knew quite well, Dr. William and Nancy Styler, driving away in their

2002 gray Jaguar sedan. This was the same couple whom she'd told the dispatcher that Nancy Pfister had "pissed off." Before talking with Gibson tonight, she'd also told Pitkin County Sheriff Joe DiSalvo about running into the Stylers at Pfister's this evening, yet she never brought this up with Gibson.

Until the past few days, Kathy told Gibson, the Stylers had been living in the Pfister home while Nancy was away for an extended trip to Australia. Nancy and the Stylers had gotten into a heated dispute over rental payments and Pfister had cut short her journey and returned from abroad to get the situation resolved. Last weekend, she'd flown into Aspen and had ordered the Stylers to move out as quickly as possible.

The couple had thought that they could stay in an acquaintance's place until they found a more permanent residence, but then a friend of his committed suicide and the plan fell through. Short on funds and squeezed for time, they'd checked into the Aspenalt Lodge, a few miles up the road in Basalt. One of the cheaper options in the Roaring Fork Valley, the Aspenalt catered to the fishing crowd and featured a multicolored painting of a rainbow trout above the lobby entrance, with the lobby itself displaying the rack of a mature elk. The Frying Pan River ran just behind the Aspenalt and you could virtually fly-fish from your room. Billing itself as a "deluxe economy hotel," the establishment offered two queen beds and breakfast for $119 a night, along with such amenities as "alarm clocks and thermostats."

Since the previous Sunday, the Stylers had returned to Pfister's house several times to retrieve their possessions and hadn't finished the job until just a few hours previously. As they were leaving the house just after noon, Nancy Styler communicated with Kathy, indicating that they'd be back later this evening to pick up some leftover trash bags. But Kathy told Gibson they never went back, which made her remarks to Deputy Turner and Sheriff DiSalvo about seeing the couple there at 5:45 p.m. all the more confusing.

With the investigation expanding by the hour, the Pitkin County Sheriff's Office contacted the Colorado Bureau of Investigation and sent Kathy's 911 call to the CBI's John Zamora, who worked on the state's Western Slope. He passed it along to fellow CBI employee Kirby Quinn Lewis in Denver. After carefully listening to the tape, Lewis prepared a transcript saying that Kathy had said that she'd seen blood on the victim's "forehead," not on the "headboard." If she'd actually viewed the victim's bleeding forehead, which was impossible by just glancing into the closet, then she'd had to have done something more with the lump of sheets than merely look at them. Something that might have included seeing the body *before* it was wrapped in the sheets—something that may also have included placing the body into the bags herself.

Why hadn't she told everyone the same story about seeing the Stylers at the house that evening? What else was she leaving out?

"When I first met with Kathy," Glenwood Springs lawyer Greg Greer recalled months later, "she said that she'd flunked her 911 call. And I told her that doesn't happen, but I guess it does. [CBI Agent] Kirby [Lewis] had sent a note back with his affidavit saying that Kathy said she saw blood on the forehead. I've listened to this tape a hundred times and Kathy says 'headboard,' not 'forehead.' The CBI said she saw things she couldn't have seen without seeing the forehead"—so they concluded she must be guilty.

"On Hunter Thompson's refrigerator," Greer went on, "was a note written by Hunter saying, 'Never call 911. This means you. HST.' The government has an enormous amount of power and with one wrong fact they can do a lot to you... The CBI's hand was in getting this case off track."

Brad Gibson contacted Deputy Alex Burchetta and asked him to locate the Stylers and their Jaguar; then Deputy Monique Merritt quickly found it parked at the Aspenalt motel. At 2:30 a.m. on February 27, Gibson learned that the couple was staying in room 122 and that Dr. Styler was apparently so disabled by a debilitating illness that he couldn't even walk to the front desk to register.

3

Nancy Pfister had long been friendly with Sheriff DiSalvo and even friendlier with his predecessor, Bob Braudis. She called DiSalvo "Joey" and Braudis "Booby"—a term of affection for a man who at first glance appeared intimidating. A former gang member in Boston who'd grown up hating cops, Braudis stood six feet seven inches and weighed in at around 270 pounds, conjuring up a bouncer for the early Rolling Stones. With his massive, deeply lined face, his thick, graying mop of unruly hair parted near the middle, and his ~~big~~, gap-toothed smile, he looked like an aging giant with a couple of bad habits. As with many others from the eastern half of the United States, he'd initially come west in 1969 to ski, but once he was in Colorado, he found something more and something harder to leave. The place felt newer and fresher than where he'd come from, more open to possibilities. The attitude toward the law was a little different in Aspen, a little looser, and he liked that. Maybe he could accomplish something in the Rocky Mountain region that he couldn't have imagined back home.

In the mid-1970s, when Braudis was relocating to Aspen, Dick Kienast was elected the head lawman of Pitkin County, after Sheriff Carroll Whitmire left office early while under investigation. Some people felt that Kienast was so soft on drugs that they called him and his deputies "Dick Dove and the Posse of Love." By 1977, Braudis was looking for work and Kienast wanted to hire him, but this required the big man taking a polygraph test in Vail.

"I was driving through Glenwood Canyon on my way to Vail, smoking a joint," Braudis recalled at a public gathering at the Aspen Historical Society in the summer of 2014. "I get to Vail and the guy wires me up with sensors. The first question he asked me was, 'When was the last time you used drugs?' which I told him was about an hour ago. I thought, 'I really screwed this up.' So I got back to Aspen and Kienast didn't have any questions about that. He said he was looking for non-deceptive personalities and told me I was pretty honest. He gradually hired a whole bunch of other freaks like me."

As Dr. Hunter S. Thompson was inventing Gonzo Journalism a few miles outside Aspen at his Owl Creek Farm in Woody Creek, Gonzo Law Enforcement was getting off the ground in the Roaring Fork Valley. More than once, Deputy Braudis and then Sheriff Braudis would find himself in the curious position of protecting the renowned author from legal trouble. It was a role Braudis was born for and one that he'd relish for decades. Aspen eventually changed its election laws in order to keep putting him back in office.

During his six terms and twenty-four years as Pitkin County sheriff, he'd pointedly called America's "War on Drugs" absurd—the perfect man in charge of local law enforcement for Aspen's longest-running party. Describing his officers as "conscientious objectors against the war on drugs," he fit into this legal landscape in ways that would have been impossible back in Boston.

The redbrick Pitkin County Jail, located directly behind the courthouse on Main Street, had twenty-six beds and annually housed about five hundred people; around 80 percent of them were booked for substance abuse. The police regularly hauled in drunk or stoned revelers, locked them up overnight so they couldn't harm themselves or others, and released them in the morning without charges. The Aspen Police Department sponsored a "Tipsy Taxi" service, paid for by donations and offering the inebriated a free ride home from any bar in town.

By contrast, the Glenwood Springs Police Department in next-door Garfield County had an officer assigned to the Two Rivers Drug Enforcement Team (TRIDENT), a task force operating throughout the Ninth Judicial District. In local parlance, Aspen was "Up Valley," while Glenwood Springs was "Down Valley," meaning that it was at the far end of the Roaring Fork

Valley and it reflected, at least to some, a much less wealthy and prestigious demographic than did Aspen itself.

One insult tossed around Aspen was that "so-and-so belonged Down Valley."

Unlike Garfield County, Pitkin County didn't embrace TRIDENT's anti-drug policies or participate with the organization, which ruffled law enforcement feathers up and down the valley. Aspen and its police force were largely indifferent to criticism of being lax about Colorado's substance abuse laws.

As the Pfister case would glaringly show—with the national spotlight bearing down on it—the town had its own way of doing things when it came to drugs, money, and the law.

"Cocaine was very prevalent," Braudis said of Aspen in the 1970s, at the 2014 historical society event. "There was a guy named Harry Swets, who we called Hooks because he lost both arms when he hang-glided onto some high-tension wires and had his arms burned off. They replaced his arms with two hooks. He couldn't really find any employment, so he sold drugs. One night, an old lady on the West End called the police because she was witnessing a bunch of guys kicking the shit out of each other.

"The Drug Enforcement Administration had made a deal with Hooks to buy drugs, and when they flashed their badges, he started swinging. Guys that were dressed in undercover clothing pulled out guns, so when the uniformed on-duty guys showed up, they didn't know who to shoot.

"Kienast called the DEA and said they needed to tell him when they were doing undercover work in Aspen because it was a public-safety issue. Immediately, they cut us off from any communications. From that day on, every deputy in Pitkin County had a target on their back. In the seventies, a grand jury subpoenaed two hundred people in Aspen trying to crucify Kienast. That incident put a wedge between the federal Drug Enforcement Administration and local police for twenty-five more years . . . the DEA has had a hard-on for Pitkin County and Aspen."

In 2011, when Joe DiSalvo replaced Braudis as sheriff, the DEA showed up at the homes of several local cocaine-trafficking suspects. Armed with guns and warrants, they arrested five Aspen-area residents, but didn't tell

DiSalvo until the bust was over; they didn't trust him because he knew some of the suspects.

Tourists from across the country and around the globe had made Aspen a money magnet; they came to town to ski and to party *après* ski. Within reason, the local police had decided to leave them alone. Most qualified observers felt that this arrangement worked well enough—until it was confronted with a high-profile murder. Like Boulder, Colorado, on the day after Christmas 1996, when six-year-old JonBenét Ramsey was found in the basement of her parents' multimillion-dollar home, Aspen was ill prepared for this kind of criminal complexity.

"The Pitkin County Sheriff's Office does a very good job of meeting the particular needs of its community," says private investigator David Olmsted, who was a cop in Denver for a decade before moving to Aspen. "But they very rarely deal with really serious criminal matters, like murder. Crimes in Aspen tend to be things like bar fights. When it comes to homicide, it's a different situation. They don't have the experience you get from working murders in a big city and they don't have the intuition or protocols that you develop when you consistently do this. In a metropolitan area, there's a chain of command in place and a set way to proceed. This isn't nearly as true in a place like Aspen."

Pausing for emphasis, Olmsted says, "To put it crudely, when a murder happens in Pitkin County, it can turn into a clusterfuck."

Once Nancy Pfister's body had been found inside her home, Braudis was interviewed by the sheriff's department and echoed some of Olmsted's thoughts.

"We don't do homicides," he said, making a pointed reference to America's most famous unsolved murder case. "JonBenét Ramsey in Boulder taught me twenty years ago when I was sheriff [that] . . . if you don't do homicides on a regular basis, you can't do it well."

4

After Kathy Carpenter had dialed 911 and spoken to the dispatcher, her message was relayed to Sheriff DiSalvo via his pager: a body had been discovered inside a closet at 1833 West Buttermilk Road. This evening DiSalvo was socializing with Braudis at the latter's home. The men had long been close friends and saw each other virtually every day. DiSalvo had also come to Aspen from the East Coast, in his case New York City. In 1979, having never been west of Pennsylvania, he visited Colorado to ski. He too fell in love with the place and wanted to settle in Aspen, but his father said absolutely not—young Joe had good, permanent, civil service employment as a truck driver, a steady job with a secure future and long-term benefits. Leaving it and leaving home were foolish ideas, but Joe packed up anyway and said good-bye. By 1985, he was working for the Pitkin County Sheriff's Office, enjoying the skiing *and* the attitude he found in the community. Like Braudis, he was a part of the Owl Farm scene presided over by Dr. Gonzo of Woody Creek.

"Aspen was more tolerant back then and less selfish," he says. "I used to go out to Hunter's place and play poker with him. I was there when he shot off guns in his backyard. That couldn't happen now."

In 2011, when DiSalvo followed Braudis as the new sheriff, he leaned on his former boss for counsel. When you were the local sheriff, parents occasionally called and discreetly asked you to sit down and speak to their adolescent or grown but unruly children—so that their offspring wouldn't run afoul of the law, get tossed in jail, and besmirch the family name. People born into great wealth were notorious for walking on the edge, taking extreme risks, and ending up injured or dead. When someone requested that the Pitkin County sheriff do this kind of favor, he did it on the down-low, the way everyone wanted things done. Aspen had an image to protect, a lot of assets, and a deep desire to preserve the feeling that it was one of the special spots on the face of the earth.

The planet at that time had 1,600 billionaires and fifty of them—mostly financiers, real estate moguls, high-tech gurus, and energy tycoons—had properties in Aspen, their collective net worth topping $335 billion. Those fifty included members of the world's sixth richest family, the right-wing Koch brothers of Wichita, whose fortunes were greater than the gross domestic product of more than half of the countries on earth. And this was after the Great Recession of 2008 and the accompanying Bernie Madoff scandal that had swept across America and wiped out the financial reserves of a number of prominent Aspenites. Media king Mort Zuckerman had considered putting his Red Mountain home on the market, while John Denver's widow, Annie, had taken a serious hit. At the height of the scandal, retailers on Main Street peddled Madoff voodoo dolls that one could jab with long pins.

Knowing the community's ins and outs, and knowing how to interact with people of privilege, was part of the job of being the local sheriff. Braudis had mastered the art for nearly a quarter of a century and now DiSalvo was following his trail.

No one could advise him better about the distinctive challenges of being the head law enforcement official in Pitkin County. There were lines one crossed and lines one didn't. There were people one treated with great respect, if not deference, because they'd played an important role in building the enormous success of contemporary Aspen. History was valued here—the history of the place and of the people who'd made that history. Grainy photos of Aspen and its founders were everywhere you turned in the village, from the walls of new businesses to the old Hotel Jerome.

The town was exceedingly proud of its past.

. . .

In the winter of 1879, a group of silver miners ignored the pleas of Colorado Governor Frederick Pitkin, who'd repeatedly tried to warn them of the dangers of a Ute Indian uprising. Loading up shovels and picks, they crossed the Continental Divide and returned to Ute City by the Roaring Fork River. In 1880, they renamed the town Aspen and it was soon America's most productive mining district. Within a decade, it had electric lights, a hospital, two theaters, a handful of banks, an opera house, and a Main Street lined with classic frontier architecture. When the Panic of 1893 wiped out the silver market, thousands of miners fled the region; by 1930 only 705 Aspen residents remained. During the Great Depression, the community faced two options: grow, or wither away like so many other mountain burgs that eventually became ghost towns. The village's greatest assets were Red Mountain to the north, Smuggler Mountain to the east, and Aspen Mountain to the south. Following the 1932 Winter Olympics, a bobsledder named Billy Fiske launched a local ski area, but lacked the money to keep it going. Other investors tried to revive his idea, but World War II intervened.

To prepare for combat in the European high country, the U.S. Army's 10th Mountain Division trained at Camp Hale in the peaks near Aspen. Fifteen thousand soldiers were instructed in rock climbing and Alpine and Nordic skiing. One of them, Friedl Pfeifer, went on a reconnaissance mission to Aspen, which reminded him of his Austrian hometown of St. Anton. The stunning reddish hills, the iconic Maroon Bells rising up and looming over Aspen's shoulder, and the rolling green summer landscape only added to the appeal of being located at the foot of world-class slopes. The place conjured up Old World Europe and its pristine beauty was almost intoxicating. The only thing missing was money.

After the war ended, Pfeifer returned to Aspen with two other 10th Mountain vets and opened Ajax Mountain ski resort. A year later, Chicago industrialist Walter Paepcke and his wife, Elizabeth, known locally as Pussy, founded the Aspen Skiing Corporation and built the world's longest chairlift. In 1950, the town hosted the World Ski Championships and modern Aspen was on the map.

Paepcke started the Aspen Institute, dedicated to "fostering enlightened leadership, the appreciation of timeless ideas and values, and open-minded dialogue on contemporary issues." The institute would eventually have satellites in Paris, Madrid, Rome, Berlin, Prague, Tokyo, and New Delhi. It had financing from the Rockefeller Brothers Fund and the Ford Foundation and a board of directors that included Condoleezza Rice and Queen Noor of Jordan. Paepcke launched the Aspen Music Festival, featuring three hundred classical music events during eight summer weeks and drawing in more than 70,000 patrons (the village has only 6,600 permanent residents). At the inaugural performance in 1949, Albert Schweitzer was a special guest and hundreds of Coloradans took the train up from Denver. Aspen added an airport, Sardy Field, making it a worldwide destination. Three new ski areas eventually came online: Art Pfister's Buttermilk and Aspen Highlands in 1958, and Snowmass in 1967. Texans invaded Aspen, then wealthy Mexicans, then rich Europeans. In the 1970s, the Hollywood crowd began arriving, with Goldie Hawn and Kurt Russell, Don Johnson, and all the rest. Musicians were next, led by John Denver, Jimmy Buffett, and the Eagles. Athletes, artists, and corporate executives followed.

"In those days," says a veteran Aspenite, "you couldn't throw a beer can without hitting a celebrity. There was a lot of schnitzel around too. Many Europeans had come here to work as ski instructors and they brought schnitzel with them. Schnitzel was everywhere."

On Aspen's small streets it was bad form to make too much of a fuss over movie stars—just take note of their fame, nod, and keep moving. It was also gauche for the celebs to make too much of a fuss about themselves. When one TV actor on a hot streak began sending out press releases about his upcoming visit to town, the locals tagged him as a phony who wouldn't last that long in show business, which turned out to be true.

Inequality may have been the lifeblood of Aspen, but relations between the classes still had a precarious balance.

"You had the millionaires and the homeless partying side by side," says a former local newspaper editor, "and everyone was having a great time. Today, it's the wealthy partying with the wealthier."

Not just partying, but also generating some very big concepts. Each June the town holds the Aspen Ideas Festival: a one-day pass costs several thousand dollars, and the event is usually sold out; the speakers have names like

Hillary Clinton, and past subjects have included the future of the American male. The festival has been described as "smart people coming in from all over the world and talking about things that matter... or not."

Aspen's first wave of growth, driven by Walter and Elizabeth Paepcke, brought in professional skiers, a world-class think tank, and high culture. The town was ruled by a small group of fur-lined grande dames starting with Pussy, Fabi Benedict, and Goodie Taylor. If you were in with them, you were golden. If you were on the outs, you were doomed to failure in trying to scale the highest peaks of Aspen society. Legend has it that Pussy and Fabi kept a secret scroll that they liked to drag out and unfurl, making fun of those in town who didn't quite live up to their standards.

The second wave of Aspen's popularity, beginning in the 1960s and fully blooming in the 1970s, attracted celebrities and massive indulgence.

"Aspen," went the local saying, "is where the fun button got stuck on hold."

Art Pfister, who wore a large white cowboy hat and had a gregarious spirit, played a major role in the initial wave, while Nancy Pfister came of age inside the endless party. Father and daughter represented the old Aspen and the new, a dividing line between the generations—between people who'd worked hard to get ahead and those who came after and enjoyed the spoils of great wealth without having as much responsibility. For years, Nancy's parents had hosted an "old-timers" get-together for several hundred early Aspenites who came to the festivities from all over the country. No one represented the old Aspen, before the fun really got going, better than Art and Betty Pfister.

No one represented the party more than their middle daughter.

5

The moment Sheriff DiSalvo saw the address for the location of the corpse, he was alarmed. He asked Bob Braudis if that was where Nancy lived and the big man looked at his computer and confirmed that it was. The first thing that passed through Braudis's mind was that someone had killed himself or herself up on West Buttermilk Road.

"I assumed it was suicide," Braudis told investigators. "We have a lot of suicides here. I think Joey was told Nancy was found in a closet. I figured she was hanging..."

In the next half hour, as more information came in, DiSalvo shared it with Braudis. Months later, DiSalvo referred to this evening in an interview with the *Aspen Daily News*, when reacting to criticism for letting anyone outside of his department know about the 911 call and its immediate aftermath.

"Of course, Bob and I discussed this," he said. "He's the only other person on the planet to have been Pitkin County sheriff when there's a homicide in town."

The two men discussed their options and concerns. By now they'd learned that the victim wasn't hanging in the closet, but had been beaten—so this likely wasn't a suicide, but a homicide.

As Braudis would one day tell the authorities, DiSalvo felt that he had to make some quick decisions because a couple of his deputies were "ready to fuck up the crime scene and Joey very shrewdly said, 'Back out, put up the yellow tape, no one knows yet.' Good decision."

DiSalvo obviously hoped that it wasn't Nancy who'd been found dead.

He wasn't ready to come to that conclusion until a positive ID had been made, calling on his ingrained sense of caution from a life in law enforcement. At the same time, he refused to get in his car and drive up to her home to take a look for himself. He'd spent years putting people he knew into body bags and then dealing with the relatives and friends of the deceased. As a deputy, he hadn't had any choice in the matter; he followed orders and did whatever his superiors told him to do. Now that he was sheriff, things had changed. He could choose what he would, and would not, expose himself to.

"I had to peel Hunter off the stool [after Thompson had committed suicide in his home in 2005]," says DiSalvo. "I couldn't go up to Nancy's house. If she was in that closet, I didn't want to see her that way."

An editor of the *Aspen Daily News* had already heard about the discovery of the body and driven up the mountain to get a sense of the crime scene and the condition of the victim. He was so shaken that he went back to the newsroom and declared that no one was to discuss what he'd seen outside the confines of the paper.

DiSalvo was simultaneously dealing with a fast-moving homicide investigation and the almost-certain loss of a close friend. He and Nancy had been part of the old guard, the ones who preferred Aspen back in the 1970s and '80s, compared to what the town had since become. She used to drop by his office to chat, as she'd done earlier with Braudis. DiSalvo's small work space featured an electric guitar on the wall and a colorful poster from when Hunter Thompson had unsuccessfully run for sheriff. DiSalvo knew the history of Nancy's family and while he'd always been respectful toward the Pfisters and their middle daughter, his most recent encounter with Nancy had been unsettling.

A few months earlier, he'd been asked to give a speech at the Hotel Jerome for the Aspen Chamber of Commerce, a staid event, a formality of the kind that someone in his position was called upon to perform. The image of continuity and stability was crucial in Aspen, and reassuring the local merchants about the steadfastness of law and order in town came with DiSalvo's office. It wasn't that difficult to keep everyone reassured because Aspen saw very little violent crime.

Fifteen minutes into his talk, a blond, middle-aged woman with unkempt hair wandered into the proceeding. Carrying a shopping bag and wearing a big hat and a bigger smile, she flashed it around the room, the way she always did, trying to make eye contact with everyone. Some people instinctively glanced away or looked down, as if they sensed what was coming or had seen this kind of thing before. Her body language suggested that she was tipsy, but one couldn't be sure until she opened her mouth.

"That's brilliant, Joe!" she yelled out in a slurred voice, breaking the flow of his speech. "That's great!"

DiSalvo, a tall man with a prominent Roman head, dark curly hair, and a face that was normally friendly and kind, paused briefly, nodded in her direction, and kept talking. His expression had hardened and he was clearly agitated by the intrusion. Maintaining decorum was also part of his job, and he couldn't let the situation get out of hand.

People were turning away from him and staring at Nancy; an awkward feeling was spreading through the crowd.

For a few moments, she was silent and the audience held its collective breath, clearly hoping she wouldn't say anything more and would just walk away.

"You go, Joe!" she cried out, giving another huge smile.

Her grin was an expression most everybody in the room was familiar with, one they'd watched alter and age over the years and decades. It was worn-looking now, especially in the wings of her eyes, almost frayed.

More people were rustling in the seats and more necks were craning in her direction, followed by more sighs.

"Beautiful!" she said. "Great."

DiSalvo paused again, uncertain what to do, but his anger and frustration were filling up the room.

The force of it reached Nancy, who didn't say anything else and soon left, so he was able to finish his talk.

Later, he took her aside and chastised her for making a scene in front of this group at the Jerome, one of Aspen's most iconic addresses (Art Pfister's picture had once hung in the hotel library). It wasn't the first time something like this had happened, but the sheriff had finally had enough—even if he and Nancy were friends and even if she was Aspen royalty.

Di Salvo told her that she'd embarrassed him and embarrassed herself in public. She needed to clean herself up and take charge of her life. He didn't want to be part of one of her spectacles in the future . . .

She said that she *was* taking control of things by getting out of Aspen for the winter and going to the beachside town of Byron Bay in the far northeastern corner of New South Wales—population 5,000 and roughly five hundred miles north of Sydney, Australia. The Arakwal Aboriginal people called the area Cavvanbah, meaning "meeting place," and British Lieutenant James Cook had named Cape Byron after John Byron, the grandfather of Lord Byron.

In mid-November, Nancy was having a sendoff party for herself, as she often did, and she invited Joe to come to it, as a way of saying good-bye and making things up to him. Would he drop by her house for the celebration?

He said he'd think about it, but days passed and he was still upset, eventually deciding not to go.

He never saw her again.

Once DiSalvo had confirmed that it was Nancy Pfister who'd been murdered, apparently inside her own home, his shock deepened. She'd been beaten so badly that she'd have to be positively ID'd through fingerprints. Her death was disturbing enough, but the savagery of it sent more waves of grief and sadness through the sheriff, his officers at the crime scene, and others in law enforcement who'd become aware of the homicide. How could anyone have unleashed such a brutal attack? Who could have hated her that much? DiSalvo wouldn't just be leading the homicide investigation but also would be taking custody of Nancy's dog until another home could be found for Gabe.

As the news spread along Main Street, the community hummed with rumor, innuendo, and speculation.

"Gossip," says a longtime resident of the town, "is a contact sport in Aspen."

The good-time girl had clearly done her share of drugs and this must have finally caught up with her. Aspen had enough of the wrong people when it came to supplying cocaine and other illegal substances to the locals. Didn't the crime look like a drug deal gone bad? Or had she been drinking again at a bar and picked up a new man, a dangerous man this time, which had led to a disastrous adventure inside her home? Or had she enraged someone because of her outspoken manner and high-handed treatment of people not in her social class? Or had she alienated someone within her own family, as everyone knew about her longstanding conflict with her sisters?

The local cocktail parties and street corners offered up no shortage of theories about the fate of Aspen's "ambassador to the world." But Sheriff DiSalvo was holding his silence, refusing to release anything about the cause of death or how long the body might have been in the closet before Kathy found it or how many people were under suspicion.

"We have several leads, but no suspects at this time," he said a few days after the story broke. "This is a homicide. We are getting support from the Colorado Bureau of Investigation. Over the last few days, CBI has sent over eight different agents. And we are getting incredible support from the Aspen Police Department and the Basalt Police Department. And we are using federal resources. We have tons of help."

Then he added something reflecting his own feelings about the victim and the small town he served.

"I loved Nancy," he said. "She was a good person."

As part of his dedication to her, he watched Gabe for a while, before the press got wind of this and there was grumbling around town that the man leading the murder investigation shouldn't be in charge of the dead woman's dog.

6

Private investigator David Olmsted came from upstate New York and eventually made his way to the University of Miami, where he studied history. He was accepted into Georgetown Law but, looking back from middle age, he says, "I wasn't ready for that." He never became an attorney, but spent the rest of his professional life working with cops and lawyers and learning to think as they do. In the Nancy Pfister case, he'd try to *out*-think the attorneys. Like Bob Braudis and Joe DiSalvo, he was initially drawn to Colorado for the skiing. After moving to Denver, he attempted to become a stock broker, but it didn't take. He was fascinated by words, language, thoughts, concepts, and the psychology of the human mind, including the criminal mind. Hired as a police officer in suburban Denver, he had the opportunity to attend graduate school on the department's dime and was soon studying English literature and the witticisms of Oscar Wilde.

Olmsted once booked a room in the Paris hotel where the playwright had died—right before he'd allegedly looked around at his surroundings, pulled in his last few breaths, and declared, "Either that wallpaper goes or I do."

Olmsted spent a decade on the force investigating major crimes before crossing over to the other side of the law and working for defense attorneys as a PI in Aspen. When Nancy Pfister was killed, he was helping the defense team on an Arizona case with Colorado connections. A once-prominent Aspen socialite, fifty-six-year-old Pamela Phillips, was on trial in Tucson for the 1996 car-bombing murder of her former husband, developer Gary

Triano, who'd made millions investing in southwestern Native American slot-machine parlors and bingo halls.

Prosecutors presented Phillips as a gold digger who'd paid her ex-lover, Ronald Young, $400,000 to execute the hit on Triano so she could collect a $2 million life insurance policy. In 2009, she was arrested in Austria and extradited to Tucson. Young was convicted and Phillips now faced first-degree murder and conspiracy-to-commit-murder charges. In April 2014, she'd be convicted of both counts and get life in prison.

Within forty-eight hours of Kathy Carpenter finding Nancy Pfister in her closet, Olmsted heard from an attorney in Boulder whom he'd worked with in the past. She'd been contacted by Will Styler, the late-twenties son of Nancy and Dr. William Styler III and a Ph.D. candidate at the University of Colorado. The lawyer asked Olmsted to go speak with the Stylers, who were clearly under suspicion and staying at the Aspenalt Lodge.

The police had already interviewed the Stylers about the murder at the Aspenalt, starting at 5:45 a.m. on the morning after the body was discovered. The next day, Friday, February 28, Brad Gibson interviewed Nancy Styler a second time at the Pitkin County District Courthouse. As he read Nancy her Miranda rights, she declared that she was stunned that the police wanted to keep talking with her or her husband about the death of Nancy Pfister; she'd had nothing to do with it and was certain that Trey hadn't, either. The couple, she told Gibson, had worked very diligently throughout the past few days to complete the transition out of Pfister's home. And at no time during this process, she emphasized, were she and her husband separated from each other.

On Saturday, March 1, David Olmsted drove to Basalt to talk with the Stylers at their motel.

When he arrived at room 122 of the Aspenalt, he noticed something and, just as important, he didn't notice something. What he observed was that a female deputy from the Pitkin County Sheriff's Office was parked at the motel and conducting surveillance on the Stylers from her car. Olmsted knew most of those in the department, but didn't know this person, who was carefully watching the door of their motel room and making notes of their behavioral patterns. This struck Olmsted as odd because following their first police interview the authorities had confiscated the Stylers' money, car, checkbook, credit cards, and anything else that would have allowed them to flee, if they were so inclined. They were without resources and had no way even to get food, until a local restaurant named Heather's pitched in to help them.

Olmsted went up to the deputy and introduced himself, making a few pleasantries. She told him that the Stylers were free to check out and leave the motel at any time, but where could they go under these circumstances?

What the private investigator *didn't* notice on this visit to the Aspenalt was something lying on the stretch of sidewalk leading up to the Stylers' room, even though he'd walked that stretch himself in the middle of the day. He hadn't seen anything at all—not a piece of trash or a cigarette butt and he was certain that he hadn't missed spotting a key with an oval tag attached to it that read "Owner's Closet."

Olmsted liked to think of himself as a naturally observant person who'd become even more observant by working as a police officer and then a PI since the 1970s. He wanted to believe that he intuited things and perceived things that others without his training might have overlooked. This isn't to say that he didn't overlook some things, the same way everybody else does, but when he left the Aspenalt that Saturday afternoon he was in highly observant mode, because this was his first encounter with people he might be representing as a PI in the near future in a first-degree murder case. These circumstances heightened his sense of awareness, yet he didn't see a thing on the way out of their room or on the walk to his car.

Twenty minutes later, motel employee Christopher Szcelina reported finding a key with an oval tag connected to it in the middle of the sidewalk, about twenty-five feet from the entrance to room 122. The tag read "Owner's Closet" and this item was passed on to the police and soon identified as the second key to Nancy Pfister's upstairs master bedroom closet, the same key Kathy Carpenter had told the police was missing from the lock when she'd first driven up to Nancy Pfister's home on the evening of February 26.

. . .

"I met with the couple," Olmsted recalls, "and they were very unlikely murder candidates. They weren't worried that much about what might happen to them and had other, more pressing problems at the time—like getting out of the Aspenalt and trying to find a more permanent place to live. In their interviews with the police, they'd said nothing incriminating and weren't feeling that the cops were about to come knocking on their door again.

"Despite how many TV shows people watch about crime, they still feel that if they haven't done anything wrong, why should they be afraid to talk to the police? They'd already voluntarily spoken to the cops without an attorney present and after their Miranda rights had been read to them. They'd left the police department and gone back to the Aspenalt. If they were guilty of murder, why would they go sit in a motel twenty miles away from the scene of the crime? And why were they actively seeking to rent another house in the region, in the area known as Ruedi Reservoir [about fifteen miles from Basalt]?"

Relying on a decade as a police officer and more than thirty years as a private investigator, Olmsted didn't see how either their personalities or their behavior was consistent with being killers. One of his favorite words when speaking about homicide was "intuition," which he maintained one could only develop over years and years as a detective. He also used intuition as a private investigator and it told him that before the authorities did anything else, like making an arrest in the case, they needed to expand their investigation well beyond the Stylers.

While he hadn't yet been hired by anyone surrounding the murder of Nancy Pfister, Olmsted would eventually play a unique role in the case. Nobody associated with law enforcement or with any of the future defense teams would speak openly to the media or the public about the death—except for this private investigator. He had opinions and, unlike most PIs in the middle of most homicides, he wasn't afraid to share them. This would become more and more important as the case unfolded, because for a long time it looked as if none of the pertinent legal documents surrounding the murder would ever be unsealed.

Olmsted was one of a tiny group of people who was about to have access to all of the evidence: 13,000 pages' worth. If you asked him probing questions, he'd talk about the case for about as long as you'd listen. Perhaps because he lived in Aspen, he had an interest in the homicide that went beyond the professional. He liked mysteries, puzzles, paradoxes, intellectual inquiries—and this particular murder, which seemed quite simple on the surface, would fit into all of those categories. Olmsted had a vocabulary that stretched out beyond the range of most cops, most lawyers, most journalists, and most everyone else; the death of Nancy Pfister would give him an opportunity to exercise it.

He enjoyed quoting Oscar Wilde, using words like "colloquy," and challenging the pat answers that would emerge in the Pfister case.

"What was done to Nancy," he says, "could not have been done easily by one person. The autopsy report said that she died without a struggle. If someone had wanted to kill her, and if they'd known her habits, all they had to do was to wait till the end of the night when she was drinking or taking drugs and had become incapacitated. Then she couldn't put up any resistance. Her lifestyle invited trouble. Many people around Aspen were aware of that and could have simply come in while she was asleep and attacked her. Nancy could be very nice to the people she thought were at her level socially and economically, but if she felt you were beneath her, she could really piss you off.

"Over the years, how many people in Aspen do you think she pissed off?"

He had a partial answer because he'd already begun digging into her background.

7

Born in Aspen on the Fourth of July, 1956, Nancy Pfister was a few years younger than her sister Suzanne and a few years older than Christina. From an early age, she was subject to allergies yet passionately drawn to horses, including wild ones. She had a special nag named Mark and rode him all over the countryside, even though the horse gave her sneezing fits. She was a small-town girl with an outdoors persona—hiking the trails behind her family home, swimming in high country lakes, searching for wild mushrooms in the mountains, fly-fishing with her mother on Woods Lake, and dressing very casually. Or occasionally dressing in the high-end, western-wear style caricatured by Jim Carrey in the comedy *Dumb and Dumber.* She'd never follow in the footsteps of Pussy Paepcke, Fabi Benedict, and Goodie Taylor.

"Nancy didn't wear makeup," recalls a woman who lived in Aspen in the 1970s and '80s. "She didn't comb her hair very often. She didn't dress up. She didn't care about any of that and could look quite disheveled, unkempt. She was like, 'I'm rich and I don't have to clean up.' She wore this attitude like a badge."

Nancy's parents had some of the same casual demeanor. Minnesota native Art Pfister had been a fighter pilot in World War II who became a file folder salesman for the Smead Manufacturing Company. In his thirties, he relocated to Aspen, but kept his sales job for decades. In 1954, he bought the 700-acre Lazy Chair Ranch for $30,000 and four years later he launched the Buttermilk Ski Area. Art was a renowned horseman, once driving his thirsty herd of cattle through the middle of Aspen so they could drink from the town's lawn sprinklers. He was also a gifted "water witcher," able to locate pools of water beneath the earth through the time-honored, mysterious activity known as dowsing; his middle daughter claimed to have these same powers.

When Betty Pfister was nineteen, her parents took her to an air show in Vermont, where her father declared that there was absolutely no way his daughter was going up in one of those small, flimsy planes. After her parents left the airfield that day, Betty sneaked back in, paid a dollar, and folded herself into one of the tiny aircraft for a ride. She enrolled in flying lessons, later studied marine biology at Bennington College, and became a Women Airforce Service Pilot (WASP) in World War II.

She later worked as a Pan Am stewardess and was a highly successful competitive pilot, retiring as a two-time winner of the All-Women's International Air Race from Montreal to Florida. In the 1960s, she helped organize the Pitkin County Air Rescue Group, flying helicopters on rescue missions during avalanches. When Nancy was growing up, her mother kept a brightly painted chopper named Tinkerbell in the driveway, at the ready to help those in crisis. In 1984, Betty was inducted into the Colorado Aviation Hall of Fame and twenty-six years later, along with more than a thousand other WASPs, she received the Congressional Gold Medal, one of America's two highest civilian honors. In her seventies, she went bungee-jumping in Australia.

Art died in 2007 at ninety-six and Betty passed away four years later at ninety. From an early age, Nancy and her sisters were known for quarrelling and this didn't change after their parents were deceased. Because Suzanne lived nearby, immediately following Betty's death Nancy drove to her mother's home, fearful that her older sister might come into the house and take things that held sentimental value for Nancy. All she truly ever wanted were some of Betty's casual clothes, like her sweaters, her carving of a wooden giraffe, and her string of pearls. Nancy and Betty had fought about many things—parenthood, money and family, and how they believed each other should live.

After Betty died, Nancy felt both abandoned by her mother and freed up as never before. She felt both sad and angry, struggling with lingering feelings of love and of friction. Many times she'd longed to get away from her mother, but now she wanted to be reminded of her and the easiest way to do so was to put on her clothes or jewelry. Nancy wore the pearls everywhere, draping them around her neck when she went into town, making them her trademark.

With Art and Betty gone, a vacuum had been created, not just inside the Pfister family, but beyond that as well. Old Aspen had lost two of its most valued members.

"Nancy's mother and father were very substantial and accomplished people," says a local man who grew up with the Pfister sisters and maintained some contact with them after they were adults. "Art and Betty were good at just about everything they did, except parenting, which they never seemed that interested in."

Like many other self-made Americans of the World War II generation, they *were* interested in protecting their assets following their deaths, so that their children couldn't squander them. In this case, the prudence of the parents was not handed down to their offspring, at least not to Nancy. You had to know something about Aspen to know how finances worked within the Pfister family, both when Art and Betty were alive and after their passing. Otherwise, you might think that their daughters were swimming in money.

The story was that when the Pfister daughters turned twenty-one, their father gave them each forty acres and a horse. The Pfister land and other assets were kept in a trust, overseen by Aspen lawyer Andy Hecht of Garfield & Hecht. Decades earlier, Hecht had come to Aspen via Astoria, Queens, in New York City. As a youngster, he'd attended the far-left-leaning Little Red School House in Greenwich Village; a couple of years behind him was class president Angela Davis. Hecht may have been studying Marx, Lenin, and Trotsky, but his eyes were on other goals.

"He never had much growing up," says a graduate of the Little Red School House. "He always wanted money."

He found it in Aspen, gradually evolving into not just a thriving attorney, but a major force in local real estate. He was known as a tennis player with a bad temper on the court and a businessman unaccustomed to losing. According to a 2007 *Aspen Times* article, Hecht and Ron Garfield, along with

Hecht's son, Nikos, developer Steve Marcus, and entrepreneur John Provine, "have been putting together a portfolio of properties that observers say rivals that of [Aspen's biggest real estate player] M&W Properties."

Before dying in 2011, Betty consulted with Garfield & Hecht so that her life insurance policy wouldn't be paid out to her daughters for more than two years, keeping nearly two million dollars from their reach until late 2013.

When people in Aspen talked about the second generation of Pfisters—the three sisters surviving Art and Betty—almost every person brought up one thing without being prompted: the women most definitely did not get along. This was as much a part of the local landscape as the certainty that snow would start to fall each autumn in the high country and build up over the long winter months.

Nancy didn't get along with Suzanne, who lived within walking distance of her, while Christina had escaped parts of the conflict by moving down to Denver (she had her own reasons for wanting to get away from her middle sister, which would emerge after Nancy's death). Suzanne and Christina felt that Nancy was irresponsible as a globe-trotter and an occasional reveler out at Hunter Thompson's Owl Farm. Her behavior had impacted Art and Betty and it may have helped prevent the sisters from getting their hands on more of the family money after their parents were gone.

At times, Art had seemed exasperated by all the female tension and disagreements swirling around him. He once confessed to Nancy that their family friend John Denver was "the son I never had."

Exasperated or not, Art and Betty made sure that even in death they were still holding the financial reins.

"Those three sisters," says another family friend of the Pfisters, "couldn't buy a roll of toilet paper without getting Andy Hecht's permission. Nancy acted as though she had access to far more money than she really did. She was like Paris Hilton, but without the Hilton."

In death, Nancy would be labeled a philanthropist. She'd given money to her twin interests of education and permaculture, which is defined as "an ecological engineering system for creating sustainable and self-maintained habitats and agriculture." But more than anything, she was a seeker, yet what she was seeking was never entirely clear. She believed in spontaneous combustion: approach a stranger, get involved instantly, roll the dice, and see what happens. It was a fun game as long as you never approached the wrong stranger. More than one Aspenite told of watching her walk into a party, spot a man across the room, motion with her finger to come hither, and close the deal for later that night in less than a minute.

"She was," says David Olmsted, "a very busy girl."

And a very bold one.

Following the discovery of her body, *Aspen Times* columnist Paul Andersen wrote an elegy about his first encounter with Nancy soon after he moved to town in the fall of 1984. One quiet day during the skiing off-season he was walking on the mall in the center of the village, minding his own business. The mall was empty, or almost so. A lone figure appeared in front of him, an attractive young woman using chopsticks to eat Chinese food from a carry-out container. He was instantly pulled in her direction, drawn to her "mischievous" eyes, but he didn't want to show her what he was feeling. To his astonishment, she came straight at him and he didn't retreat. When they were face-to-face, Nancy "scooped up a clump of rice with her chopsticks and pushed it toward me. I opened my mouth, accepted the morsel and knew I had arrived."

Dumbfounded by the "flirtatious serendipity of the moment," Andersen was captivated by Aspen and Nancy Pfister.

Her sense of daring didn't lessen with age. Where others saw insurmountable problems, she found opportunities. She helped build schools in Nepal and India, and in the 1980s she brought a twelve-year-old boy named Hemlal back to Aspen and educated him in her hometown. Later she flew to Argentina and picked out the man she wanted to be the father of her only child, Juliana. Once she'd become impregnated by ex-polo player Ashley Kent Carrithers, his job was finished and at age twenty-nine she returned to Aspen alone to bring her daughter to term. Nancy and Goldie Hawn had their baby showers together.

A Perfect Hostess

8

As Olmsted continued looking into Nancy Pfister's background, the Stylers also filled him in on their past and what had brought them to Aspen. For twenty-eight years, the couple had lived in the upscale Denver suburb of Greenwood Village. Everything about this city of 10,000 conveys newness, cleanness, exclusivity, and distance from the grittier parts of the urban experience. Nothing seems out of place or scruffy. The streets are lined with still-young apple trees, the lawns are precisely manicured, and the imposing brick houses are impressive, if not quite mansions. Even the names of the neighborhoods ("Heritage" and "The Preserve") underscore the arrival of the upper-middle class, just one step below the older and more established wealth of nearby Cherry Hills Village.

For a good part of those twenty-eight years, Dr. William Styler III—because of the III, everybody called him "Trey"—was a highly respected physician who eventually became chief of the St. Joseph's Hospital Department of Anesthesiology. His peers had put him in that position.

"I met Trey thirty years ago, when I first came to town," says Denver anesthesiologist Dr. Laurie Haberstroh. "Everyone told me to go to Trey and talk with him because he was a very skilled doctor who really knew his stuff. Everyone in the operating room wanted to work with him because he was a warm and generous person."

And one with considerable financial resources.

As other residents struggled along on eleven or twelve thousand dollars a year, or as young doctors made small down payments on starter homes,

Trey was soon buying a three-story house in Greenwood Village. He was born in Tulsa (Nancy came from Massachusetts) and had graduated from Oklahoma State University's College of Osteopathic Medicine. There was oil money in his family and he was in line to inherit sums that some people believed ran into the millions.

While he headed up a department in a major metropolitan hospital, his wife would become even more widely known. By age sixteen, Nancy was a makeup artist whose skills put her through college and then nursing school. She'd attended the latter in France, where she received training in general medicine and anesthesia, meeting Trey shortly after he arrived in Denver for an anesthesia residency in 1980. As a nurse anesthetist, Nancy was a young member of the faculty at the University of Colorado and he was the newest resident. From the beginning she was wowed by several things about him, starting with his brilliance as a physician.

He'd been valedictorian of his med school class and was "the smartest resident I ever had," Nancy later told the Pitkin County deputies. She liked to brag that his DNA held exceptional intelligence. In February 1982, the two were married and a few years later they had a son who would become the fourth to bear his father's name, though they would call him Will.

In the early 1990s, Nancy Styler saw an image of a woman in Victorian England standing atop a giant floating water lily. When she showed the picture to seven-year-old Will, he urged his mother to start growing these plants so he could snap pictures of people riding on them. He'd already decided to charge his customers a few dollars apiece to build up his college fund. Will obtained a handful of the small plants from the Denver Botanic Gardens and nurtured them in a pond in his backyard. He and his mother kept a seed bank in their basement and as the plants got bigger, Nancy expanded the ponds, until there were five. The lilies became a neighborhood sensation and Nancy loved nothing more than having the local kids and their parents come over so she could show off their exotic masterpieces.

"It was a really great thing for her to do for the children," recalls a woman who took her kids to see the plants. "Nancy was very open with the children and very kind."

She was evolving into a world-class expert on the Victoria lily, which reached up to eight feet in diameter, supported fifty pounds of weight, and could change color and sex overnight. Traveling back and forth to the Amazon, she and Trey collected lily DNA samples and more seeds. As founder and codirector of the Victoria Conservancy, she began providing the plants to gardening entities around the globe, while at Denver's Botanic Gardens, just as Will had once envisioned, she had visitors perch on a specially built platform, creating the illusion of people standing on a floating leaf. Before long, Nancy was featured on HGTV, decked out in waders and making jokes about her outfit being "the latest in pondwear."

The interior of the Stylers' home was as colorful as the lily ponds out back, at one time decorated with ornate, papier-mâché wallpaper, pink furniture, lavender carpet, huge bouquets of plastic flowers, massaging chairs, and fake-rock water fountains. Their three-car garage held a Jaguar and a Mercedes SUV, and the couple entertained as lavishly as they lived. Trey was the more reserved of the two; with an intellectual air, he bore a passing resemblance to novelist Salman Rushdie. At social gatherings, Nancy was a gracious presence, a perfect hostess, with her outgoing personality, her flowing, platinum-dyed hair, and her expensive outfits that evoked a mixture of Zsa Zsa Gabor and Dolly Parton—complete with gold lamé shoes and French manicure. She enjoyed telling people that she was drawn to Trey because of his superior mind, but some of their friends felt that she was just as drawn to his significant inheritance.

"To be honest," says a woman who on numerous occasions visited the Stylers at their Greenwood Village home, "I felt sorry for Trey. The style of the house was definitely Nancy's taste, not his. He was not an attractive man and I think he just couldn't believe that someone who looked like Nancy would date him and then marry him. She was a social climber and my gut instinct was that she was just very interested in money."

And makeup.

She also moonlighted for Lancôme, the cosmetics and skin-care giant, at a suburban mall. She devoted considerable effort to mascara and eye liner, and if she didn't feel that one of her customers or a female guest in her home or a friend at someone else's house had done her liner properly, she'd take the woman aside and go to work on her. When people recalled Nancy years after being around her, they didn't talk about her medical skills or even much about her giant water lilies. They brought up her iridescent eye shadow, with one Denver anesthesiologist labeling her *oysgeputst*—Yiddish for "glammed up."

Some of their acquaintances found the Stylers a little odd, but not that unusual. They had financial resources and spent them freely, and there would be more after his mother was gone. Money was not a problem.

Initially, Trey went into private practice with the Denver Anesthesiology Group. In 1990, he joined Colorado Anesthesia Consultants and his fellow CAC doctors made him chairman of their department at St. Joseph's Hospital. Then the *Denver Post* wrote a laudatory article about Nancy's talents with water lilies. The Stylers were thriving.

"I first met Trey in 1982," says Dr. Ron Stevens, one of CAC's founders. "He was in training to be an anesthesiologist and looking to get into private practice. I was a resident at University of Colorado hospital and a couple of years behind him. He was a little quirky—quirkier than most people in the medical field. He was opinionated and had a temper. Nancy was also working at the University of Colorado as a nurse anesthetist. What I remember about her was that she put on way too much makeup. Very flashy. She also thought she knew more than I did because at that point she'd already been in the trenches with patients and I hadn't gotten there yet."

Dr. Stevens became CAC's first president, while Trey sat on the board of directors. Things went along well enough for about a decade before the Stylers' good fortune began to turn.

First, Nancy was diagnosed with breast cancer and had reportedly had a double mastectomy.

Then, according to Dr. Haberstroh, one day Trey was digging a new lily pond in his yard when a backhoe fell on his leg. He was seriously injured and had a number of surgeries for the wound, but never fully recovered. For months he used a scooter to get around the hospital and operating rooms, while suffering with chronic reflex sympathy dystrophy, a condition resulting from crushed nerves. He'd become very sensitive to pain and to intense heat, and had trouble standing for any length of time. For a while, he tried to keep working in the operating room, but couldn't react quickly enough and decided to give this up.

Over the past decade or so, some doctors have described his condition as being "like Lou Gehrig's disease." One symptom, Trey told people, was that he kept breaking the small bones in his feet. Occasionally, he used a wheelchair. In his sixties, he stood five feet eleven inches and weighed between 140 and 150 pounds, a frail-looking, bespectacled man with white hair and a white beard. When he sank his body down into his wheelchair and collapsed his shoulders, he looked seventy-five instead of sixty-five.

Not everyone readily accepted that he was too severely injured to continue functioning as an anesthesiologist.

"Some people claim to have a disability to get out of practicing medicine," says Dr. Stevens. "Trey had inherited money from his mother, who was quite well-to-do. I don't know if he was just looking for an out from being a doctor. He said to me, 'I can't work." I asked him, 'What's your problem?' He gave me an answer and it's hard to say if this was a ruse. I've dealt with many ruses over the years from people making disability claims. I felt sorry for him. He began walking with a cane and didn't look good."

Trey wrote the CAC board of directors a letter stating that he was suffering from "idiopathic sensory-motor peripheral neuropathy . . . Between some help from medications, and significant limitation of physical activity, I was 'coping.'"

The term "idiopathic" means that this particular illness had no known cause, but could result in, among other things, nerve damage. Trey gave up his medical practice and the Stylers attempted to start a printing business so they could generate income and have a new health insurance program, but it sputtered. Trey knew that CAC had forty-six doctors serving ten hospitals around Greater Denver and that it could use a more efficient method of putting patients together with physicians. The anesthesiology group offered this challenge to him and he took it because, he later wrote to CAC's board of directors, "I was bored, depressed and broke (having been out of work for a year, and disability insurance not having paid much, if anything)."

"Trey wanted to take charge of our scheduling," recalls Dr. Stevens, "and he said he'd help make us a computerized system. Talk is cheap. Most of the talk about this kind of thing is not about hardware or software. It's just vaporware—people blowing smoke. We looked at some other possibilities for computerizing our scheduling system, but these companies wanted several hundred thousand dollars to do this. Trey said he could do it for much less."

CAC hired Trey and a computer outfit named Intraprises, run by Odell Isaac. Their mission was to create a software program (called ASAP) to bring CAC into the digital age. Trey was given a date to deliver the software, but allegedly missed his first deadline of April 15, 2002, and then missed a second one, as the CAC doctors and administrators became more impatient and exasperated. The once-admired physician was different since his accident, morphing into someone whom his former colleagues didn't understand. Had living with pain caused this change? Or was it something else? His stubbornness, if not his arrogance, was something that they tried to accommodate, but it was becoming too obvious to ignore.

"At the start of this new scheduling process," says Dr. Stevens, "he was reasonably diligent, but then..."

In late 2001, Dr. Stevens left CAC and moved to Wyoming to practice medicine there. He wouldn't see Trey again for nearly eight years. In his absence, things deteriorated between the medical outfit and Styler, and on December 31, 2002, CAC took the initial steps to fire him for not delivering what he promised to deliver. It was the first significant stumble in Trey's career and the start of a long downward spiral, the first time that his professional judgment seriously came into question.

Nancy Styler had her own spin on what had gone wrong between her husband and those he'd once successfully worked alongside. Many years later, her anger at CAC slipped out when she told Pitkin County detectives that after Trey had developed a spreadsheet for CAC, it "was opposed by a few in the group because it did automatic billing... A few were trying to pad their bills... [and] they were flipped out [because] this program was going to take away their 'fat.'"

While the conflict between Trey and CAC would produce a copious case file, no court records substantiate his wife's allegations.

In January 2003, Dan Egan, the chief financial officer of CAC, issued the following memo to their anesthesiologists:

> I was informed by Judy Craft, Executive Secretary ... that the scheduling program was inaccessible to the scheduling department ... She stated that Dr. Styler had called Carrie Williams, Scheduling Manager ... stating ... he would turn off CAC's access to the scheduling program ... Later that morning, I called Odell Isaac and inquired as to what the problem was ... I then reminded Odell that Dr. Styler was no longer an employee of CAC's and that I did not want him to allow Dr. Styler any access to our system once the correction was made.
>
> I then received a phone call from Dr. Styler gloating over the sabotage of our system ... I also understand that Mrs. Styler had called members of the scheduling department informing them that they would reestablish their passwords ... This was something that I had not anticipated would be required ... I then called Odell and reiterated that I did not want Dr. Styler involved in our business ...

Four months later, CAC insisted that Trey was in breach of contract on software delivery and had thirty days to remedy this. He missed that deadline as well, but in July 2003 he announced that the product was finally ready. CAC had stopped listening and started accusing him of what they labeled "unjust enrichment."

On August 19, 2003, CAC filed a lawsuit against Styler, but he countersued them, seeking damages. A trial date was set for November 15, 2004, but to avoid litigation, CAC made a settlement offer of $135,684.60, which seemed to them and their lawyers a decent payout for Trey's efforts. He rejected the deal. In late 2004, Intraprises reached an agreement with CAC, but again Styler refused the terms. He was now claiming half ownership of the software—and contending that half of his half was held by his wife.

As the stakes got higher, the legal tactics got harsher. CAC engaged a special investigator to look into Trey's past and an allegation regarding his behavior toward a female doctor within their group—a charge he dismissed as nothing more than a momentary fit of anger, a shouting match between two adults.

9

For years the dispute between Trey, CAC, and Intraprises dragged on, creating thousands of pages of legal documents. CAC alleged that not only had Trey missed multiple deadlines for delivering the ASAP scheduling program, but had improperly attempted to market the software to other medical practices. Styler countered that his intellectual property rights had been violated and he'd been betrayed by both CAC and Intraprises. As the case approached half a decade, he was represented by Denver lawyer John G. Powell (e-mail handle "friendlyshark"). While Powell had charged him more than $600,000 in legal fees, Trey had stuck with him and paid this bill in full, but the combination of ongoing physical problems, daily bouts of pain, financial worries, and stress over the lawsuits caused him to confess to another attorney that at times he felt suicidal.

In May 2008, Styler finally declared that he could no longer pay his lawyer and dismissed Powell from the case, which continued to grind forward. The income he'd made as a physician and his other financial resources were gradually evaporating, which surprised some observers.

"To someone in Trey's position," says Dr. Laurie Haberstroh, echoing the sentiments of other physicians who'd worked with Styler, "six hundred thousand dollars doesn't seem like a lot of money."

In August 2008, while driving his Audi to yet another legal conference, Trey rear-ended a Volkswagen, unleashing a new lawsuit. Styler suffered a "closed head injury" and the woman in the Volkswagen had medical bills in excess of $300,000. This case was settled in 2009.

That summer, District Court Judge Larry Naves was finally ready to bring *Dr. Styler v. CAC* to a jury. By now, Trey was acting as his own lawyer and before the trial commenced he pleaded with the Colorado Supreme Court to help him with some legal procedures that he felt had been mishandled. Serving as your own attorney is called *pro se.*

"It is not arrogance," he wrote the state's seven highest justices,

> that causes me to Petition this Court as a *pro se* litigant—it is a simple question of desperate necessity. It is important for the Court to know that I did not begin this action *pro se*, nor did I come to this status by choice. From April 2004 until May 27, 2008, I was represented by John G. Powell. He withdrew as my attorney when told I was out of funds—the $600,000 I had paid him thus far had exhausted my assets... (I report this to you only for context. Mr. Powell's actions are not in question here—they have been referred to the appropriate disciplinary body).
>
> With three months to trial, and no assets, I made multiple attempts to obtain other representation, but without success. I then had to decide whether to abandon my claims and assets, or to attempt to proceed *pro se.* Some basic research quickly showed me two things: first, that I could not possibly acquire the skill and knowledge required to litigate a case such as this, but secondly, the nature of the legal system and its Rules of Civil Procedure should make it possible for me to obtain the information necessary to negotiate an appropriate settlement of my claims...
>
> Naively, I thought that if I informed the Court... the Court would intervene in some corrective fashion. This, I hoped, would lead to the information I needed and the settlement I desired.
>
> When I first read these Rules of Civil Procedure, they gave me hope, as well as the tools I would need to pursue my goals. When I experienced the reality of those Rules as practiced by judges and attorneys... I was rendered both hopeless and helpless...
>
> My rights to due process have been trampled. Without this Court's strong affirmation of those Rules and their universality, no litigant, whether *pro se*, private attorney, public defender, or the Attorney General of Colorado, can feel secure in their own rights to due process.

I thank Your Honors greatly for your consideration.

Sincerely, William F. Styler III, D.O.

The Colorado Supreme Court denied Trey's request.

The jury trial Trey was seeking began and on the first morning he presented his side of the case. A few hours later, the lawyers opposing him asked Judge Naves to dismiss Trey's suit, and Naves did. That afternoon, Trey called the scheduler at CAC and said that he was thinking of killing himself. When the police came to check on his condition, he appeared to have calmed down.

He sued Powell for legal malpractice, believing the attorney had severely overcharged him. After another lengthy court battle, Trey won a judgment of $896,056 and it looked as if his financial troubles were at last over, but Powell declared bankruptcy and Styler was unable to collect a nickel.

By 2009, he was hardly the only one facing massive money problems. Like countless other Americans, the Stylers had been caught off guard by the Great Recession starting in September 2008. Bad investments and a lost inheritance, along with failing health and misfortunes in court, hounded Trey at every turn. His family was so alarmed about his state of mind that they were considering staging an intervention and the Stylers eventually did get suicide counseling.

Nancy Styler was now looking for work in the jewelry-making business or wherever else she could find it. At her age, she hadn't expected to be the couple's main source of income, but her husband was ill, their resources had dwindled, and they'd possibly lost assets in the recent stock market crash and financial scams. The *Blue Jasmine* phenomenon wasn't merely a fictional plot in a 2013 Woody Allen movie, in which a formerly wealthy woman falls into poverty and has to go live with her working-class relatives in California. It was a desperate new reality for many people, some deep into middle age.

10

Outside the Styler family, former colleagues of Trey could see how much he'd deteriorated. In 2009, he asked CAC cofounder Dr. Ron Stevens to testify on his behalf at his upcoming trial—a request that alarmed the physician. One Sunday night, Trey showed up unannounced at Dr. Stevens's front door, having driven his Jaguar from Denver the hundred miles north to Cheyenne, where Dr. Stevens now lived. He wanted to talk with the physician about his lawsuit against CAC. Like others who'd worked with Trey in the past, Stevens was befuddled by the former anesthesiologist.

"I left CAC on good terms," he told Trey, "and I'm still on good terms with them. I'll speak with you, but if you choose to go forward with your lawsuit, I won't testify for you."

Trey spoke at length about his problems with the lawyers he'd earlier hired to help him and said that he was now representing himself.

"It sounds like you're in trouble," Stevens replied, feeling more and more uncomfortable with his visitor.

Styler again asked him to testify.

"C'mon, man," Stevens said, finally showing his discomfort. "What are you doing here? I hired you to do this job and it went south and I don't have too much else to say about it. CAC paid you to do this work and if you didn't have a clear agreement with them on the ownership of the software, I don't see where you're coming from."

For another hour the men went round and round. Trey tried to change Stevens's mind, while the latter attempted to ease out of the situation without offending his former colleague. This wasn't the same person Stevens had once worked with, but someone who'd been altered by his experience with the legal system or by physical pain or by the stress that he seemed encased in. As politely as he could, Stevens ended the conversation and moved toward the front door.

Styler left, but called the doctor once or twice more, their discussions going nowhere.

Stevens didn't think much about Trey until five years later, when he heard about the Stylers' potential involvement in the Nancy Pfister case. The memory of the conversation with Styler in Cheyenne came rushing back.

"Trey had a messianic complex and the gift of being right," Stevens recalls. "He didn't compromise well. When he got angry, he turned red and yelled. He very much wanted to be in control of things, but that's the way anesthesiologists are. It comes with the job. The more in control you are in the operating room, the better doctor you are.

"He was always odd, but the CAC lawsuit definitely made him odder. It turned him from odd to desperate and then perhaps to deranged. Once he got on a mission about something, he had to succeed."

In July 2011, two years after Trey had dropped in on Stevens in Wyoming, the Office of the Presiding Disciplinary Judge approved a "Conditional Admission of Misconduct" and suspended his former lawyer, John G. Powell, for six months for overcharging his client. The suspension was stayed pending the successful completion of a two-year period of probation. During this period, Trey sought the assistance of other attorneys to help him recover some of the settlement money from his former counsel.

"In my opinion," wrote lawyer Paul Gordon in a 2013 affidavit on Trey's behalf, "Dr. Styler was unusually vulnerable to being victimized by an attorney over-billing a client. Dr. Styler repeatedly expressed suicidal thoughts. Dr. Styler also told Ed Aro [a lawyer representing CAC] that Dr. Styler was fantasizing about 'suicide by cop . . .'"

In 2014, Gordon would tell the *Aspen Times*, "The Stylers paid every penny of that $600,000. It's an extraordinary amount of money, perhaps the largest I've seen paid by an individual or corporation. But he never got to the point where he said, 'I'm not going to pay my bill.' He was being a responsible citizen, but this particular lawyer was taking him to the woodshed and beating the crap out of him."

In June 2013, Powell himself wrote to the Colorado Attorney Regulation Counsel about his ex-client: "For a period of time, a person I have good reason to believe was Mr. Styler was personally keeping my house under intermittent observation. In fact, his presence was such that my wife told me that she had filed a police report. Further, a neighbor of mine reported that he confronted Mr. Styler as he, Mr. Styler, was rummaging through my home mailbox one afternoon... It is true that I have stated that I will not pay anything toward the satisfaction of Mr. Styler's judgment."

A month later, Trey acknowledged that he'd observed Powell's house "to see if Mr. Powell still lived at his address of record."

As Trey conducted surveillance on Powell, he and his wife had long since vacated their elegant Greenwood Village address and were renting a more modest suburban Denver home. The change had brought Trey even more health problems, from a leakage of carbon monoxide in the house. His legs had continued to weaken and he sometimes walked with the assistance of a round-headed metal cane, strong enough for him to lean his full weight on.

They relocated once again, this time to a rental property in Castle Rock, twenty miles south of Denver. By the summer of 2013, the couple had begun looking for new business opportunities and turned their attention to places outside of Greater Denver, where they could start their lives anew. As they did, Trey continued petitioning the Colorado legal system to get his $600,000 back from John Powell.

After examining the demographics of Pitkin County and Aspen in particular, the Stylers decided to relocate to the small mountain town because, as one of their acquaintances put it, "That's where the money was."

In this setting, where so many people had so many financial resources, they could surely recover. Nancy would move on from the medical profession and do what she really wanted to—get her aesthetician's license, do facials and Botox and provide spa services for wealthy clients. The couple took weekend trips to Aspen looking for rental properties big enough to hold their prospective new venture. Nancy had other skills, five industrial sewing machines, and could compete with the town's other two seamstresses. It would be the right change at the right time.

While they made plans to resettle in the mountains, Trey wouldn't leave everything behind him in Denver, but would carry one thing above all to the high country—the rage that he felt toward lawyers and the legal system that had "robbed" him of so much money in recent years. "Robbed" was the word he used when bringing up his former attorney or the conditions that had pushed him to the edge of poverty in his sixty-sixth year. Sometimes he let his bitterness seep out, without filtering it for those who didn't know him or his background. He and his wife, he told friends and strangers alike, were victims of circumstance. He'd been cheated by life, or at least by a conniving lawyer, and the wrong was unresolved and unending.

In the fall of 2013, the Stylers began making their transition to Aspen. Trey was apparently in such poor health that he was confined part-time to a wheelchair. At sixty-two, Nancy was fitter, stronger than her husband, and ready to go to work. She had more than $100,000 in equipment and spa products, but they lacked capital and Aspen was an increasingly tough place for small, independent entrepreneurs. Its streets were now lined with internationally known retailers paying very high rent: Ralph Lauren, Dior, Louis Vuitton, Prada, Gucci, Fendi, Bulgari, Burberry, and Ermenegildo Zegna.

Nancy began approaching hair salons and Aspen hotels, including the Jerome, offering her services to guests, including eyelash extensions, facials, laser skin care, and Botox, but the plan was slow to develop. They needed help, some new connections, a toehold in order to work their way into the community. They were soon to meet two strangers—who also felt like victims of circumstance—and their worlds were about to collide.

"You Can't Afford Me"

11

Unlike Nancy Pfister, Kathy Carpenter had a lower profile in Aspen, settling there after living in a series of other Colorado towns: Aurora, Glenwood Springs, and Rifle. The only stain on her financial résumé was a 1999 filing for Chapter 7 bankruptcy, although she'd gotten into a scrape or two because of alcohol and had spent more than one night in the Aspen jail sleeping it off. She was typically pleasant and rather shy, often staying in the background. However, when she was drinking, she could be loud and belligerent, edging out of control. Kathy always seemed to be scrambling for another dollar, although for years she'd drawn a steady paycheck as a teller at Alpine Bank. In its November 2013 newsletter, the business recognized her for her twenty-year anniversary of service at various branches in the region. She worked hard, was diligent, and made a good impression on customers. At the same time, the bank had demoted her a few years earlier—from supervisor to teller.

One day after Art Pfister died in 2007, Nancy came into the bank and Kathy helped her open an account. Something between the women meshed and from then on, whenever Nancy needed to make a withdrawal or another transaction, she sought out Kathy as her exclusive teller.

Kathy had given Nancy her business card and Pfister called her at work.

"You're a really nice lady," Nancy said. "I'd like you to quit your job and become my personal assistant."

She offered her fifteen dollars an hour.

"I'm honored," Kathy told her, "but you can't afford me. I've got my benefits, my housing, my insurance..."

Nancy invited her to lunch and their relationship moved outside of the bank. Kathy was flattered that someone with Pfister's background—someone with money and from one of Aspen's most respected families—wanted to spend time with her. Nancy began inviting her to parties around town that she'd never otherwise attend; she was meeting people she'd only seen in passing at the bank. For years, Pfister had been an Aspen A-lister. When the Kennedy clan had come to town, she'd hung out with them. When Steve Martin was performing locally, she shared laughs with the comedian. When His Holiness the Dalai Lama showed up in the Roaring Fork Valley, Nancy drove him to his appointments in her red Porsche. She had a way of being where the action was or of generating it herself.

Aspen's intense economic stratification—with a few super-rich at the very top, the just plain rich in the middle, and all the workers and service people far below that—had grown more severe in recent decades, but Nancy was going in the opposite direction. If she'd once leaned toward Aspen's upper echelon, as she'd aged, she'd moved away from that stratosphere and was socializing more and more with people who had less money than she did, or not much money at all. Kathy Carpenter was the latest example.

Despite their class difference, the women struck up an acquaintanceship that developed into a friendship and turned into an informal business relationship. The closer they became, the more responsibility Nancy gave Kathy, in part because she didn't get along with her own sisters, even though Suzanne lived nearby. And Nancy's own daughter, the twentysomething Juliana, rivaled her mother as a world traveler. She blew in and out of Aspen at irregular intervals and one could never be sure how long she might stay or where she'd go next.

One morning, Nancy phoned Kathy as she was getting ready to leave for an extended trip to Hawaii.

"Why don't you come to my home?" she asked the teller. "I can teach you how to eat and lose weight."

Nancy had no compunction about letting her new friend know that she needed to drop some pounds, but softened this by adding that she was pretty.

"I went up to her house," Kathy recalled much later, "and we drank some wine. We went over to her mother's and she had a birthday present for her."

They drove to Betty's in Nancy's Porsche. It was great fun to ride around town in this status symbol.

Back at Nancy's, they "drank some more," Kathy remembered. "Nancy loved to drink and I started to develop that drinking habit..."

When Nancy went abroad, Carpenter oversaw the house and began handling other duties, as their informal business relationship deepened.

At times Kathy felt it was too informal because she often didn't get paid for running errands, but she did get taken to lunch at expensive local restaurants and got to stay in Nancy's multimillion-dollar home. Nancy herself was known for her casual attitude toward money—her own and other people's. She had a well-earned reputation for ordering the most expensive champagne on the menu and then leaving the restaurant without chipping in. She was born rich and entitled, so what did it matter if someone else picked up the check?

Kathy had watched her friend withdraw substantial amounts of money from Alpine Bank, unaware of what the funds were being used for. Nancy enjoyed attending fund-raisers with the town's elite and nonchalantly writing checks to those running the events. She could hand a hostess thousands of dollars with a flair rivaling the richest people in town. She loved playing the wealthy philanthropist in public, but those who'd known Art and Betty Pfister were aware that things weren't that simple.

Garfield & Hecht didn't just hold the paper on Nancy's house; they'd also, according to her sister Christina, put her on an allowance of $7,000 a month, not exactly a bounty in Aspen. For the past eight years, Stacy Stanek, an employee of the law firm, had made a monthly deposit into Nancy's Alpine Bank account. She might be able to withdraw more funds for a contribution to a charitable organization, but was never in full control of her finances.

When she was gone from Aspen and renting out her house, Kathy had access to Pfister's safe deposit box and could put money from tenants into an account. Or she could wire money overseas to Nancy. Or send it via FedEx. Kathy knew that when Nancy went abroad, she made vague, oral agreements with those occupying her home and always wanted to be paid in cash. Cash was important to her, especially cash that she took under the table without Garfield & Hecht being in charge of it.

Some members of Pfister's family hoped that Kathy would rein in Nancy's substance abuse; she tried to for a while, but then joined the party herself. The women evolved into drinking buddies and certain people assumed they were more than friends, as Nancy had a taste for experimentation of all kinds. They made an odd couple: the blond, worldly looking Aspen native and her dark-eyed, dark-haired companion with the bushy, unruly locks. In spite of her drinking, Nancy was fit, with a good complexion and perfect teeth, while Kathy was square and stocky and didn't seem overly concerned with her appearance. At five feet tall, she weighed 140 pounds.

Nancy's eyes conveyed a sense of calm and kindness (when she wasn't high), but Kathy's were skittish, uncertain, never quite comfortable, as if she were someplace she didn't really belong. She'd often been rootless, while Nancy, despite all of her globe-trotting, was grounded in Aspen and its past. No matter how far from home she'd ventured, she'd always returned to the place she knew best and to those who accepted her.

Kathy was accepted in Aspen, too, despite having been picked up more than once for causing a disturbance in town. By 2014, she was attending meetings of both Alcoholics Anonymous and Bible study, and people in her support groups felt that *she* was making progress, while the conflict around Nancy was intensifying.

12

In July 2012, Pfister filed a lawsuit against her then tenant, Gayle Golding, who'd been growing marijuana inside the residence: the address up on West Buttermilk Road was secluded enough to avoid detection and its greenhouse and large skylights were perfect for horticulture. Pfister sued Golding for breach of lease and statutory civil theft, claiming that she'd left pot plants strewn about and made off with several of her valuables. She also hadn't paid the $3,500 rent for September 2011. It was the failure to pay the rent, not the pot growing itself, that had triggered the clash.

Golding filed a countersuit, accusing Pfister of "extreme and outrageous conduct, trespassing, battery, and slander," alleging that the row began after Nancy decided to raise the rent to $6,500 a month. If Golding refused to pay the extra $3,000, Pfister "would evict her or report her to law enforcement for conducting an illegal grow operation."

Golding fired back, asserting that she'd "always fully complied with Colorado's regulations regarding the cultivation of medical marijuana."

For those who knew Nancy, the episode revealed just how important rent money had become to her.

"Sure, Nancy liked pot," says her friend Teresa Wyatt, "but she didn't grow it. I never saw her as angry as she was at Gayle Golding."

Nancy threatened her tenant or had others do so on her behalf, saying that if the woman failed to terminate her lease, Nancy would write the *Aspen Times* and expose her and her pot business.

During the height of the conflict, Kathy Carpenter later recalled, "Nancy was staying with her mom, Betty Pfister, on Tiehack mountain... She was living with her mother because Gayle was still in the house and then she called the sheriff on pot girl... The agreement was that she [Gayle] could use the greenhouse for pot... [but] it turned out that she expanded it to downstairs...

"I used to go over there to start the Porsche once or twice a week and Gail wouldn't allow me in the house... After kicking Gayle out, she [Nancy] stayed with her mother a short time because she was ill... I stayed with her at her mother's in the back room... Nancy begged me and pleaded with me to..."

Golding paid the extra $3,500 for September, but claimed that she was in emotional distress because Pfister's conduct was causing her "anxiety-related heart problems." Despite this, Nancy did not back down from her threats, calling the Pitkin County Sheriff's Office and telling the authorities that Golding was growing "thousands" of marijuana plants in her home. The sheriff's office contacted the U.S. Drug Enforcement Administration and the Medical Marijuana Enforcement Division of the Colorado Department of Revenue.

In September 2011, Golding checked into the Aspen Valley Hospital, certain that she was having a heart attack.

Three months later, the women met by accident in Aspen's Little Nell hotel. An inebriated Nancy strolled up to Golding and, when she refused to talk to her, Pfister reportedly gave her a push.

"The following day," wrote Golding's lawyer, Scott Grosscup, in a legal motion, "Ms. Golding began suffering pain in the shoulder Ms. Pfister had shoved. The shoulder pain prevented Ms. Golding from skiing and interfered with her sleep and ability to dress and perform basic tasks."

Golding was diagnosed with a rotator cuff strain and underwent physical therapy for her injury. Thereafter, the women went out of their way to avoid each other, but more trouble loomed for Pfister.

In August 2012, after a long night of carousing with Kathy in Glenwood Springs, Nancy asked a clerk at the local Hampton Inn to dial 911. Carpenter was supposed to be the designated driver this evening for the hour-long trip from Aspen to Glenwood and back, but that plan had fallen through. Nancy, Kathy, and two pilots they'd just met had eaten dinner together at the Pullman restaurant in downtown Glenwood, but then the women forgot where they'd parked the car.

"Prior to dinner," Kathy once recollected, "we went into the hot springs pool in Glenwood . . . We met these guys. They had some booze in a flask and so I started drinking this stuff and I got really inebriated and I couldn't drive . . . By the time we got to the restaurant I was really hammered . . . Nancy was mad at me."

Outside the Pullman, Pfister met Amanda Holley, a waitress who'd just gotten off work, and enlisted her to help them find her car. They spent an hour wandering around the streets together, trying to locate the vehicle. Holley was struck by Kathy's "annoying, crass, and rude" manner toward Nancy, constantly putting her down with barely coherent mumbles. Once they found the car, Nancy offered Holley sixty dollars to drive her back to Aspen, but she refused. Instead, she drove them to the Hampton Inn, where Nancy insisted that Kathy get a room. The two women began arguing in the lobby and Pfister had the clerk call 911 so that Kathy could dry out.

When Officer Drew Hatch arrived on the scene, he saw the women in the parking lot in Pfister's Toyota Prius. Nancy told him that Kathy was drunk.

"Pfister," Hatch wrote in his report, "stated she was just afraid because her friend does not drink very much and she thought she might get violent."

Hatch took note of both Kathy's condition and Nancy's slurred speech and the smell of alcohol on her breath.

"Throughout the entire time I was in contact with Pfister and was able to see Pfister's friend," Hatch noted about Carpenter, "I never once heard her say anything or act aggressively."

Because Nancy was in the driver's seat, Officer Hatch decided to arrest her for DUI. Pfister pushed back, saying that she'd called 911 because Kathy was inebriated, not because of her own condition.

Hatch took Nancy into custody and impounded her car. One of the airline pilots got Kathy a room. The next morning Pfister demanded that Kathy pay to get her released, which she did.

"I picked her up..." Kathy said later. "She apologized to me and said it was my fault but because she loved me, she took the bullet for me... That's Nancy for you. She's very, very, very tight. Very, very frugal."

Nancy's attorney, Richard Ivker, was able to lower the charge because Amanda Holley had driven the Prius to the hotel rather than Pfister. Nancy pled guilty to driving while ability-impaired and received probation and community service, along with not being able to leave the state.

Although Kathy had paid to get her out of jail, Pfister was unsatisfied and suggested that she now pay her attorney fees. Carpenter asked if they could split the cost, which they eventually did, but not before Pfister—as she'd done earlier with Gayle Golding—threatened to put an ad in the local paper denouncing Kathy.

"I didn't even know if she would really do it," Kathy remembered, "but that's how she is... She's always threatening people... I paid $1,500... She respected me and said I was really a great friend..."

In November 2012, Kathy wrote the judge in the case a letter asking him to let Pfister get out of Colorado for the winter: because of a prior injury, Nancy had had metal plates inserted into her arm and cold weather aggravated them. In her letter, Kathy described herself as Nancy's "close friend, house sitter for six years and personal banker." Allowing Pfister to travel to a warmer climate would help ease Nancy's physical ailments from wrist and shoulder surgery five years earlier.

"I live with her and witness the daily pain and trauma..." Kathy had written. "I have been her guest in Hawaii and have witnessed the difference in her physical, emotional and overall well-being when she is in her element."

The women were reconciled, at least for now, and in the fall of 2013 Nancy planned to escape the Aspen winter and spend the next six months in Australia. She'd need a new set of renters to replace the last ones. The conflicts with Gayle Golding and Kathy were a prelude for everything to come.

13

Teresa Wyatt was engaged to Daniel Treme, a French chef who'd cooked for celebrities all over the world before finding work in Aspen preparing meals for the kind of people who owned $45 million homes. One evening in 2011 the couple ran into Nancy Pfister at a local restaurant, il Mulino, where she was out with Kathy Carpenter. The first thing Teresa noticed was the casual interaction between the two women, even in public.

"Kathy was lying down on a couch, with her feet resting on Nancy's lap," Teresa remembers. "Nancy immediately began talking with us and making us feel comfortable. We appreciated this because we hadn't lived in Aspen very long and didn't know many people. She was definitely 'Aspen's Welcome Wagon.' She was very friendly and liked to giggle. Once you'd heard her giggle, it was hard to get that sound out of your head. I keep hearing it whenever I think about her."

The first thing Daniel noticed was that Kathy's finger was bleeding. He offered to get her a Band-Aid and asked what had happened.

"You don't want to know," she told him.

He never forgot this response. His intuition told him that something about the women's relationship was complicated, and maybe something wasn't right. In the future, he'd try to keep his distance from both of them.

Teresa did the opposite, getting close to Nancy and becoming part of one of her favorite rituals: going to her house in the afternoon and watching Ellen DeGeneres's TV show. Nancy loved to sit on the couch with her friends and drink Prosecco, a sparkling Italian wine. Sometimes, she pretended that she was a producer for *Ellen* and approached strangers on the street or in airports, conducting fake interviews with them about appearing on the program.

Occasionally, when Nancy had women or men friends over, she served them tea laced with marijuana without telling them, just to see what happened. She always seemed so carefree—until a visitor violated one of her rules or quirks.

If anybody said anything during the *Ellen* show, she'd glare at them and snarl, "Don't talk!"

If she felt anybody was taking advantage of her financially in any way, the carefree side of her suddenly disappeared.

And if the household ran low on booze, it was always a mini-crisis.

One day Kathy, Teresa, and Nancy were on the sofa waiting for *Ellen* to come on, when Nancy learned that all the wine was gone.

"Kathy," she demanded," run down to Roxy's and get some Prosecco!"

Kathy didn't move or say anything.

"Oh." Nancy turned to her and sighed in her snarkiest tone, "I guess we're not having Prosecco today."

Kathy didn't budge, but looked visibly nervous, coiled, as if ready to strike.

Pfister wouldn't let up.

"She's madddddd," Nancy said mockingly.

Kathy sprang off the couch, stomped out of the house, jumped in her car, and tore down the mountain to the liquor store, maintaining her silence when she got back with the wine.

Everyone who spent time with Pfister either learned how to deal with her imperious attitude—or didn't last long in her circle.

"Nancy," says Teresa, "could be very bossy. She liked to order people around. She'd say to me, 'Come rub my feet' or 'Go get this or that for me.' She asked a lot of people to rub her feet. I didn't think anything about it, but not everyone was like me. She really liked Kathy, but they fought like cats and dogs. A love-hate relationship."

In some ways, Nancy was easier to love from a distance, when she wasn't running the world from her couch. One e-mail exchange (there are others like it) between the two women as Pfister was traveling abroad reveals the affection.

On February 9, 2012, Kathy wrote her friend, "Hey Sista... It was really nice talking to you this morning. I'm sending you a flower and a daily quote. Have a beautiful day darlin... luv ya Kathy xoxo."

Teresa did not believe, as some did, that her friend was bisexual.

"When Nancy had had too much to drink or had smoked too much pot," she says, "I'd have to put her to bed. I took naps with her and slept in bed with her several times and we never came close to having a physical relationship. Nothing ever happened between us."

14

When Betty Pfister died in November 2011—both of Nancy's parents were now gone—Teresa became more aware of her friend's entangled finances.

"Nancy told people she was rich," says Teresa. "She liked to throw this around, but nobody who really knew her believed it was true. She didn't have much control over her money situation and said that it was controlled by attorneys. This had been set up by her father so she was on a tight leash and incredibly frustrated by this arrangement. She was always trying to get someone to buy her a bottle of something or to take her to dinner. It made her crazy. When she traveled, she usually stayed with friends, not in hotels. She and I shopped in thrift stores in Carbondale [half an hour Down Valley from Aspen]. She wore secondhand clothes. She never wore a bra if she could help it and she was never that concerned about her appearance. But she *always* wore her mom's pearls."

Teresa, like everyone else in Aspen, had learned that Nancy was notorious for ordering big in restaurants and skipping out on the tab. Teresa joked about this with references to old TV episodes of *Lost in Space.*

"Warning! Will Robinson! Will Robinson!" she says, mimicking dialogue from the show. "Nancy Pfister on the block! The check is coming!"

All of this was entertaining and amusing enough . . . until you were the one stuck with the bill.

. . .

In 2012, Teresa asked her parents if Nancy could visit them in St. Croix, in the Virgin Islands, where they had a winter home. The things that had once tied Nancy to Aspen—Hunter Thompson's Owl Farm, raising Juliana at least part of the time, her attachment to her mother and father—were gone. She and her sister, Suzanne, had been estranged for decades and Christina had left home as a young teenager, in part to escape her middle sister. The only person in her family she'd consistently gotten along with was her dad.

"Nancy adored her father," Teresa says, "but more than once after Betty died she sat on her couch and just sobbed and said in the voice of a young girl, 'I hate my mother! I hate my mother! I'm an orphan now!' I thought it was a very strange thing for a woman in her mid-fifties to say."

Of the three Pfister daughters, Teresa says, "Nancy was the one most in need of mothering, but Betty wasn't the kind of woman who made you cookies and milk. After Betty died, Nancy missed her as much as she hated her."

Nancy seemed adrift and Teresa thought it would be good for her to be around her own parents, Else and David Weborg, in the islands. They agreed to have her come down for a while and stay in their guesthouse.

Things did not start well.

"I picked Nancy up at the airport in St. Croix," Else recalls, "and showed her where she was staying with us. The next morning she asked me if I could bring up her suitcase. I thought to myself, *I'm not your servant*, but I didn't say that. I had to keep her at a distance and not let her too far into our world."

That was difficult because Nancy came into the couple's living quarters and flirted with David, asking him to rub her feet, in front of Else. Nancy talked a lot about having money, but she didn't spend any, not paying for her own expenses at the Weborgs or offering to. When she mentioned an interest in buying a property in St. Croix, Else set her up with a local real estate agent.

"She drove that broker crazy," says Else. "After a few days, the woman called me and said, 'The next time you set me up with someone, make sure they have some money.'"

Nancy hoped to spend months with Teresa's parents, but Else had other ideas.

"My mother," says Teresa, "is the smallest thing in the world, but you don't mess with her."

After Else found Nancy sitting on David's lap a few times, she tossed her out of the guesthouse.

Nancy quickly found a man to live with in St. Croix.

"She just moved in with him," Else says with astonishment in her voice. "In my world, you don't do that. She didn't even know this person. He could have been anybody—he could have been some kind of weirdo. Her lifestyle was just so . . ."

Nancy continued to drift, thinking about buying property in St. Croix or in Aspen or in Costa Rica. None of these ideas came to fruition, even though she was about to come into a sizable chunk of money from her mother's life insurance policy.

In the spring of 2013, when the French TV show *Access Privé* came to town looking for an Aspen tour guide to the rich and famous, initially the French TV producer didn't want Nancy to be the host, but Teresa and Daniel convinced the woman to use her. Daniel Treme had French connections and he and Teresa wanted to do something good for Nancy. Teresa felt that her friend suffered in comparison to her sisters and had never lived up to her parents' expectations. Being featured on *Access Privé* would give her a much-needed boost in confidence and self-esteem.

"Nancy was the star of the show," Teresa says, "and the program was a real success."

That spring was relatively calm until the production was over, and then Nancy and Kathy had another blowup.

"Nancy got upset and fired her," says Teresa. "They were separated for a while, but then she hired her back. Nancy had complex relationships with women, just as she did with her sisters and her mother. She was very generous with me. She'd take me to lunch and pay the bill, but she *made* men pay for her—always. She liked the attention of men, but I'm not sure that she actually liked *them*."

Not long after the *Access Privé* show was completed, Teresa and Daniel obtained a DVD of the program. They were very proud of Nancy's performance and thought she would be, too. They took the disc up to West Buttermilk Road to present it to their friend, eager to watch it with her.

The three of them sat down on the sofa and opened a bottle of Prosecco, but the DVD failed to work in Nancy's television. To their surprise and then shock, she exploded, enraged at them for bringing her a faulty product.

"Everyone has anger fits," recalls Teresa, "but she was *really* angry. It was a temper tantrum."

Teresa suggested that they view the DVD on Nancy's computer, which they did without any trouble, but the explosion wasn't over.

When Teresa said that she'd order more copies of the show, at six dollars apiece, Nancy threw the DVD across the room.

"Everybody wants my money!" she told them. "Everybody wants my money!"

Trying to calm her down, Teresa quietly explained that she and Daniel had had to pay for their own copy.

They left the house shaken and the incident continued to reverberate, especially the throwing of the DVD and the part about the money. Daniel was very upset and Teresa became more cautious about interacting with Nancy.

One day that summer they spotted her at the downtown Aspen Farmers' Market, a lively Sunday morning gathering of townspeople who supported the local growers. She was wearing a cowboy hat, which had been a trademark of her father's for decades. Teresa and Daniel had seen her here many times before and always looked forward to running into her. Today, they thought about approaching her, but she hadn't seen them yet.

Months earlier, Daniel had been standing outside in Aspen waiting for a bus ride home. Nancy drove by and picked him up, insisting on taking him to the Mezzaluna café. He went along to be polite and she stuck him with a bill for several glasses of expensive chardonnay and an order of pasta. When they were back in her car, she lit up a joint, which frightened him so badly that he started to tremble and made her stop the vehicle. He jumped out in the middle of traffic and ran off.

That Sunday at the farmers' market, Teresa and Daniel looked at

Nancy and then at each other and decided to slip away before she noticed them.

"We felt that she'd have asked us to go out and eat," recalls Teresa, "and we didn't have the hundred dollars it would have taken to cover the meal."

Later that afternoon, they ran into her with some other people, including Bob Braudis, at Little Annie's restaurant. After chatting a bit, the couple said good-bye and broke away from the group.

Teresa would later speak with Nancy on the phone but she and Daniel never saw her again.

Trolling

15

In October 2013, Teresa and Daniel were in downtown Aspen when they spotted an aging woman with a lined face, staring in the window of the Queen Bee salon, not far from the Hotel Jerome. She had dark hair and wore a darkish wool cape, not the usual outfit for the fashionable streets of Aspen. Next to her were several cases of cosmetics. As Teresa gazed at the woman, she thought she looked haggard, weighed down, and out of place in this setting.

Teresa had twenty-five years of training in tae kwon do, the Korean martial art that combines exercise with self-defense and combat techniques. Her training had taught her to have "eyes in the back of my head" when it came to assessing people and situations. On occasion she'd spied certain individuals in town and sensed trouble or danger swirling around them, feeling this strongly enough to call the local police and have the people questioned. More than once, her instincts had been right; they *were* troubled or on the verge of starting trouble. On this particular afternoon, watching the figure staring in the Queen Bee window, she experienced something similar.

"Oh, my," the woman said, turning to Teresa and approaching her, "your hair is so beautiful."

Teresa knew it wasn't true—her unkempt blond locks were blowing in the autumn wind and she badly needed a haircut.

She asked the woman if she trimmed hair, but the answer was no. She'd come to Aspen looking for a job in a spa.

"I do facials and things like that," Nancy Styler explained to her.

What she didn't say was that a few months earlier she'd traveled to Aspen with her husband and tried to launch herself in town by working at Queen Bee's. She already had a connection there, having attended the beauty school of Rita Bellino, the salon's owner. When Nancy had asked Rita if she could do her treatments at Queen Bee's, the salon owner was open to the idea. She let Nancy bring in her equipment, but it wasn't long before she wondered if she'd made a mistake. Her new employee was loud with customers, too aggressive, and constantly touting her skills in cosmetics, Botox, skin care, sewing, jewelry making, upholstery, and other areas. She suggested painting one of the walls pink, but Rita felt that the salon was pink enough. While Nancy kept her husband waiting outside in the car for long periods of time, she filled up Queen Bee's with her machines and her personality.

"It was too much, too fast," Rita once told the police. "I felt a bit imposed on by her. I said, 'Nancy, calm down. This is Aspen. People want you to be an expert at what you do. Don't be talking to the clients about all your personal stuff... They want you to put their eyelashes on. That's all they care about.'"

Another problem was her clothing: Nancy dressed too loud for Aspen—mostly in purple or all in turquoise. And she kept bringing more and more things into the salon, including blankets and pillows, while Trey waited out in the car. Style was important in town, especially if one wanted to do business with the wealthy. A woman's wardrobe was as much a status symbol as a car or a house with a prestigious Aspen address. Local fashion ran the gamut from East Coast preppy to European haute couture to high-end western, but all of it had to be contemporary and chic. Nancy Styler, try as she might, was once described as "more Vegas than Aspen."

And the blankets and pillows, said Rita, were "like stuff she'd gotten from Target. Really tacky stuff."

When Rita told her to remove the items, Nancy got irritated, but offered to make things right by giving the salon owner a special microdermabrasion treatment. Rita didn't feel that Styler was qualified to do this, or at least not on her, and said she should try it out first on "some girls that work in restaurants." That remark left Nancy more irritated. When she announced to Rita that she wanted to start a Queen Bee mobile service outside the salon and run it on her own, the end was near.

"She knew I had great clients, wealthy clients," Rita has recounted, "and she wanted to get her fingers in there."

Nancy never actually started working in the business, even though it had taken her weeks to put her equipment in place at the salon. Just as quickly as she'd decided to join Queen Bee's, she pulled out and began looking for other places to ply her trade. According to Rita, she didn't need much help in clearing out the space she'd been occupying.

"She's a very strong woman," Rita has said, "physically strong. She was lifting the heavy stuff by herself. Trey was around, but he can't even walk... He doesn't say too much. Kinder and gentle-spirited... She ran the show."

On that windy October afternoon in downtown Aspen, Teresa and Daniel spoke briefly with Nancy Styler and then Daniel, known for his friendliness, gave her his business card and they parted. The encounter lingered with Teresa; when she thought about it during the coming weeks she felt that Styler had been deliberately standing in the middle of town on that cool day, waiting for someone to pass by, trolling for business connections and looking for anyone to latch on to.

Because Daniel and Teresa had been out of touch with Nancy Pfister lately, they didn't know that she was searching for someone to rent her home while she spent the winter in Australia. Two months earlier, she'd sent out a mass e-mail to friends and acquaintances: "I would love to rent or trade my Tibetan ski chalet long term on Buttermilk Mtn. please let me know if anyone has warm water climate with a great dog friendly place for longer term, oct through August..."

On October 14, 2013, she sent out another one: "Please help me find a great renter for my home."

This wasn't producing results so she placed an ad for her residence in the *Aspen Times*.

The Stylers, who'd come up from Denver and were staying in town at a condo while trying to find housing, saw the ad on October 16. Nancy Styler immediately called the number.

"I was just out in the greenhouse watering," Pfister told her on the phone, after they'd introduced themselves.

"Greenhouse?" Nancy Styler said, the word evoking some of the best memories of her past life in Greenwood Village, where she was the star of the neighborhood because of her outsize water lilies. "That's my thing."

"Really?"

"I grow organic vegetables."

"Well, I'm an organic gardener."

The women sensed an instant connection.

Pfister told Nancy Styler that another couple was about to come view the house, so if they were interested they needed to act.

"You sound like a good match for me," she added.

"We've had a big house," Styler told her. "We know how to respect nice things. We'd be a good match for you. We're solid people."

"Then get over here right now."

She hung up, herded Trey out to the car, and they quickly drove up West Buttermilk Road.

Pfister greeted them in a bathrobe, holding a glass of pink champagne and ushering them inside.

"Oh, my god," Nancy Styler said, looking around at the house, which wasn't flashy, but a very comfortable three-bedroom, three-bathroom, 4,102-square-foot home, with more than enough space for the couple. The only potential problem was that one had to negotiate two stairways to get into the house and up to the master bedroom, where the Stylers would be sleeping if they rented the property. For years Trey had told people that on some days he could barely walk without a wheelchair, but this didn't seem to be an issue now. There was no holding his wife back.

"This is incredible," she said to Pfister. "I love it!"

As a landlady, Nancy Pfister was a veteran at renting out her home, but not much experienced in negotiating firm deals with written contracts. A verbal agreement and a handshake had long been good enough for her. She and the Stylers seemed compatible and she was ready to talk business.

To seal their arrangement for the winter, she wanted $12,000 in cash. That included the first month's rent of $4,000, the last month's rent of $4,000, and a security deposit of the same amount. The Stylers agreed to these terms and also offered to pay $300 a month for the use of Pfister's Prius.

Pfister explained to them that after she left the country for Australia, they'd give their monthly rent money to Kathy, who'd put it in Pfister's safe deposit box at Alpine Bank, where Carpenter worked. They'd also be expected to pay the utility bills through Kathy.

The couple agreed to all the conditions. Then their new landlady brought up her dog.

This past July, Pfister had gotten Gabe, her young black labradoodle. While she was spending the next six months away from home, a trainer was supposed to start working with Gabe in Arizona, but that plan had gotten derailed after the dog had gone on a rampage at Jack Nicholson's house and ended up in his hot tub. The trainer was present when Gabe had dived into the water and had decided then and there not to take the labradoodle to Arizona because he was too much work. Kathy, whose fondness for the dog probably surpassed everyone else's, was greatly relieved. She wanted Gabe in Aspen for the winter because she'd be his part-time caretaker.

Pfister asked the Stylers if they would mind watching the dog while she was abroad, but just during the week. Could they keep him in her house Monday through Thursday and hand him to Kathy on Friday evenings for weekend duty? Although Trey, with no prompting, bluntly described himself as not being a "dog person," he and his wife also agreed to this plan.

During their first conversation in Pfister's home, the labradoodle got hold of Trey's camera and began chewing it, along with his wife's phone, and whatever else he could get his teeth into. They were so thrilled to have found Nancy Pfister and to be moving into her home that they pretended not to be annoyed.

As they were finalizing their arrangements, Pfister made a pronouncement about the three of them coming together so quickly and solving each other's problems.

"It's karma, darling," she said.

The Stylers nodded and smiled.

Pfister invited them to start moving in their things (which included spa equipment and industrial sewing machines) before she flew to Australia on November 22. In return, the couple could help her pack for her trip. As the Stylers prepared to leave that day, already making plans to drive to Denver and retrieve the rest of their belongings, Pfister told them, "You can stay in the room downstairs. You can do your spa work here and in the other room you can put your sewing stuff... I'm a Buddhist. I have no attachment to physical possessions. You can take my furniture and put it in the garage. Do what you want with it."

Nancy Styler couldn't believe their good fortune. Sometime later, when she remembered her feelings at that moment in Pfister's home, she said, "I thought, that's cool. A nice gig if you can get it."

16

Not long after the Stylers decided to move into 1833 West Buttermilk Road, Teresa got a call from Pfister, who was standing inside her house with a visitor.

"Guess who I have here?" Nancy asked Teresa.

"Who?"

"You won't believe who's with me right now!"

"Who *is* it?" Teresa said.

She handed the phone to Nancy Styler.

"Guess what?" she said to Teresa, explaining who she was and what she was doing at the Pfister residence.

Gradually, Teresa came to the realization that she was speaking with the tired-looking woman whom she and Daniel had had a strange encounter with in front of Queen Bee's on that windy October day.

"Now," Nancy Styler told her over the phone, "I have the money to *open* a spa!"

Teresa, whose instincts were again on high alert, remembered that Nancy Styler had said that she'd been looking for a job in a spa—not to open a business. Something had obviously changed and she now had the resources to run her *own* shop. Teresa didn't say anything, but her stomach muscles had tightened.

Oh no, Nancy, she thought, already feeling concern for her friend. *Don't tell me you got involved with this woman.*

She had, and who could be surprised? Wasn't it just like Nancy Pfister to jump into something new, hardly getting to know the situation or the other people at all? She'd been doing this for years, decades, with strangers and strange men, and nothing had ever gone wrong. She'd done it with business ventures and never been seriously burned, or at least not seriously enough to make her break this pattern. She'd told Teresa and Daniel that she'd helped start Takah Sushi, one of Aspen's most popular restaurants, and then cashed out her interest. She'd talked about launching a café right next to her house; it would be perfect for the cross-country skiers who used her property to begin their treks into the mountains. She wanted Teresa and Daniel to partner with her in this venture, but they sensed it wasn't a good idea and backed away as gracefully as they could.

After Teresa and Nancy Styler chatted on the phone, the latter handed the receiver back to Pfister, but Teresa couldn't stop thinking about what she'd just heard. How was it possible that Nancy Styler, who only weeks earlier had looked destitute, had come into enough money to open a spa? Where could the funds have come from—other than Nancy Pfister?

This brief conversation with Nancy Styler would haunt Teresa for months, and then even longer.

"It's entirely plausible," she says, "that my friend Nancy loaned them some money for what they were going to do in her house. She may have later held their spa equipment as collateral against the loan—and that could be where the problems really started."

Following Pfister's murder, Teresa was convinced that sooner or later somebody in law enforcement, from either the Pitkin County Sheriff's Office or from the local district attorney's office, would call or come knocking on her door to interview her about the crime and the four principals around it. She knew or was at least aware of three of them: Pfister herself, Kathy Carpenter, and Nancy Styler. In the past few years, she'd interacted numerous times with Nancy and Kathy inside the former's home and beyond. Then there was that odd encounter with Styler in downtown Aspen and the subsequent phone call.

Teresa waited a long time, but no one in authority reached out to her or sought her views. She began to believe that if she didn't speak up, Pfister might never receive justice as a homicide victim and the truth behind her murder might never come out. If she did in fact know something about the case and if she didn't try to convey it to the authorities, she could never live with herself and the resulting guilt. Didn't she have an obligation to share anything she may have known or observed or perceived?

She finally called the DA's office herself and spoke to Deputy District Attorney Scott Turner, one of the prosecutors on the Pfister homicide. He listened politely and seemed to agree with some of what she said about how no one person could have murdered Nancy and put her body in the closet—and how no one who was disabled would have ever moved into the Pfister residence, with its multiple levels and staircases. She felt there had to have been more in play between Pfister and the Stylers than just a spat over the rent, but Turner didn't appear interested in pursuing her hunches.

"My sense," says Teresa, "was that they'd made up their minds early on about the case and didn't want to hear anything else."

When Rita Bellino, the owner of Queen Bee's, learned that the Stylers were moving into Nancy Pfister's house, she had a similar reaction to Teresa's. She knew Pfister quite well—well enough so that when Pfister had given one of her pet dogs too many treats and it had developed diarrhea and soiled the carpets all over her residence, she felt no compunction about calling Rita and asking for help in cleaning up the mess (while asking her mother, Betty, to pay for this).

"That's probably not a good combination," Rita has said about the two Nancys sharing living space for any length of time. "Nancy Styler is very strong and Nancy Pfister is an alcoholic and can be moody. I didn't think that would go together."

After Pfister was murdered, the police interviewed Rita and she gave them her assessment of the crime.

"I don't think Trey was involved in anything," she said. "He was, if anything, just trying to protect his wife... The guy can't even stand up. He's physically not capable of anything. I think she's very smart. If they wanted to get away from here, they would have left [the Aspen area], but by staying here it makes them look like they're not guilty."

Nancy Styler, Rita went on, is "intense. He was always waiting on her, waiting in the car, waiting on her decisions . . . He looked at her like she was Miss America."

17

Nancy Styler loved living with a greenhouse. As a master grower herself, she felt that moving into the Pfister residence was like coming home. The place was perfect and to her delight her new landlady was also becoming her friend. Pfister was so lively, so open with them—so generous and nice. The two women made big plans for the future.

Nancy Styler was also "very nice," according to people who'd interacted with her in suburban Denver. The interior decorators who'd worked on her home said that about her, as did those in the medical community, in the cosmetics business, and in horticultural circles in the Mile High City. She was very nice to those she opened her home to and entertained, especially the kids, and Trey was nice, too, except when his temper flared in the hospital or in meetings with lawyers.

Besides gardening and greenhouses, the two Nancys shared an interest in travel and holistic medicine. Pfister was exactly the kind of person Nancy Styler had hoped to meet in Aspen—an interesting native with lots of connections and resources. The Stylers knew very little about their landlady or how the Pfister family had been instrumental in creating Buttermilk Mountain as a ski resort. They didn't know how much money Art had made from this and other investments, or how he'd protected those assets not just when he was alive, but after he and Betty were dead. They didn't know that the Pfister sisters weren't free spenders, but on a tight leash controlled by the law firm of Garfield & Hecht. They couldn't have known that they were getting involved with someone who didn't have access to nearly as much money as she pretended to, and someone who really needed their monthly cash payments.

Likewise, Nancy Pfister had no real understanding of what the Stylers had been through during the past decade. She might have known a little about their medical history, but not the details of their legal struggles in Denver, which had started more than ten years earlier. She didn't know how much money the couple had spent or lost since Trey had inherited substantial sums or how quickly the assets had evaporated. She didn't know how bitter Trey was about his recent dealings with attorneys or how much he still thought he was owed from one in particular. The Stylers were so relieved to have met Pfister and so happy to be moving into her home that for the moment their past faded and they could finally relax.

All that mattered now was that Pfister had paying tenants and the couple had a place to stay and run their business from. Who cared that 1833 West Buttermilk Road wasn't zoned for a commercial enterprise? If you were Aspen royalty and well connected at the sheriff's office, you didn't have to worry about such trivialities. Pfister had always found ways of sidestepping the minor inconveniences or rules in her hometown. She wasn't subject to the things others were, like the service people who commuted from Down Valley to their jobs in Aspen. Among her friends, Pfister jokingly referred to nearby Carbondale as "Carb-*andale*," as in the Spanish word *andale*—the only place where South-of-the-Border emigrants or others in the working class could afford to live.

The elitism of Aspen was never as obvious as when it came to one's physical location, and you hadn't arrived until you occupied a mailing address in Pitkin County. One of Nancy Pfister's e-mail handles was dirtyblondezg @aol.com, the "zg" signifying the coveted two letters on a Pitkin County license plate (not unlike the zip code 90210 for residents of Beverly Hills). Even online, she constantly reminded everyone that she was an Aspen native.

In any tourist town, tension exists between the locals' desire for the money that visitors bring in and having to deal with those intruders face-to-face. This was especially true in small, isolated mountain towns, where newcomers or *arrivistes* were often looked upon with a certain suspicion, if not disdain.

Says one longtime Aspenite, "Outsiders come here because they're attracted to the lifestyle, the wealth, the beautiful weather, and the culture. They want to be part of it. But it's hard to gain a foothold on this little island. Some people come with money, egos, dreams, and the belief that they can fit in. In most cases, it doesn't work out that way. They come and go around here, but the mountains endure. The Aspen envisioned by Walter and Pussy Paepcke and the ideals of the Aspen Institute collide with harsh reality."

Says a woman who worked in the Aspen service industry in the late 1970s and early '80s, "We'd always look for places where the tourists wouldn't go, just to escape them for a while. The people who come to Aspen are usually privileged and act entitled and if they get in trouble, they have the money to get out of it. This behavior and attitude get old really fast.

"Once a month, we'd dress up and go to a movie theatre on Main Street and watch porn films. We had noisemakers and had a great time getting away from the invaders. While the tourists were out dancing at clubs, we'd go to the Rocking Horse Bar in the basement of the Jerome and do cocaine in the bathroom. This was in Hunter Thompson's heyday, when he was shooting at everybody out in Woody Creek. One time I was pedaling past his place at Owl Farm on my bicycle and he came out and fired a shotgun right over my head. Scared the living shit out of me. I thought he was trying to kill me."

Because of Aspen's enormous wealth, the fear of gold diggers was even more pronounced. You couldn't walk into town and get invited to the A-list parties unless you had a tremendous reputation or vast financial resources or knew someone who was a native or, even better, Aspen royalty. In years past, Nancy Pfister had traveled in the community's highest circles, but the seventies, eighties, and nineties were long gone now. Many of her friends had gotten married, had children, and settled down or moved on from the hard-partying lifestyle. She never had and because of this some old acquaintances now kept her at arm's length, or further, never quite certain how she might behave in public.

She'd begun developing friendships with those on a lower social level, like Kathy Carpenter. In the snobbish world of Aspen, there were people who also distanced themselves from Nancy because of her new associations.

"Everybody liked and enjoyed Nancy," says a Denver private detective who once lived in Aspen, "but at the same time they were cautious with her."

Everybody, that is, except for people who knew nothing about the community or the Pfister family or Nancy herself. In meeting the vivacious woman up on West Buttermilk Road, the Stylers believed that they'd settled into a "mountain oasis." This impression only deepened after Pfister took them to parties around town and introduced them to people with money and more connections, people they could never otherwise have met. Here was the "wonderful opportunity" that had eluded them for so long. With their living quarters stabilized, Nancy Styler could finally start working and making money. She'd brought in her spa equipment, her several tubs of sewing material, and her sewing machines, along with her jewelry-making tools. She'd perform facials and other cosmetic services for customers in the Pfister home—a perfect setup because in Aspen it was especially important to conceal the work done on your face, the Botox injections or fillers. Concierges would quietly drive guests up to the house from Aspen's finest hotels; it would be much more private and discreet to do this kind of thing a few miles outside of town rather than near Main Street, where people might see you and start to gossip. Two rooms on the bottom floor could hold Nancy Styler's work area, but Pfister was already talking about building an addition onto the house to accommodate the new business. In return, she'd get a piece of the action.

To celebrate their future success, Pfister opened a bottle of champagne and, as Trey once put it, "We had a symbolic toast to our new friendship and our new relationship... We thought we'd struck gold."

The Stylers soon got a taste of Pfister's dizzying lifestyle. On a flight into Aspen, she'd just met a Hollywood producer and told the Stylers that the man had recently done *The Dallas Buyers Club.* Pfister bragged about wanting to invest in his next film, but had another agenda: she hoped the producer would give her daughter, Juliana, a job in L.A.

While preparing her landlady for her trip to Australia, Nancy Styler altered Pfister's clothes and tried to be helpful in other ways. In the afternoons or evenings, Pfister would usually leave the house, come back around nine p.m., and always seemed high. The couple, despite some misgivings about her alcohol intake, began meeting her for drinks at the Hotel Jerome and its famous J-Bar.

On Halloween night, the trio got dressed up—Nancy as a geisha, Trey in a Russian military uniform, and Pfister donning a prison outfit.

The former doctor was awkwardly trying to play the Aspen hipster, in order to stay in his landlady's good graces until she was finally out of the house. The physician who'd once had all the money he'd needed was now scraping to get by, in part to satisfy his wife's desire to live in Aspen and tend to wealthy ladies and their whims. Some of the stress that Trey had tried to keep at bay was creeping back in, but he did his best to disguise it. For years he'd felt bad that he hadn't been able to support his wife in the manner she was accustomed to. It had fallen on Nancy to take up the slack, getting odd jobs wherever she could to pay the bills and to hold things together. Trey felt bad about that too.

On Halloween Bob Braudis showed up at the Jerome, joined their party, and for tonight anyway, the good times were rolling. Before long, the Stylers gave Pfister a first payment of $6,000, while promising her the other $6,000 as soon as they could come up with it.

“Rub My Fingers!”

18

Despite the couple's best intentions, trouble started before their landlady left for Australia.

"Most people who had only a casual relationship with Nancy Pfister," says Aspen PI David Olmsted, "didn't know her well enough to be abused by her. Only the people who got to know her better had that experience. When the Stylers first met her, they really thought she was their friend. They believed this right up until they became her tenants."

Once Pfister had their initial $6,000 payment, Nancy Styler would later tell the police, she became dramatically different.

"While I was getting her ready for her trip..." Nancy Styler said, "she was nice. She treated me as an equal... We went to the Redstone Inn and hot springs together. She said she'd introduce us to people we should know... For two days she was good until she got our money and the deal was sealed and then she treated me like a slave! It was, 'Darling, get my champagne, rub my feet, rub my neck, rub my fingers!' "

She also asked Trey to rub her back and shoulders. And she boasted about the money her family had made from selling off parts of Buttermilk Mountain. What had seemed to Nancy Styler like a budding friendship suddenly turned into subtle warfare, an Aspen version of *Upstairs, Downstairs* or *Downton Abbey*. If this was galling for both Stylers, it was especially so for Nancy Styler, who'd once known the feeling of being the grande dame of her Greenwood Village neighborhood. Not long ago, she and Trey had lived in a four-bedroom home of just under 6,000 square feet. Built in

1983, the house sat on 1.14 acres and had magnificent gardens spread across the backyard. In 2012, the property had sold for $840,000 in a Denver market still recovering from the Great Recession. By contrast, Nancy Pfister's home, built in 1990, had just over 4,000 square feet, had three bedrooms, and a price tag of around $4 million in 2014. The house may have cost nearly five times what the Stylers' previous residence did, but it was considerably smaller and had less curb appeal.

The trouble deepened when Pfister planned a going-away party for herself on November 16, six days before she was to fly to Australia.

"Come to my party on the sixteenth," she told folks around town. "It's going to be all A-list people."

Initially, the gathering was supposed to raise money for the next film of the Hollywood producer she'd recently met. This fell apart after Pfister asked him to pay for the party, being held in her home, which resulted in a shouting match on the telephone.

"Fuck you," she told him. "You're trying to jerk us around."

Then she began telling people that the celebration would generate funds for a crisis in the Philippines; the rationale for the party changed from day to day. As November 16 approached, Pfister hired some maids to clean the house and expected the Stylers to pay for half of this.

"We're not even living there yet," Nancy Styler later told the police. "The maids haven't done a great job [because] I found dead mice downstairs in the room we were staying in."

Despite her reservations about the money and the mice, Styler told Pfister not to worry, she'd help her clean for the party. But time was tight because the couple was still traveling back and forth to Denver to get their possessions and finish the move to Aspen.

According to Nancy Styler, every time she'd leave for Denver, Pfister would tell her, "'You little scoundrel, I need you here to work!' When she got me up there, it was, 'Do this, do that, hold the dog like this, not like that, get this, don't do that' . . . She disabled the ice machine . . . The dishwasher didn't work: 'You can just wash 'em by hand.' Four thousand dollars a month and I don't have ice, a dishwasher, a dirty house. I said to my husband, 'I don't know if I can take this woman. She's really crazy and really drunk . . .' "

The Stylers paid around $1,000 for four cases of champagne for the party and chipped in another $600 for the caterer. They expected to deduct these costs from the rent.

"She went through the cases of champagne we'd brought up before the party," Nancy Styler later told investigators. "I'm deducting this from the cash we were going to give her... When we brought the last cases for the party she said to Trey, 'Oh, so this is your donation to the party!' He was dumbfounded... We're not in great financial shape. You know it, we've told you, but rather than start trouble, he said to me, 'She's going to be gone, Nance. We'll hang in there...'"

After a long two weeks together, Pfister was ready to leave for Australia. Nancy Styler was enlisted to help her pack her clothes and her copious bags of pills, while Trey would drive her the nearly five-hour trip to the airport east of Denver. She'd taken so many drugs that she barely spoke to him on the ride, sleeping most of the way. Trey had to order a wheelchair to take her to her gate.

With her out of the house and out of the country, the Stylers thought they could relax and settle into their new home. Nancy would work on her spa business and Trey would assist in any way possible.

Almost as soon as Pfister arrived in Australia, she alleged from Down Under that Nancy Styler had bought clothes with her credit card and hadn't paid her back. One morning Nancy Styler turned on the water for a bath and black liquid came squirting out of the nozzle; the water heater was broken. The Stylers would have to go through Pfister's trust to get the money to hire local handyman Merlin Broughton to fix the problem. They wouldn't have a working heater for the next four weeks. How could they open a spa if the water in the house was filthy?

From Australia, Pfister demanded they give her the $6,000 she still felt she was owed. Three weeks after leaving Aspen, she began making threats via the Internet about tossing them out of her home.

On December 12, 2013, she e-mailed Trey, "Nancy [S.] charged almost $670 to my card... expect to hear from my lawyer! U guys have a lot of nerve to move in with no payments, making me upset, I have other people to take care of Gabe, better get a moving truck and return to Denver."

Trey was stunned by Pfister's tone and her accusations. They'd barely had a chance to settle in and now she was trying to undermine their stability and all their plans. He decided that he didn't want to communicate directly with her any longer—she was too volatile—so he started writing and calling her Aspen lawyer, John Beatty. In mid-December, Beatty informed the couple that they had three days to pay what they still owed Pfister or the attorney would commence proceedings to evict them.

On December 17, Trey realized the seriousness of Beatty's words and tried to lower the tension by e-mailing the lawyer and apologizing "for losing my temper on the phone today ... for anything personally offensive I may have said in the heat of passion ... Ms. Pfister was fully aware of our financial situation ... and had agreed to allow some flexibility and informality, and finally, my recent legal experiences have involved highly immoral and corrupt attorneys ... these people have robbed my family of over a half million dollars ..."

In late December, the Stylers rectified the conflict, at least in their own minds, by giving Kathy Carpenter the second payment of $6,000 in cash, plus an additional $650 for utilities. The money had come from a loan from a friend in Texas. They were expecting another $10,000 check soon. Having given the funds to Kathy, they believed they were free and clear until the next payment was due.

On the last day of 2013, the Stylers and their landlady communicated again, and Pfister suggested that they find another place to stay—by going Down Valley and living in a trailer. It was poignant moment for the aging couple. The Stylers were not only angry, but deeply hurt, realizing just how far they'd fallen since their heyday in Denver and just how shaky things had become. Nancy Pfister wasn't their friend—she was hostile, snarky, and threatening everything they'd hungered for when relocating to Aspen.

Hadn't they given her the money they owed her? They had, but for some reason it hadn't made any difference and she was still enraged with them.

19

On January 1, 2014, Trey wrote John Beatty again: "At this time, we don't feel we can trust her [Nancy Pfister], or rely on anything she says (to us or to you). That is why we have requested assurances from her that she intends to honor the original agreement. I don't believe that any such assurances were present in her statements regarding her intentions. I hope that she will provide them, as we will not continue to live and work here without them.

"To clarify any issues regarding rent due, as I explained to Kathy Carpenter today: 'Just to be clear, we have paid you $12,000, representing first month, last month, and security (we hope).' As you know, we did not get possession of the house until Nov. 22, 2013."

Three days later, Nancy Pfister wrote to Carpenter: "Kathy, the deal is there is no lease signed, they moved in about October 15, so they were living in my house and moving shit from Denver into my house starting early so they have to pay, where is the money for this month's rent and then next month then you know they are not going to get back the damage deposit because they've taken advantage of my generosity, all I can say is Trey is lying about the lease. Where is the 585$ for the use of my credit card to buy her clothes??? They have had heaps of electronics plugged in sense mid-October when they did begin using the room downstairs!!!"

Pfister went on Facebook to tell people in Aspen and beyond that her tenants couldn't get their monthly payments together or cover their utility expenses and they weren't even taking good care of Gabe. Trey was her Facebook friend and aware of what she was sharing with others in a public forum, but that did nothing to stop Pfister's posts. She sent out pointed e-mails and texts, and her message was abundantly clear: the Stylers were "deadbeats," the worst possible development for people trying to launch a local business.

On January 7, Pfister wrote to her Facebook friends, "Love from down under I need a tenant for my Aspen house if you know anybody. Also need a dog sitter for my 8 month old Labradoodle... Happy new year."

She e-mailed Sheriff Joe DiSalvo and Bob Braudis about her ongoing problems with her tenants, saying that the couple wasn't living up to their agreement and seeking advice from the men about evicting them.

Aspen private investigator David Olmsted contends that the couple justifiably felt wronged:

"The Stylers paid Nancy some money before she left for Australia and then paid her some more in December. They were never paid back for the champagne they bought for Nancy's going-away party. This kind of maneuver was very typical of Nancy Pfister. Order the best of something, but don't pay the bill. Despite what's been widely reported in the media, the notion that the Stylers weren't paying their rent to Nancy is not accurate. In the past, renters had not given her a check every month. The arrangements Nancy made with people were always more vague than that."

Part of Kathy Carpenter's job was to collect the rent from tenants and deposit it for Pfister in a safe deposit box at Alpine Bank. Olmsted was not the first person to suggest that all of this money may not have found its way to Nancy Pfister.

"A property manager," he says, "who was watching her house while she was away could use this money for her own benefit, thinking she could pay Nancy back later on. A manager would have access to the cash or could make the checking account deposits. Kathy Carpenter seemed to have a lot of access to Nancy Pfister's personal property."

Trey had tried to explain to John Beatty that while he and Nancy may have been a little late with the rent, they'd eventually paid up. Yet none of this had softened Pfister's vitriol toward them.

On January 16, 2014, Trey sent another e-mail to Beatty: "I don't know why Ms. Pfister is distressed. Perhaps she expected more communication from us—but there is no cause for concern here... We recognize that we owe Ms. Pfister some money, and fully intend to pay fully. The $10,000 check we expected to receive last week has not arrived here in Aspen, and the moment it clears, Ms. Pfister will be paid in full."

He wrote again to Beatty: "There is no formal or written agreement of any kind (much less a lease) ever executed between, myself, my wife, and Ms. Pfister that would create any debt or obligation, much less a 'due date.' We believe that there should be no need for any formal actions, legal or otherwise (nor lawyer's fees for such). We expect to resolve the situation and Ms. Pfister's concerns before you could draft (much less resolve) any such."

With the conflict unresolved, Kathy regularly drove up to the Pfister residence and met with the Stylers, as they handed off the dog to Carpenter for the weekend. The trio gradually got to know one another and on occasion they indulged in lengthy "bitch sessions" about the current state of their lives. The more they talked, the more they discovered they had one thing in common: in some ways they were all dependent on Pfister and were always looking for the next dollar or the next plan to improve their station in life. Trey was too old and frail to work and Nancy's schemes for making money in Aspen hadn't developed as she'd hoped. Kathy was always hustling to pay her bills.

One day at work Kathy was having trouble breathing. Trey picked her up, gave her some epinephrine, a hormone and neurotransmitter, and took her to the emergency room. The epinephrine helped, and Kathy believed Trey had saved her life. After her stay in the hospital, Nancy invited Kathy to the house and gave her a makeover, straightening her hair and putting on eyelash extensions. The couple had even begun telling her that they loved her.

According to Kathy's comments to police, Trey asked her to use the knowledge she'd gained at Alpine Bank to look into some local accounts to see who had money in Aspen and how much. He was also interested in learning more about Pfister's finances and occasionally logged onto the laptop she'd left behind in the closet of her upstairs master bedroom. Pfister was always telling people that one day she'd write a book about her experiences in Aspen. Before leaving for Australia, she'd asked Trey to read over some journals on her computer so he could help her compose her life story, which she intended to call *My Mother Parked Her Helicopter in Our Driveway.*

Trey had the key to the upstairs closet and when Kathy saw him working on Pfister's computer in the master bedroom, it made her uncomfortable. He'd attached his computer to Pfister's through a cable, as if transferring information from one laptop to another. Kathy became worried and told Nancy in Australia that they should change both her passwords and the lock on the closet door. Nancy didn't want the Stylers rummaging through her closet; she asked Kathy to get her personal computer out of the house and to hire a local locksmith to change the lock. Kathy followed orders and had two copies of the key made, keeping one in Pfister's home and the other in her condo on Main Street.

On January 19, 2014, Kathy sent an e-mail to Nancy saying, "Your closet is locked I have the keys. Your computers are stored safely at my place."

Two days later, Pfister again wrote her friends: "I am still in Byron Bay [Australia]. I have just found most beautiful place on earth and I really want to buy it first of all I need somebody to rent my place in Aspen because the people that I was letting to did not come through they are out of there Feb. 22 I believe and I do not want to say much more."

In February 2014, Stewart Oksenham was a fifty-year-old, much-beloved photographer and editor of the *Aspen Times*. In addition to his writing, he'd shot a treasured series of photos of musicians performing in town: B. B. King, Ray Charles, Lyle Lovett, Carlos Santana, David Byrne, and Grateful Dead bassist Phil Lesh. On February 2, Oksenham killed himself by jumping off a bridge outside of town, leaving behind a wife and son. Pitkin County is small enough that every death of a local citizen becomes an intimate event and sends ripples of mourning and grief throughout Aspen and up and down the Roaring Fork Valley. The way that these stories are covered in town makes you feel that you know the deceased even if you never met the person.

Pitkin County's suicide rate is roughly double the rest of Colorado's and three times the national average. When this statistic comes up, people often talk about Aspen's substance-abuse issues, but also mention something less obvious. From all over the country or abroad, seekers come to the mountains looking for paradise. Undeniable physical beauty surrounds Aspen, but in some cases that doesn't solve their problems. When bliss fails to arrive, depression can set in.

"If you can't be happy here," goes the saying heard in the community, "where can you be happy?"

Some people's gradual disillusionment with Aspen, or with its isolated setting, especially in the winter, and or with its overwhelming presence of wealth—if you don't happen to have a lot of money yourself—can be debilitating.

Oksenham's suicide shook up a lot of people, including Nancy Pfister, half a world away. On February 6, she posted to her Facebook friends: "really sorry to hear about Stew. Still in shock! terrible tragedy, suicide!!!" Yet, Pfister was undeterred from her hunt for new tenants and continued the post, "Please rent my house someone, it's a great deal because it comes with my beautiful labradoodle Gabe, a very well-behaved gentle dog! I would like to travel until end of May or June . . . Kathy carpenter from alpine Bank will show anyone interested the ropes, watering greenhouse, Gabe's stuff, etc. Very easy to contact me via email, thanks in advance!!!

"The rent is 4 thousand a month plus utilities, which Kathy picks up at the Alpine Bank and deposits for me. It's Kathy's birthday if u know her, give her a shout out!!!"

In addition to sending out cyber-messages to her contacts in Aspen and elsewhere, Pfister reached out to her friend Patty Stranahan about changing her Australia plans and coming home early. If she decided to do this, she wondered if she could stay for a few weeks with the Stranahans before getting back into her own home. That would give everyone more time to deal with the rental situation, but this arrangement wasn't made and the conflict intensified.

On February 17, Trey wrote to Pfister: "You keep repeating your allegation that Nancy (Styler) never repaid for the clothes bought with your card. This is false. You were repaid in excess between the money paid to the caterer on your behalf and the more than $1000 spent buying you your special champagne (which was never intended to be a 'gift' to you). If you ever mention it again, we will make a list of the expenses we have incurred on your behalf, and require you to repay them all (beginning with the $500 plus for personal belongings destroyed by your dog, and the expenses of caring for him). Be careful what you ask for—you may get more than you expect."

Pfister fired back, "I'm coming home and don't be there. And if you have to get a hotel room you do that."

20

From Australia, Pfister e-mailed her friend Teresa Wyatt, saying that she was frightened by her troubles with the Stylers and she needed help with Gabe. She sent the same message to Bob Braudis and to Hunter Thompson's widow, Anita.

"I was copied," Braudis later told the police, "on scores of e-mails from Nancy bitching about their non-payment of rent, utilities, leaving her car out in the snow."

Sheriff DiSalvo was also aware of the dispute, but didn't think it was of a threatening nature. Nancy's friend, Michael Cleverly, was in the same position—he knew she was struggling with renters, but not the details.

From a distance, Teresa had watched Pfister's relationship with the Stylers evolve over the past several months and she had her own take on why things had so quickly gone sour. She felt that Gabe had played a critical role in what was happening between all of them—and what was about to happen. Pfister had long had the same attitude toward dogs that she'd had with certain people. She loved them as she'd loved her daughter when Juliana was a child, but when it was time for Nancy to pick up and leave Aspen on a whim, to fly off to Europe or Asia or the islands in the winter, someone else could take care of whatever she left behind. Somebody was always there to finish what she'd started.

While she was in Australia, on Monday through Friday afternoon, the Stylers watched Gabe and then Kathy drove up to the house to get him for the weekend. The exchange of the dog gave them time to talk and get to know one another.

Kathy and the Stylers, says Teresa, "would never have been thrown together without Gabe."

On February 18, after hearing from Kathy that Pfister was coming home four days from then on the twenty-second, the Stylers knew they had to act as quickly as possible. Trey went to Aspen's Alpine Bank, Kathy's employer, and applied for a loan, speaking to branch president Scott Gordon and asking him for an advance of between $25,000 and $50,000. He needed the money, he explained, to pay his first month's rent, last month's rent, and a security deposit on a new place to live because he and his wife had to vacate their current situation immediately. Some of the cash would also be used for a new business venture. In the course of their discussion, Trey confessed to Gordon that his landlady was mean and had mistreated him and Nancy—and if something were to happen to Nancy Pfister, that would be best for all involved.

Styler made a strong case for receiving financial assistance, but he had a low credit score, no assets other than his car, and was unemployed. His wife wasn't earning a living, either, so his loan application was denied. His long descent from upper-middle-class comfort into relative poverty, which had begun in Denver more than a decade earlier, was culminating in Aspen in the winter of 2014. His decision-making, considered excellent in the operating room, had failed him outside of a hospital setting. He'd been incapable of walking away from lawsuits when he still might have been able to collect on a settlement or avoid paying more attorney fees. Throughout all those years, he'd clung to the belief that eventually he'd collect what was owed him, but he never had.

In the aftermath of his rejection at the bank, Trey told Gordon that one of the options left to him was committing suicide. The remark was not off the cuff; it was clear that he'd thought about this from a financial point of view. In the past, he'd taken out a million-dollar life insurance policy on himself, which would ensure some security for his wife if he were found dead and she could collect the payout.

After getting rebuffed at Alpine Bank, Trey began calling his old contacts in the Denver medical community, frantically looking for a loan. His former colleagues at CAC wanted nothing more to do with him.

On February 19, Pfister announced that she'd be home in three days and the Stylers had that long to vacate her house and remove all of their possessions.

"I have never known anybody worse then [sic] you," she wrote the couple.

While they were certain that meeting this demand was basically impossible, they started looking for a moving van, storage locker, and a place to stay. They found a room at the Aspenalt Lodge, while trying to get their belongings, including their hundred thousand dollars' worth of spa equipment and five industrial sewing machines, out of Pfister's residence.

On February 20, Trey went to Aspen's W Jewelries and spoke with employee Steve Wiseley. Trey hoped to pawn a ring he'd given his wife for their tenth anniversary, a three-carat, pear-shaped diamond with two one-carat diamonds on either side. He told Wisely that he needed the money to open a spa at the Hotel Jerome. Wiseley informed him that the cut of the ring was out of fashion so the diamonds had lost some of their value. He made an offer, but Trey thought he was being lowballed. If he'd been discouraged walking into W Jewelries, he felt worse now; the ring was one of their few remaining assets and even it couldn't command much respect in the marketplace.

Sitting in front of Wiseley, he fell silent and hung his head, saying nothing for quite a while. This was not what the merchant was used to in Aspen and neither was what happened next. Styler began mumbling and threatening to kill himself, before getting up and shuffling out the door. In the coming months, Trey's son, Will, the Ph.D. candidate at the University of Colorado in Boulder, would try to sell the ring in Denver to raise money for his parents.

On February 21, Nancy Styler texted Kathy with a request intended to speed up their transition out of Pfister's house, because Kathy's Subaru had considerably more interior space than the Stylers' Jaguar.

"Could we switch cars tonite," she wrote, "so we can use your car to move with tomorrow give me a call when u are heading back Xo take some Advil for your arm."

By the morning of the twenty-second, Nancy Pfister was in the air, leaving Australia and returning to Aspen, changing her plans on the spur of the moment, as she was known for doing, deciding to deal with a problem that no one else had wanted to clean up for her. Neither Braudis, DiSalvo, nor Cleverly had volunteered for the job so she'd do it herself. She'd sweep in and resolve things quickly and find someone new to live in her home and there would still be enough winter left in Colorado for her to take off again. Folks like the Stylers were always showing up in town and trying to get closer to the people with money and to get some of it for themselves. They always wanted to take advantage of those who tried to help them...

Sometime later, Nancy Styler recalled Pfister's last communication with them in this way:

"She said to us, 'If you're not out of my house, then you have to book me a room at the Hotel Jerome and pay for all of my food and drink.' We called [the Jerome] and if it was $200 a night, that might be easier than us rushing, but they only had a $900/night room. I wasn't doing that for her... She left a message on my phone, 'Have my sheets ready on my bed. I've messed up my shoulder really bad, I just want to come home, get in my bed and be with my dog. You guys get out of there. Get a room.'"

The Stylers had initially told Kathy that they'd found a house to rent on Red Mountain and Kathy had passed this along to Pfister, heightening her expectation that the couple and their possessions would be gone when she got home, but the deal fell through.

"They never started packing..." Kathy later told the police. "I thought that was odd... I personally thought that they just planned on staying there... They said they had zero money and lost the money on Red Mountain...

"There was the drama, crying... They were really upset with her... She was unfair, unbelievable... They never started packing till the very end..."

According to Kathy, Trey asked her what Pfister would do if she got home and they were still there.

"That would get really ugly," she told him.

21

As Pfister flew into Sardy Field that wintry Saturday evening, the tarmac was relatively bare and the small airport quiet. During December's holiday season in Aspen and June's Food and Wine Classic, G-4 and G-5 private jets lined up at the terminal, bringing in the money-and-power crowd from around the nation and the globe. On those occasions, rows and rows of shiny black Escalades were parked at the airport, primed to take the celebrities and other VIPs to their destinations in town. Tonight there was no rush of activity, no push to get through the checkpoints. It was a good time for Nancy to return to the place she always came back to, no matter how far away she'd gone or how exciting or even dangerous some of the locales she'd visited. Among many other adventures, she'd smuggled marijuana into St. Croix, against the strongest possible advice from those who were close to her. Trouble had never reached Nancy—she'd lived as she'd wanted to and damn the consequences.

Earlier this evening, Trey had told Kathy that he was going to drive to the airport and pick up Pfister, but Carpenter had pushed back hard, saying everything she could think of to change his mind.

A few days later, Kathy would tell detectives that when she'd asked Trey why he was so hell bent to get Pfister at Sardy Field, it was Nancy Styler—not her husband—who'd answered this question with: "Because she needs to disappear forever. This is just a horrible woman. I never wanted to kill anyone like I want to kill her."

Kathy would later tell the authorities that she should have called the police that Saturday, but "I just thought they were speaking out of anger... They were running around slamming doors."

As Kathy and Trey argued about going to the airport, Pfister called Carpenter on her cell and demanded that she get the Stylers out of her house.

If the couple wasn't gone when she got back, she repeated, they'd have to book her a room at the Jerome, at around $900 a night. When Trey heard this, he reiterated that he *was* picking her up tonight.

Kathy relayed this to Pfister, who told her, "I don't want to see those fuckers. I want to see you and the dog."

After much persuasion, Kathy was able to talk Trey out of going to the airport and she picked up Pfister in the Stylers' Jaguar so they could continue putting their possessions into her roomier Subaru and return to the Aspenalt.

Later that night, Nancy Styler phoned Kathy to see if Pfister had made it home.

"Yeah," Carpenter told her, explaining that on the flight to Aspen Nancy had met two Australians and they'd followed the women to the house, helped them unload the luggage, and then left.

At the house, Kathy helped Pfister unpack and Nancy asked her to spend the night. Kathy was tired and conflicted about staying, but she said yes and they stayed up late watching videos and talking.

In the next few days, Kathy would tell investigators her version of what had happened after Pfister's return and how the two women had gotten along extraordinarily well. Before going to bed Saturday night, she recounted, they "made a pact that we would just love each other as sisters [because] she didn't have relationships with her sisters. I was her sister and... all she had and couldn't live without me... She sat down with me and hugged me, just so grateful to me for everything I've done, more so than she ever has been. She just shared that with me as I was unpacking her clothes... She told me just appreciated everything [and] gave me a big hug."

As Kathy had prepared for bed and Pfister settled into being home, she looked around at the Stylers' possessions still cluttering her space and texted one of her friends: "I have a big mess on my hands."

Then Pfister lay down, slipped plugs in her ears, and covered her eyes with a mask, eager to sleep off her jet lag.

In the morning, Kathy made Nancy breakfast and prepared to do some chores for her later in the day, after meeting with her Alcoholics Anonymous sponsor around noon.

By that Sunday, the Stylers had rented a moving van from Alpine Motors in Glenwood Springs and driven it to Pfister's residence to load up as much as they could. They didn't yet have a space in which to store their belongings, but Trey was certain he could find one in Basalt on Monday morning. While working on the lower floor of the house, they avoided their former landlady, who was above them in the master bedroom still trying to catch up on sleep.

From time to time she awakened and sent out more text messages, one of them going to her Aspen attorney, John Beatty, after the Stylers had left for the day:

"John my house is a total mess they [the Stylers] broke my bed putting it back in the room they deconstructed my entire house I can't find a thing I don't know if they've stolen stuff... they're not here and I think I should get a restraining order till I get $6100 that would be the last two months of the utilities..."

In early afternoon, Kathy met with Megan Mulligan, her AA sponsor. The two of them had been doing the twelve-step program together, with Megan assisting Kathy in each part of the process. They were working on setting boundaries with people, starting with Nancy Pfister. It had taken more than a few volatile incidents—some of them between Kathy and Nancy—to get Carpenter to acknowledge her drinking problem, go into AA, and then confront her own behavior and her earlier blowups with Pfister.

On February 11, 2006, the police had come to Carpenter's home after Kathy and her son Michael had gotten into a scrape over *his* drinking. When the cops showed up, he had scratches on his neck.

On December 29, 2009, the police were called out to Nancy Pfister's home at 11:20 p.m., after she accused Kathy of trying to break into her bedroom, where she was watching a movie. Nancy told the officers that Kathy was "having a mental breakdown" because that's what happened when she drank. Nancy wanted her out of the house, but Kathy kept trying to barge into her room.

Carpenter told the police that Nancy had been "using her" and that she couldn't go home to her Aspen condo because her son was there partying with his friends. She asked the officer to take her to jail so she could sleep it off. They resisted her suggestion and escorted her downstairs to another bedroom, but she quickly broke out and charged the cops and threatened to punch them so they'd be forced to take her into custody. They handcuffed Kathy and transported her to the jail, holding her in protective custody until she was sober enough to be released.

On July 11, 2010, Deputy Jim Hearn—who four years later would be the first person in law enforcement to come to 1833 West Buttermilk Road and see Pfister buried under a pile of sheets in her closet—was called out to the Pfister residence. Kathy had taken a "handful of pills," including prescription drugs and a sedative, and was reeling around the house, unsteady on her feet. She told Hearn that she hadn't tried to kill herself and that she hated Nancy Pfister. An ambulance took her to Aspen Valley Hospital.

On February 26, 2011, at 12:30 a.m., the police found Kathy at Paepcke Park in downtown Aspen, drunk in a snowbank. Again, they put her in protective custody. On August 4, 2011, the authorities received a call from her son, Michael, telling them that he'd received a call from his mother in San Francisco. She'd swallowed a number of pills because she "could no longer take it."

On November 20, 2011, she was found on the ground in Aspen, curled up near a white picket fence. Betty Pfister had died a few days before and Nancy and Kathy had been out drinking that night and talking about Betty's death and mourning their loss—until Nancy met a man and ran off with him.

Once more, Kathy landed in protective custody.

Megan Mulligan, Kathy's AA sponsor, told investigators that ever since Nancy Pfister had gone to Australia for the winter Carpenter had been spending a lot of time up on West Buttermilk Road. She knew that Nancy Styler had been giving Kathy beauty treatments and Megan was worried that Kathy was around the Stylers more than was "normal" or "reasonable." She'd later tell investigators that their interaction was "extreme" and that because Trey had once helped Kathy with a breathing problem, she felt indebted to him "for her life."

Megan also told police about the conflict between the Stylers and their landlady because, she said, Kathy had talked about this with her sponsor and even joked about the couple killing Pfister. Megan was very disturbed by this piece of information, letting Carpenter know that it wasn't funny and that if she'd heard discussions like this, she should go to the police.

When Kathy arrived at Megan's home that Sunday afternoon, Megan immediately sensed that something about her was "off." For one thing, Nancy Styler had given her a dramatic makeover involving hair treatment and eyelash extensions; the effect of all this was that Kathy had started to "feel creepy" to her sponsor.

Megan wasn't shy about confronting the situation.

"What's going on?" she asked Kathy.

"Oh, you know me so well," Carpenter said.

No, Megan replied, she didn't know her that well. What was happening with her to make her act so different?

Kathy avoided giving a straight answer.

It wasn't the response Megan wanted.

A feeling was "energetically" coming from Kathy that day that Megan had never picked up before.

Earlier, the two women had worked on setting boundaries. Now they'd arrived at the fourth step of the twelve-step process. The "Big Book" of AA describes the fourth step this way: "One of the requirements for sobriety is the need for confession of personality defects, a moral inventory, and step four is designed to be just this." The fourth step involved taking a personal inventory of all the things that had been done to you by others—along with all the things you'd done to them.

This was not "a fun process," Megan later explained to the police, but the point of it was to free yourself from repetitive, painful, and destructive emotional and psychological behaviors. Part of the fourth step was admitting to your sponsor that you felt resentment toward certain people. During their session that afternoon, Kathy confessed to Megan that Nancy Pfister was one of those individuals.

As the women moved through this exercise, Kathy began to waver and stall, which wasn't uncommon, given the difficulties of what they were doing together.

"My instinct told me there's something up with Kathy..." Megan recalled to officers. "There's something she doesn't want to look at."

By the end of the session, Megan's discomfort had grown stronger.

22

Leaving Megan that Sunday afternoon, Kathy met Trey near the Pfister residence so they could exchange cars. As the two of them parked beside one another and prepared to make the switch, Kathy began frantically looking for something, first in the Jaguar that she'd been driving and then in her Subaru, bending over to look around, getting down on her knees and searching on the floor, under the seats, and in the glove compartments.

"What are you doing?" he asked.

She'd lost a piece of paper and had to find it.

Before meeting with Trey on Sunday, Kathy had sat down with Pfister, who'd said to her, "When you pick up your car, tell them they better not come near my property or I'm going to get a restraining order...'"

As Trey watched Carpenter search for the paper, he was struck, as Megan Mulligan had been an hour earlier, by how nervous, overwrought, and even afraid Kathy seemed. In the Jaguar, she finally located what she was looking for—an envelope with some scribbling on it, the words spelling out Pfister's latest round of demands on the Stylers. She was asking them to pay $4,000 for her to hire someone to rearrange the furniture in her house, once they'd finally moved out (four days later, Trey would admit in his first interview with the Colorado Bureau of Investigation that when Pfister was returning from Australia, he'd wanted to arrange her furniture in a way that would anger her, but his wife had overruled him and hadn't let him do this).

On the envelope, Pfister had written that they'd chipped or broken her bed, which they'd slept in while she was gone, so they'd have to buy her a new one. After listing a few more demands, she'd concluded that they owed her a total of $14,000—in back rent, utilities, and money for snowplowing, etc.—money that she had to have before releasing all of their belongings back to them. Once she had this amount in hand, they were free to get on with their lives without any more interference from her or her lawyer.

Carpenter handed Trey the envelope, which he briefly studied. He looked at Kathy with bewilderment, then disbelief, and then disgust.

Since learning that Pfister was on her way back to Aspen, he and his wife had been trying to resolve the problem by getting out of her home as quickly as they could. They'd rented a truck, were in the process of looking for a storage space in Basalt, and had thought that once the move was behind them, their troubles with their ex-landlady would go away. Now she was holding their possessions hostage and asking for money they didn't have. Now she was taking steps that were not only putting more stress and pressure on Trey, but also on his wife, whom he was already worried about.

Kathy could see how upset he was.

"I'm just the middle person here," she said to him, according to what she later told the police. "I hate being involved, but Nancy wanted me to give this note to you. You owe this money and you are not allowed on the premises and you will not be able to come and retrieve any of your personal belongings until this is rectified. Why don't you guys call or e-mail and just try to work it out. I'm really sorry."

"The bitch is crazy," Trey said. "I'm going to sue her for half a million—for every fucking dime she has."

If Pfister wanted to play games with him, he went on, he had a lot of experience with lawsuits and was more than willing to go down that road with her. The couple had grounds to sue her for breach of promise, libel, slander, and maybe some other things. As a veteran of courtroom wars, he'd gladly enter into this one... if she pushed him any further.

He got in the Jaguar and drove off, returning to the Aspenalt and telling Nancy about Pfister's new demands. He knew that his wife would react badly and tried to soften the message, saying that these were idle threats and Pfister couldn't get the $14,000 from them. In the next few days, they'd find a way to retrieve all of their possessions and begin their lives anew, in a different location, with this nightmare behind them. He spoke very carefully to Nancy, worried about her own "suicidal leanings," as he would soon put it. She'd been even more depressed lately than he had, more crushed by what had happened between them and Pfister.

Despite Trey's efforts to bolster his wife, she responded worse than he'd expected: they were finished in Aspen, with basically no resources and nowhere else to go. They were defeated and too old to start over…

Trey gently disagreed, trying to stay positive. They'd already begun looking for another place to live on the Roaring Fork River, by Ruedi Reservoir. They had plans to visit the house tomorrow afternoon and speak with the owner. All they had to do was get their very expensive sewing machines and spa equipment out of Pfister's home, find a new rental, and they could relaunch themselves in Pitkin County. Their dream wasn't dead; they just needed to get away from Pfister and out of the Aspenalt. He couldn't let his wife slide any deeper into despair, and was committed to offering her the same kind of support she'd been providing him for years. She'd taken care of him and protected him and become the breadwinner for their family, and now it was his turn to keep her from letting go of hope. In the past, he'd let down both her and their son and he didn't want to do that again. Her stress compounded his own discomfort and he needed to find a way to relieve it.

After giving Trey the envelope, Carpenter returned to Pfister's house, which had no groceries. Pfister gave Kathy her credit card, along with a specific set of orders, and sent her off to shop at Aspen's downtown City Market, while Pfister went back to sleep. Kathy was instructed not to be gone too long, not to spend more than $100 on food, and to bring back the receipt. While she was at the store, Pfister called and reiterated these things, telling Kathy to put the supplies away in the kitchen.

Pfister was a notoriously finicky eater, so Kathy diligently picked out the things she knew Nancy would enjoy, swinging by Whole Foods and buying salmon. After driving up West Buttermilk Road, she went into the master bedroom, where Nancy was still in bed, and gave Pfister her credit card and the receipt. Nancy asked her to get her some pills from her nightstand, and she did, also bringing her a cup of tea. Kathy unpacked the groceries. By now it was evening and she was more than ready to go home.

Nancy again asked her to stay the night.

Carpenter was tired, after a long weekend of dealing with the Stylers and running errands for her friend. She hesitated in answering.

"Please, Kathy, stay here," she said.

"Well, I have to work tomorrow."

"Please stay here. You can even sleep in the bed with me."

"Oh, Nance," she said, giving in. "I'll sleep in the living room on the couch. You get a good night's rest."

According to what Kathy would soon tell investigators, the two women watched TV in Nancy's bedroom for a while and Pfister once more made a point of thanking Kathy for all she'd done for her recently, especially during the conflict with the Stylers. She'd kept her informed about the couple while Nancy was in Australia and had acted as the intermediary since she'd come home.

"I love you," Pfister told her, hugging Kathy before going to bed alone.

Exhausted, Kathy fell asleep with Gabe on the living room sofa.

As Sunday night became Monday morning, Officer Joshua Bennett picked up Trey for speeding across the Midland Bridge in Basalt in his Jaguar sedan. It was 12:15 a.m. and the officer told Styler to produce his driver's license and registration. Trey couldn't come up with the latter or proof of insurance for the vehicle. He must have misplaced them in the move. He didn't mention to the officer that for the past several days a friend of his named Kathy Carpenter had been using his car and had had access to these missing documents. The police report generated by this incident didn't indicate where Trey was going or what he was doing out after midnight.

While sleeping on Pfister's couch, Kathy was awakened by Nancy sometime between three and four a.m. She'd turned on the kitchen light and was eating a snack and looking at her computer, sending out e-mails and texts. Kathy pulled the covers over her head and tried to go back to sleep.

Before they'd said good night, Pfister had instructed Kathy that prior to leaving for the bank in the morning she was to put a "Do Not Disturb—Nancy Sleeping" sign on the outside door so that no one would show up and wake her. Kathy followed these instructions and, after making sure that Gabe had food and water and letting the dog outside to relieve himself, she locked the external door and slipped quietly out of the house, driving into town to get dressed for work.

That morning at 9:49 a.m., Bob Braudis would later tell the police, he received a text from Pfister saying, "I can't sleep, are you free manana, xox."

23

Because the Stylers hadn't yet rented a storage unit, on Sunday they'd left the moving van holding their possessions at the bottom of Nancy Pfister's driveway, before driving back to Basalt in their own car. One of Buttermilk's many cross-country trails abutted the Pfister property; that evening a handful of skiers came to the trailhead and parked their vehicles in the driveway behind the van. One was blocking it in. When the Stylers came back to the house on Monday, they couldn't move the truck and the cross-country skiers were nowhere in the area, so they filled up the Jaguar this time and returned to the motel, a number of their belongings still inside the Pfister home. Their exit was taking longer than anyone had hoped.

That Monday, the Stylers called Kathy and told her that after considering Pfister's latest demands they'd consulted with a lawyer who'd said that their landlady had no legal right to kick them out of the house in this manner or to hold on to their possessions.

Later that day, or possibly on Tuesday (the specific date was never determined), Kathy had an appointment with her psychotherapist, Dr. Frederick "Bo" Persiko, in Basalt. Persiko's office was within two blocks of where the Stylers were staying at the Aspenalt. It was also near where a black plastic bag holding Trey's car registration would later be found, and near where the "Owner's Closet" key would be spotted.

. . .

On Tuesday, the Stylers and a crew of hired helpers from Aspen Workforce made plans to go to Pfister's house to continue moving, but the couple was worried about a confrontation with their ex-landlady. They hadn't responded to Pfister's demand for $14,000 and were afraid that if they ran into her inside the house, things could get ugly. After speaking with the attorney about their legal rights, they'd phoned the Pitkin County Sheriff's Office and asked it to provide a "civil standby" at the Pfister residence starting on Tuesday morning—an officer who'd be on the scene or monitoring the move, in case problems erupted.

The sheriff's department said they'd provide this service, but felt that their personnel should not be on the premises, as this might further provoke Nancy Pfister. Instead, a deputy would park nearby and come to the house very quickly, if necessary. The Stylers agreed to this and returned to the house on Tuesday morning to continue packing.

When they arrived, Nancy Styler later told the police, the door was locked, which was unusual, because Pfister "never locked it. My husband opened the door, the dog came bounding out. The doggie door was also shut, but Gabe had a big bowl of food."

This detail would call attention to itself later on because of the critical timeline issues that developed around the case. Kathy Carpenter would say that she'd left Pfister's twenty-four hours earlier and the dog would surely have eaten something during the course of the day just passed. That left only Nancy Pfister to have filled the bowl—but where was she?

On Tuesday, the Stylers didn't see or hear Pfister in the house and the dog had relieved himself all over the place. The residence, according to Nancy Styler, had developed a bad smell. The movers didn't seem aware of this odor and Trey later claimed that an injury to his nose in his youth kept him from smelling much of anything.

Because Pfister was perhaps gone from the house, Nancy Styler called Kathy at work and posed what struck Carpenter as a very strange question: did Kathy think that Pfister had gone off somewhere and killed herself?

No, Kathy said, taken aback. And even if she had done something like that, wouldn't she have done it in her master bedroom? Had the Stylers gone upstairs and looked for her?

They had, but she wasn't there.

During the moving on Tuesday, a friend of Pfister's named Patrick Carney showed up looking for her. The day before, Pfister had asked him to come by and pick her up on Monday, but he'd broken his collarbone skiing yesterday and couldn't get there until Tuesday. In the past, Carney had taken Nancy out for dinner on Thursday evenings (he always paid) and had reputedly gotten upset on occasion when he'd felt that other men were paying too much attention to her.

According to Carney, he went upstairs to Pfister's bedroom to look for her, with Nancy Styler trailing right behind him. She later claimed that she'd stayed downstairs and he'd gone up alone.

Carney called out his friend's name, but received no answer.

He soon left without mentioning to anyone that he'd smelled anything unusual, either.

When Kathy Carpenter later began speaking to the police, she remembered Tuesday another way:

"Nancy Styler called me Tuesday at work between eleven a.m. and one p.m. She said, 'Nancy's not here, it's strange... But Gabe is here all alone and he's peed on the floor. He's locked in. He left a mess here in the house... Patrick was here when we arrived and he was upstairs.'"

Kathy was struck by this last detail and told the authorities that she then said to Nancy Styler, "'That's odd, because I locked that front door.' I didn't think anything of it... I e-mailed Nancy Pfister, but never heard back from her..."

On Tuesday evening Kathy went to an Alcoholics Anonymous meeting, and on Wednesday, the movers were back at the Pfister residence, getting the last of the Stylers' possessions out of the house. Around noon Wednesday, Nancy Styler called Kathy and repeated that Pfister wasn't there and Gabe was alone. Dog excrement was all over the rooms and the labradoodle's water bowls were dry. Styler said that she'd gone up to Pfister's bedroom to look in, but there was no evidence of her anywhere. And the strangest part was that there weren't any sheets on the bed.

According to Kathy, Nancy Styler then said, "There's no sign of her... Maybe she took off with someone. Her pills and everything are here."

Also about noon, Patty Stranahan who, along with her husband, George, had helped raise Juliana, came into Alpine Bank and spoke with Kathy. Carpenter said she was worried because she hadn't heard from Nancy Pfister during the past two days. She wanted Patty to make some calls to look for Nancy, but Stranahan was busy and felt that Kathy was overreacting.

At 12:56 p.m., after the Stylers had at last finished packing, Nancy Styler texted Kathy at work. She wanted to assure Carpenter that the items they'd left behind at Pfister's would soon be picked up:

"We just left the house we will come home later to get the trash tonight and the snow blower Gabe is locked in I opened a window because it is warm, we got her car in the garage and the furniture put back we are out of here. I cleaned up the Gabe mess... and put her dishes in the dishwasher. So if anything is out she has been there and I'm glad that you are getting Gabe. I can't believe she left him alone for that long our poor baby xo..."

Kathy would later tell the police that she found it odd that Nancy Styler would be doing all of these things for a woman she professed to hate, but she didn't mention this to Styler herself.

At 12:58, Nancy Styler phoned Kathy and said they'd be back that night to retrieve some black trash bags and a snow blower. According to Kathy's account, the Stylers intended to drop the bags in the dark at a public trash can at the base of West Buttermilk Road, so that no one would see what they were doing or question the couple for disposing of their garbage in this manner.

Kathy said that if they came around six p.m. she'd be off work and could be there to help them get their bags and blower, but no definite plans were made.

At 4:05 that afternoon, Nancy Styler phoned Kathy once more and they spoke for roughly two minutes.

At 5:30 p.m., Kathy left for Nancy's home and fifteen minutes later walked into her bedroom, but no one was there. She said she called Patty again, and told her that something about the house was weird. For one thing, Nancy's bed was neatly made and that never happened. She didn't say to Stranahan, as she would later that night tell a deputy and Sheriff DiSalvo, that she'd seen the Stylers leaving the house a little after 5:30, as she was pulling into the driveway.

At approximately the same time that evening—5:30 p.m.—the Stylers were on their way to Glenwood Springs to drop off the rental truck and Nancy had also unexpectedly gotten an appointment in the town for eyelash extensions at Lovely Nails. Despite the Stylers' constant complaining about being broke, Nancy was going to have this work done on her appearance, one way of lessening her stress.

Kathy went downstairs and opened the refrigerator, but none of Pfister's champagne had been drunk, which was peculiar, as she was known for downing a bottle or more a day. Her purse and her cell phone were missing, and the air held a bad smell. When Kathy walked back upstairs and decided to check the closet in the master bedroom, the key wasn't in the lock, which was also weird.

Because she'd known that Nancy was coming home from Australia on February 22, Kathy had left one of the two closet keys she'd recently had made in the lock. It was clearly marked with a tag saying, "Owner's Closet."

On the phone, Kathy asked Patty if she thought that the Stylers had done something to Nancy and Patty reiterated that Carpenter was overreacting. Kathy said she was leaving to go back into town and get the second closet key from her condo.

At 7:30 that evening, the Stylers were in their Jaguar returning from the appointment at Lovely Nails. While there, Nancy's cell had rung and a friend of Kathy's named Susan Wasko had left a message for her.

According to Nancy Styler, Wasko told her that her boyfriend had just driven by the Pfister home and seen "five sheriff cars and two police cars and an ambulance... I haven't heard from Kathy and that woman [Nancy Pfister] is so crazy, who knows? I'm really nervous."

By now, police cars were in fact stacked up in the Pfister driveway, with their lights flashing.

Nancy Styler had earlier told Kathy that they'd swing by Pfister's place to pick up the bags and snow blower, but the couple changed their minds and decided to return to Basalt.

After getting Wasko's message, Nancy Styler began making a series of calls, back to back to back. She dialed Kathy Carpenter, a connection that lasted only fifty-one seconds. She called Kathy's mother, Chris, who sounded frazzled and said that she was on the other line and couldn't talk. She phoned Kathy again. She called Nancy Pfister's lifelong friend and handyman, Merlin Broughton, who'd earlier suggested that the Stylers get a room at the Aspenalt when they'd quickly needed a place to stay. She called Kathy again, before phoning a woman named Kacey Pelletier, the spa coordinator at the Hotel Jerome, for reasons that were unclear. She called Susan Wasko and then she phoned Megan Mulligan, Kathy's AA sponsor, three times in a row. Mulligan didn't know Nancy Styler and would later wonder how she'd gotten her number. Nancy called Kathy's mom twice and, finally, she phoned Susan Wasko once more. All thirteen calls were placed between 7:56 p.m. and 9:11 p.m.

As Nancy Styler later explained to the authorities when reconstructing Wednesday evening for them, "We were realizing something was funky.... I went to bed at midnight."

“Absolute Disbelief”

24

On Wednesday evening, once Kathy had driven away from the house after seeing the white lump of sheets rolled up in the closet, she made a 911 call and then initially spoke with Deputy Ryan Turner by the side of West Buttermilk Road, who detected that she'd been drinking. After talking with other officers well into the night, she was released and left the courthouse. Based on information she'd provided to investigators, they planned their next move.

At 5:45 the next morning, less than twelve hours after the body had been found, Pitkin County Deputies Levi Borst, Jeff Lumsden, and Marcin Debski arrived at room 122 of the Aspenalt Lodge. Knocking on the door, they awakened Trey and Nancy. The trio of deputies entered the room, followed by Pitkin County Peace Officer Brad Gibson and CBI Agent John Zamora. The deputies had brought with them two search warrants, one for the motel room and another for the Stylers' Jaguar sedan. They'd caught the couple completely off guard and nearly unclothed. After handcuffing both suspects, Gibson helped Trey get out of bed, as he seemed to be having trouble doing this himself. Lifting the frail, sixty-five-year-old man under his left arm, Gibson got him into a standing position and steadied him. Trey's legs, the officer couldn't help observing, appeared emaciated.

At sixty-two, Nancy Styler was five foot three and weighed 125 pounds. She looked better and stronger than her husband, but nothing like the woman seen in pictures taken of her in the 1980s and '90s. Her face was a tightly drawn set of wrinkles, her dirty blond hair no longer shining and bright. Hard times had left their stamp around her eyes, in the set of her mouth, and in the creases of her skin.

After the deputies secured the motel room, they took the cuffs off the Stylers and asked them to strip so they could take pictures of them front and back, looking for defensive wounds or any other unusual markings. Humiliated, they complied.

When Nancy needed to relieve herself, the officers kept her waiting for about half an hour, until a female officer showed up and could accompany her into the bathroom. The deputies placed a buccal swab inside each of their mouths and collected a DNA sample. They asked the couple to ride into Aspen for questioning and the Stylers complied again, but it would take Trey awhile to get ready.

By now, Gibson had learned from CBI Agent Jack Haynes that the queen-size mattress in Nancy Pfister's bedroom had been turned over and the underside of it contained large, fresh bloodstains. Following his initial observations at the crime scene and of the aging doctor on the morning of February 27, Gibson would write: "Knowing the physical and medical state of William Styler, it is difficult to believe that he alone could flip a queen-sized mattress from one side to the other . . . While one person may be able to drag a body across a bedroom carpet, based on my experience with dead bodies, even dragging a dead body a very short distance is extremely difficult."

In separate cars, the Stylers were driven to Aspen. On the way Nancy heard something on a police radio about the murder of Nancy Pfister. When the couple arrived at the courthouse, they were escorted into different rooms and interrogated for roughly nine hours apiece. Given the option of having attorneys present or remaining silent and refusing to be questioned, they chose neither. Their stories of the recent spat over rent with Nancy Pfister were quite similar, as were their accounts of what they'd done in the days leading up to the finding of the body. They did not incriminate each other or Kathy Carpenter or anyone else in the murder of their former landlady. Instead of blaming her for their dispute, Trey explained to his inquisitor that when they first came to Aspen in the fall of 2013, Pfister seemed like the long-awaited answer to their prayers.

"After all these bad things that have happened," he said, referring to their health problems and earlier legal troubles, "we finally met the right person, and she's going to help us instead of hurt us..."

In the long, rambling, and disjointed interview that he did with CBI Agent John Zamora, which ran to 181 typed pages, Trey repeatedly stated that he and Nancy had had nothing to do with Pfister's death and knew nothing about who or what had caused it. More than anything else, he seemed concerned with protecting his wife from allegations of wrongdoing and with portraying her as a kind and gentle person. When they were moving out, he explained to Zamora, it was his spouse who'd insisted that they leave Pfister's house in a way that would please her upon her return from Australia.

Trey was less concerned with portraying himself as gentle or mellow.

"I kept telling my wife, 'Don't do the bitch any favors...'" he said to Zamora. "I used to be a nice guy, but you can only get fucked over so many times... We weren't looking for revenge or pity or any of that bullshit. We just wanted the fuck out of there."

During the interview, Sheriff DiSalvo walked into the room and didn't seem at all interested in coming off as gentle or mellow. He clearly was taking the death of his friend personally and wanted a shot at questioning Trey. DiSalvo came in close to the suspect and aggressively accused him of being involved in the murder.

Trey just as feistily protested that the sheriff was wrong: it was impossible for him to have done something like this because he was an invalid and physically incapable of killing anyone.

His wife, he said, did *everything* for him.

DiSalvo left and Zamora continued the interrogation.

The last time he'd seen Nancy Pfister, Trey recalled, was three months earlier, on November 22, when he'd driven her from Aspen to the Denver airport for her trip abroad. He told Zamora that on February 22 she'd flown into the Aspen airport with two men, although he didn't elaborate on who they were or what had happened with them after they'd all landed together.

As Zamora constantly tried to focus and refocus Trey on the timeline of the past few days, Styler traced and retraced and then traced again in a roundabout way his actions between February 22 and Kathy finding the body on the evening of February 26. On Monday morning, February 24, he told Zamora, he'd phoned Pfister to settle things between them regarding her demands for $14,000, so they could finish moving out of her house. He explained that he'd made the call on his wife's cell phone, while he was away from the Aspenalt and Nancy Styler was still asleep at the motel. He'd taken her cell with him this morning so that no one would call and wake her up.

Since he wasn't able to reach Pfister, he'd left her a message, saying that he'd spoken with an attorney and that he and his wife had the right to retrieve their possessions from the house without any more resistance from her.

The gist of the message, he said, was "don't give us any crap or you will get more crap than you ever wanted..."

That was their last communication, he told the CBI agent, and at no time after her return from Australia did he see or speak directly to Pfister.

"I don't want anything to do with that bitch," he emphasized to Zamora.

25

Nancy Styler's story of the past few days was very much like Trey's, with no significant discrepancies between the two accounts. She told investigators that her first thought after learning about the demise of Nancy Pfister was that she'd killed herself. She also said that she and her husband were never separated during the moving-out process.

Trey echoed this to Zamora, "Neither my wife nor I were at the house alone at any time."

Nancy Styler mentioned that the past autumn she and her ex-landlady had discussed how Pfister would soon be getting a substantial amount of money from her mother's life insurance policy—something over $600,000 was coming her way in November 2013—and she'd asked the Stylers for investment advice. Nancy said that Pfister was always talking about buying a property somewhere and had mentioned purchasing a condo in Pavones, Mexico.

While Trey had seemed angry and edgy speaking with Zamora, Nancy was calm and chatty during her police interview, joking and acting in charge of the process. Her demeanor didn't change until the detectives suggested that Kathy Carpenter had begun talking with them about the Stylers' conflict with Pfister over money and their possible connection to the crime. The jokes stopped and her body language tightened.

"Kathy has kind of been our savior..." she told the investigators. "She said don't worry about this. She's [Nancy Pfister has] done this to so many people before . . . I thought my relationship with Kathy was very good. My husband saved her life . . . I wouldn't hurt a fly."

During Trey's initial interview on February 27, Zamora picked up Trey's volatile emotional state and suggested that the doctor might never have intended to harm Pfister, but they'd had a confrontation inside her home and things had slipped out of control.

"I don't think this was premeditated . . ." Zamora said. "It was just a bad situation that happened right there. It was just a lot of anger and it's just like all of a sudden the mind blew up . . . It suddenly just raged . . . and it just lost it."

"I don't know who would do that," Styler replied. "I don't know who's responsible, but what we have learned is that there are a lot of people in this town who actively dislike her [Nancy Pfister] . . . My condition is such that I don't think I could beat up a kid."

"Right now," Zamora said, based upon the multiple interviews being conducted around the crime and its potential suspects, "we absolutely have somebody lying to us . . ."

"If I was going to kill somebody, it would be that fucking lawyer on the other side of the mountains," Trey said, referring to the attorney, John G. Powell, whom he'd battled with in Denver.

Zamora gave Trey several more chances to talk about his possible involvement in Pfister's death, but he repeated that neither he nor his wife had had anything to do with her murder. Before releasing Trey, Zamora wanted him to take a polygraph exam so he could clear himself once and for all. Trey said that he was willing to do this, but explained that because of his physical infirmities and his dependence on various medications, the test results might be inaccurate.

Zamora was undeterred.

CBI Agent Rosa Perez administered the polygraph to Trey, but before she could get started, he told her that he was overdue for taking his meds and in no condition to be examined. The test went forward anyway. Perez asked him if he'd caused the death of Nancy Pfister or knew who had. He answered each question with a "no" and Perez concluded that in both instances he was being deceptive.

The next day, Perez administered the same test to Kathy Carpenter. She also answered each question with a "no" and Perez felt that she too was being deceptive with both answers. For reasons that were never explained, Nancy Styler wasn't given a polygraph.

Zamora zoomed in on the two suspects who'd failed their exams—telling Trey and Kathy that one of them had to be lying and that he or she should be the first to speak the truth about the crime, in order to protect themselves from what might happen with the case later on. Steadily, the agent ratcheted up the pressure on both, playing them back and forth against each other. He hinted to Trey that there were inconsistencies in Kathy's story, especially the part about her seeing the Stylers leaving the Pfister home right before she found the body. Wasn't she pointing to them as the killers? He hinted to Kathy that the couple was talking about her and saying things that could be damaging.

Kathy held to her basic story—that she was completely innocent—and Trey did the same.

Following Trey's polygraph exam on February 27, the Stylers were released from custody, but weren't exactly free to go wherever they pleased. As they were being questioned, the police had done a Luminol test to look for blood in their Jaguar and gotten what they believed was a positive reading. The Jag was impounded and numerous carpet swatches were cut out of it and sent to the CBI for further testing, along with other swatches from their motel room and a storage locker. All of their cash, their checkbook, and their credit cards had been confiscated by the police so they went back to the Aspenalt without transportation or financial resources.

When a local Basalt restaurant, Heathers, learned that the couple was staying at the motel without any money, they sent food over to the Stylers until other arrangements could be made.

On the afternoon of the twenty-seventh, Gibson learned from another deputy that the autopsy on Nancy Pfister had been completed. She'd died from "multiple severe blunt force trauma" to the head and from an open skull fracture on the right temple. Her body revealed no defensive wounds, showing that she hadn't struggled with her assailant before dying. She'd been attacked in bed while unconscious and had been wearing a sleep mask and ear plugs (those close to her knew that she'd long had trouble sleeping and before getting into bed she liked to wash down an Ambien or Soma with champagne). According to Pitkin County Coroner Dr. Steve Ayers, she'd been dead for twenty-four to forty-eight hours when Kathy Carpenter called 911. This meant that she'd died sometime between Monday evening, February 24, and Tuesday evening, the twenty-fifth.

"It was rapidly fatal," Dr. Ayers said of the blows that had killed Pfister.

The toxicology report showed "low to therapeutic amounts of commonly prescribed muscle relaxers and sleep aid" in the victim's system. To the surprise of many, the report did not reveal any other drugs or alcohol in her body.

After Trey and Nancy had returned to the Aspenalt, she made a point each morning of walking across the parking lot to the lobby and getting copies of both the *Aspen Times* and the *Aspen Daily News* so she could read about the latest developments in the Pfister murder. While standing in the lobby, she made an offhand comment to some people about having been interrogated by the Pitkin County Sheriff's Office.

"We're the criminals in room 122!" She smiled.

During the ongoing police interviews in the days after Kathy found the body, the authorities asked her a question that others around town had posed after learning about the crime: were she and Nancy Pfister lovers?

Kathy answered them casually, matter-of-factly, saying that the women had been intimate, but only once. The police apparently found this story more intriguing than Kathy did and pressed her about it. Was sex a part of motivation behind the murder? Had Nancy somehow used their physical connection as a weapon against Kathy? Because they'd been a couple, had rage or jealousy erupted between the two of them and led to violence?

Not really, Kathy shrugged, and this line of inquiry didn't go much further. Nancy had been intimate with a lot of people... and it had never seemed to mean that much one way or another.

On the evening of the twenty-seventh, George and Patty Stranahan drove to the Aspen airport to pick up Juliana Pfister, flying in to meet and grieve with friends and family after getting the news about her mother. Patty had helped raise Juliana and over the years George had become a local legend: an heir to the Champion spark plug fortune; an award-winning cattle rancher; a successful restaurateur who'd founded the Woody Creek Tavern; the force behind the world-renowned Aspen Center for Physics; the founder of Stranahan's Colorado Whiskey; a pioneering microbrewery owner and creator of Denver's Flying Dog Brewery; and a former business partner of Colorado governor John Hickenlooper. Stranahan used his Flying Dog labels to keep alive a message from his late neighbor and friend, Hunter S. Thompson: "Challenge authority!"

Also waiting at the airport on that evening were Kathy Carpenter, her mother, Chris, and Gabe (Kathy took custody of the dog after Sheriff Braudis had been criticized for doing so). They were there to pick up Kathy's son, Michael, whom the police would soon be questioning regarding his knowledge of his mother's recent activities. Within twenty-four hours of finding the body, Kathy had gone to Nancy Pfister's safe deposit box at Alpine Bank and removed $6,000 in cash and some jewelry belonging to the dead woman. Law enforcement wanted to know where the $6,000 had come from and what she'd done with the jewelry. In the coming days, Juliana would ask Patty Stranahan to get the key to this box back from Kathy.

Outside the airport, a snowstorm was building and flights were delayed, so both of the parties were compelled to wait together for a couple of hours at Sardy Field, and forced to be around one another much longer than they wanted to inside the small airport. The Stranahans couldn't help but view Kathy with some suspicion, while she was eager to deflect any blame away from herself.

Patty would soon be interviewed by detectives and tell them that at the airport Carpenter appeared shaken.

“Kathy looked like she was a hundred years old,” Patty recalled. “She was visibly tranquilized ... They [the police] wouldn’t let her go home, because they [the Stylers] knew where she lived ... She said, ‘I know they did it ... They hated her ... He had such a bad temper ...’ ”

As they all lingered at the terminal, Kathy spoke to Patty about how Trey had wanted to pick Pfister up at the airport the previous Saturday night, but Carpenter had felt this was a bad idea and talked him out of it.

Before either of the planes landed in Aspen, Patty texted Juliana to warn her that Kathy and her mother were at the airport.

“She never really cared for Kathy,” Patty said of Juliana. “I didn’t want her to think they were her welcoming committee ... She didn’t love Kathy ...”

26

The following morning at 9:30, Kathy returned to the Pitkin County Sheriff's Office for a second interview, which lasted nearly twelve hours. She told police that during the past few months the Stylers had asked her a lot of questions about Pfister's financial accounts and that Nancy Styler had said multiple times that she wanted to kill her—or that Pfister might simply disappear. Kathy would later mention one occasion in particular, when Nancy Styler was very upset and crying and talked about putting cyanide in a piece of chocolate for Pfister to eat. Dr. Styler, she told them, had a bad temper and walked around the house slamming doors and cursing under his breath.

Investigators took note that Kathy told them that when she'd first looked in the master bedroom closet and seen what turned out to be the body of her friend, she'd observed a strand of blond hair with blood on it.

The detectives pounced on this detail, believing it to be an obvious falsehood because Pfister's entire body had been wrapped up and not visible.

"Based upon what I viewed at the scene," Deputy Brad Gibson wrote in his report about the murder, "it would not have been possible for Katherine Carpenter to have seen Nancy Pfister's hair and blood, and she could not have been able to identify the body as Nancy Pfister."

Again and again, the interrogators would return to this discrepancy and to Kathy's 911 call, asking about the figure in the closet and what she'd seen or hadn't seen lying on the floor. They circled around her relationship with Pfister and what had happened after her friend had left for Australia and the

Stylers had moved into her home. They went over and over these basic elements, looking for inconsistencies or for any information she hadn't yet given them, prodding her to change or add to her original story.

Wasn't Kathy the last person to see Nancy Pfister alive and didn't that alone make her a suspect?

Throughout the twenty-eighth, Kathy held to her narrative, repeating the same pattern on March 1 and then two days later, on Monday, March 3, when she was intensely questioned for another four hours.

"I just wanted to help her [Nancy Pfister]," she told her inquisitors. "I was always there for her. She shared a lot of her sadness and stories with me through the years. I'm a people person. I care about people and always want to help people probably too much. I need to take care of myself, to take care of Kathy. I'm a caregiver..."

If she wasn't guilty of killing her friend, the detectives pressed her, who was? What was her theory of the case? Who'd beaten Nancy Pfister to death and why had they done it? Were the Stylers angry at Pfister over their rental dispute or was there more to the conflict than that? Did they have a sufficient motive to murder her?

Kathy kept saying that she didn't know anything more than she'd already told them and she didn't have a theory of the case.

But the questions and accusations didn't stop: Pfister had humiliated her in public, hadn't she? Or used her sexually and then ignored her? Or called her names and ordered her about and made her run her errands at all hours of the day and night, treating her like a servant or a slave—the way she'd done with many others after befriending them? She felt superior to Kathy, didn't she? The same way she felt toward most people in town because she was born into the Pfister family?

She and Nancy had fought in the past, when the police had been called out to the Pfister residence to keep them apart. Nancy had said something or done something to enrage Kathy and she'd finally snapped and—

It wasn't like that, Carpenter said, not like that at all.

What about her lies regarding the body? Kathy had gone into the closet and pulled the coverings off of Nancy and seen her head, hadn't she? She'd viewed her face and hair—and it wasn't the way she'd described it in her 911 call, was it? If she'd lied in her first encounter with the authorities, what was she lying about now?

No, no, and no, Kathy said, but the interrogators kept at her, hoping to push her into a confession or at least an admission.

Part of the reason for pressuring Kathy was that both the CBI and the Pitkin County Sheriff's Office were feeling pressure to make an arrest. This was not the sort of publicity Aspen wanted, especially not in the middle of the ski season, when something like this could hurt the town's image and be bad for business.

"Aspen's a very small place," says a female private detective from Denver snooping around the edges of the case from the beginning. "Everybody knows everybody else's business or at least they think they do. When Nancy got killed, people were genuinely stunned and saddened that something like this could happen to one of their own. You could feel the pain and the grief inside the whole town and you could also feel the fear. Was a killer on the loose? Was it a serial killer? That was one rumor at the start of the investigation. Older people in Aspen were really frightened and started locking their doors. All of this put heat on law enforcement to act quickly to quiet people down. It became one of the driving forces for doing what they did after the body was found.

"In Aspen, you don't kiss and tell. After Nancy died, people got very angry that some of their fellow citizens started speaking openly to the media about her past as a wild child. There were stories of people getting paid by news organizations to talk about these things. We all knew about Nancy's past, but the town didn't want to dwell on it so they shut down to outsiders. They wanted to honor Nancy's memory and to protect her daughter. They wanted to control the narrative of the murder."

But the narrative had a life of its own.

As Kathy's questioning progressed on that Friday morning, February 28, Robert Larson, a Basalt facilities maintenance worker, found a black trash bag inside a bear-proof municipal Dumpster at 137 Midland Avenue—near the local Alpine Bank and just behind room 122 of the Aspenalt Lodge, where the Stylers had been staying. The only bag in the Dumpster, it was tear-resistant, but with some effort Larson was able to open it and look in. Every Monday and Friday, Larson emptied these containers and he was known for getting aggravated if a civilian had dropped some personal garbage in one of these city-owned receptacles, which was against the rules in Basalt. The Roaring Fork Valley, including Basalt, was highly conscientious about environmental matters and the disposal of trash, and Larson could not ignore this violation. He dug deeper into the twenty-five-pound bag, thinking it might reveal who'd left it there. Then he could track down the offender and see that the individual got fined.

Rummaging in the bag, he found a jewelry box and an old photograph. He picked up an empty medicine bottle and read the label, seeing that it had been prescribed to a Nancy Pfister. The name was familiar—wasn't she the woman who'd just been murdered outside of Aspen and whose name was in the paper every day now?

Larson called the Basalt Police Department and was told to wait in place with the bag for an officer to come and take it into custody. CBI Agent Jack Haynes arrived and began examining the potential evidence, finding a smaller white bag within the larger black one. The white one held an old hammer that appeared to be marked with "red flakes." Haynes saw more prescription bottles for Nancy Pfister; a string of pearls; a United Airlines boarding pass for Pfister; numerous credit cards registered to her, her health insurance card, her passport, and information for some Westpac bank accounts belonging to the dead woman. Matching bank account information had been recovered from her bedroom.

Amidst these items was the car registration for William Styler and a vehicle inspection sheet for the couple's Jaguar sedan, plus a receipt for Trey's Aspen post office box.

The police quickly sent the evidence along to the Colorado Bureau of Investigation. CBI tests would reveal that the red flakes on the hammer matched the DNA profile of Nancy Pfister. DNA on both the black and white plastic bags did not exclude William Styler or any of his paternal male relatives from being the source.

. . .

Later that Friday, patrol vehicles from the Aspen Police Department and the sheriff's office began a stakeout of Kathy's small condo on Main Street, but the bank teller was gone, spending more and more time at her mother's.

Using Luminol on the Stylers' Jaguar, forensic specialists swabbed some reddish-brown stains on the interior driver's side door and rear driver's side seat. Luminol reacts with fluorescent lights in the presence of blood and other materials, but one cannot determine from the reaction if the substance is human blood. The Jag held nine stains in all, with the Luminol producing a hit on the right side of the driver's seat between the cushion and the console. In the trunk were cleaning supplies: paper towels and ceramic tile cleaner. Covering the floor of the rear driver's side passenger area were black trash bags made of tear-resistant material, like the one just found in the Dumpster in Basalt.

Two days later, on March 2, Pitkin County Sheriff Deputy Grant Jahnke executed a search warrant on a safe deposit box at Alpine Bank, opened in 2003 in the names of both Kathy Carpenter and Nancy Pfister. In November 2010, this agreement had been superseded and the new one was in Carpenter's name alone. In the deposit box were a 2000 Garfield County court order for a name change for Katherine Carpenter; Nancy's Pfister's birth certificate; Social Security cards and birth records for Carpenter's son, Michael; an expired driver's license belonging to Carpenter; Kathy's passport, and a Chase Bank credit card apparently issued in both their names.

CBI Agent John Zamora interviewed Kathy's mother, Chris, who said that Kathy had told her that the body of Nancy Pfister had been wrapped in sheets, a detail that Carpenter hadn't mentioned to Zamora. It also took her awhile to confess to the authorities that within a day of finding her friend in the closet, she'd removed $6,000 in cash and two rings from Pfister's safe deposit box at Alpine Bank—one ring made of gold with an emerald diamond and the other with a single small diamond.

Kathy's son, Michael, told Zamora that Kathy had taken the money to pay for his plane flight home and to cover his college tuition payment of $825.

He said that his mother had asked him what to do with the ring and he'd advised her to give it to the Pfister sisters. She told Michael to stash it for her, so he put it in a storage shed near Kathy's condo.

Deputy Jahnke searched Kathy's apartment for personal property belonging to Nancy Pfister; for DNA evidence; for "any and all human remains;" and for weapons, ammunition, bludgeons or any other objects that could be used "to inflict injuries and/or death." Inside the condo, Jahnke located documents holding the victim's name, along with bank account information and a safe deposit box key labeled "Nancy" stuffed inside a red envelope. Jahnke found a notebook, a notepad, and other documents with Nancy's personal information on them. Similar documents were recovered from Carpenter's bedroom, plus a ripped-up business card belonging to Nancy Styler.

From a Basalt storage unit that Kathy had rented deputies retrieved a small hammer, a lint tray from a clothes drying machine, a light blue towel with a stain, a pillow with a red stain, a left shoe with a red stain, and a hose with a red stain. They recovered surveillance footage from the storage business from February 21 to March 4, 2014, and keypad access data from the same time frame.

On March 3, District Attorney Investigator Edward Piccolo executed another search warrant at the Alpine Bank branch where Kathy worked, seeking records for Nancy Pfister's account from October 1, 2013, to March 3, 2014. The records included incoming wire transfers, checks deposited and written, bank statements, safe deposit lease agreements, and credit card information. Piccolo wanted "any and all records and transactions involving a transfer of funds in the amount of approximately $600,000 on or around November 15, 2013," a week before Pfister left for Australia and when the Stylers were already living in her home.

On November 15, $664,837 had been deposited into one of Pfister's Alpine accounts, as she'd finally received the life insurance payout from her mother's estate. A week later on November 22, the day she flew to Australia, she transferred $830,000 from Alpine Bank to an account at Charles Schwab.

While executing their warrants, the authorities seized from the Stylers two iPads, three iPhones, three laptop computers, three cameras, a glass jar holding marijuana, and a bag with "narcotic accessories." Forensic testing would reveal a gap in the data of Nancy Styler's cell phone between January 30 and February 24, 2014 (a crucial date in the timeline surrounding the murder), making it harder to track some of her movements and the position of the phone itself during this three and a half weeks. The police tracked down the Stylers' records from Verizon, American Express, Chase Bank, AOL, Facebook, and Google from October 14, 2013, to February 27, 2014. They retrieved voice mail, text, cell tower, and other information from phone calls involving the Stylers, Nancy Pfister, and Aspen attorney John Beatty.

In a storage locker Trey had rented in Basalt, detectives found a wadded-up piece of cloth about four inches wide and long enough to wrap around an adult's wrist. Inside the material was a pill identified as the prescription medicine ketamine. On the street the drug was known as "Vitamin K" or "Special K," and was used for a variety of stimulating effects, including euphoria. Within the medical community, it was utilized for pain management and anesthesia and was potent enough to render a patient unconsciousness. Trey hadn't held a medical license since 2005 and the drug would have been challenging to get without one. Had he been taking it recreationally? Had he wanted to use it to render someone unconscious?

Following the initial police questioning of the Stylers on February 27, they were interrogated again the next day, a Friday. That evening, Merlin Broughton went to visit the couple at the Aspenalt. Since Nancy Pfister had been away in Australia, Merlin had gotten to know the Stylers and to like them. He'd been helpful to them, including fixing the hot water heater in Pfister's house in January. He knew they were being interrogated about the murder, but didn't want to think of them as suspects in the killing of his lifelong friend. Broughton himself would go through a police interview and the story he told detectives on March 2 would stand out from many others in one critical aspect: the time frame around the victim's death, which would become increasingly controversial as the case unfolded.

While others had spoken for the last time with Pfister on Monday, Broughton mentioned that a "girl" he knew had talked to her on Tuesday, suggesting that she was still alive then, a significant detail.

This, Broughton said, "could be important because everyone who I knew talked to Nancy on Monday... She [the girl] had talked to Joe [DiSalvo] and let him know that Nancy called and left a message on Tuesday... I tried calling Nancy on Monday, left a message in the afternoon. Tuesday I was over there to pick up my trailer two-ish, which Trey had loaded up... I was there about twelve minutes... Wednesday I tried to call Nancy... It was odd she hadn't gotten back to me... Wednesday I went to Nancy's to pick up the snow blower... That's what's been bothering me... I was there... Thursday I found out about Nancy's death... by text."

On Friday, February 28, Nancy Styler had reached out to Merlin to assist them in getting food and medication for Trey, since the police had impounded their car. He offered to do what he could for the couple.

"I felt sorry for them," he told the police, when recounting his meeting with them that Friday evening at the Aspenalt. "Their whole world was falling apart... They were in a bad way... They were very much in love... Nancy told me that after thirty years of marriage she was still in love with him...

"Nancy said that many times she hated Nancy Pfister... Not that she had hatred for the woman, but she hated all the things that Nancy had put Nancy Styler through.... I felt that was a little strong at the time, quite insensitive..."

To his surprise, if not shock, Nancy Styler now told him that she "really did hate Nancy [Pfister]."

The words unsettled Broughton. His friend had been dead only a few days—not to mention that Nancy Styler was being questioned by the police about her possible role in the murder.

After he told the couple it was a shame that Pfister was dead, Nancy Styler "got on her soapbox again about all the things she had done to her... There were issues with Nancy Pfister about moving stuff in her house..."

Merlin explained to the Stylers that he didn't want to hear this now in the wake of Nancy's death.

As he recounted for the authorities on March 2, "If they [Trey and Nancy] could be involved in something like this... I wanted to distance myself from them."

After leaving the motel, he never spoke with the couple again.

27

As the police were conducting numerous interviews, private investigator David Olmsted first met with the Stylers at the Aspenalt on Saturday, March 1, and they'd laid out for him Trey's medical problems. They were waiting for his prescription to be filled at the City Market pharmacy in Aspen, but with their car impounded they didn't know how to get into town and pick up the drugs. Olmsted said that he'd be happy to do this for them, but by the time he was able to run this errand, the pharmacy was closed. He suggested that on Sunday morning Nancy ask the Pitkin County deputy, who was conducting surveillance on the couple from her patrol car parked outside the Stylers' motel room, to drive her into town. No matter what you do on the ride, Olmsted insisted, don't say anything to the officer about Nancy Pfister or the past few days. She followed the PI's advice, the deputy agreed to the plan, and Nancy was able to get the meds for her husband. On Monday, March 3, Olmsted had to leave town for the Pamela Phillips trial in Tucson, where he was working with the defense team. Before departing, he stopped by the Aspenalt and spent another hour with the Stylers. He had a sense of what was coming next.

"I hate to be the bearer of bad news," he said to them, as the deputy continued watching their doorstep, "but don't be surprised if they arrest you. If you do get arrested, don't make any statements to anyone—especially to anyone inside the jail."

Olmsted flew to Arizona and when he landed in Tucson, he had a message waiting from the lawyer in Boulder who'd first contacted him about the case. He didn't have to pick up the message to know what had happened.

That Monday, Brad Gibson finished putting together an arrest warrant for Nancy Styler and submitted it to Ninth District Judge Gail Nichols. Another warrant was being prepared for Trey. The Pitkin County Sheriff's Office had earlier shown similar warrants to the judge, but she'd asked them to gather more information before she'd sign them, as the case against the couple had been too thin. The deputies did as Nichols requested, until she was satisfied with the results.

"I have probable cause," Gibson wrote in the final draft, "to believe that Nancy Styler conspired to and was complicit in the murder of Nancy Pfister. Nancy Styler had the motive to kill Nancy Pfister because the Stylers were experiencing significant financial hardship, they had an ongoing rental dispute involving thousands of dollars with Nancy Pfister, Nancy Pfister refused to allow the Stylers to retrieve their belongings until the rental dispute was resolved, Nancy Styler made comments to Kathy Carpenter that she was going to kill Pfister and that something bad was going to happen to her."

Gibson also pointed out that in his interview with Kathy's mother, Chris Carpenter, she recalled hearing Nancy Styler say that she was going to kill Pfister.

"Nancy Styler," Gibson continued writing, "had the opportunity to kill Pfister and attempt to cover it up because she had access to Pfister's home and was removing her belongings there during the alleged timeframe of the murder.

"When Patrick Carney [a friend of Nancy Pfister's] came to Pfister's house on February 25, 2014, Nancy Styler initially indicated that Pfister was at home upstairs, and that she had had problems with Pfister. Nancy Styler followed Carney upstairs and after he called for Pfister, Nancy Styler said Pfister was not home.

"Nancy Styler is linked to the murder and attempted cover-up through physical evidence which includes but is not limited to: her husband's DNA was found on the white trash bag which contained the suspected murder weapon and on the black outer trash bag which contained the white trash bag with the murder weapon. Several of the Stylers' personal documents were inside the black trash bag, which contained Pfister's possessions and the alleged murder weapon—all of which were found in a public trash can in close proximity to the Stylers' hotel in Basalt, Colorado.

"The Stylers' Jaguar contained trash bags similar to those used in the murder and cover-up, had two reddish-brown marks near the driver's side doors, and there was a Luminol reaction inside the car near the driver's seat. It is unlikely that the murder and cover-up could have been completed by only one person due to the physical difficulty of such a task, and especially considering Trey Styler's physical infirmity. Nancy Styler stated that she and Trey Styler were together at all times while moving out of Pfister's home. Trey Styler was deceptive when asked under a polygraph about whether he knew for sure who had killed Pfister.

"Wherefore, I believe and have probable cause to believe that Nancy Styler . . . committed the crime of Murder in the First Degree . . . and Conspiracy to Commit Murder in the First Degree . . . on or between February 24, 2014, and February 26, 2014."

With both arrest warrants completed, members of the Pitkin County Sheriff's Office drove to the Aspenalt and knocked on the Stylers' door again before taking them into custody. Nancy was led from the hotel in tears, while a very frail-looking Trey was brought out wearing his wife's bright blue terrycloth bathrobe and calling Nancy's name as they were put into separate squad cars and driven to Aspen. They were booked into the small jail right behind the courthouse and were both about to be charged with first-degree murder and conspiracy to commit first-degree murder.

An hour after the arrest, Sheriff DiSalvo announced that the investigation into Nancy Pfister's murder was ongoing and his office was casting "as wide a net" as possible.

The new developments were broadcast across Colorado and startled Denver's medical community. Anesthesiologists and surgeons all over the Mile

High City who'd worked with Trey could not imagine that there was any truth in what they were hearing. The Stylers had always been a little eccentric, with that lavishly decorated home in Greenwood Village and those giant water lilies in the backyard . . . and they'd clearly had health and financial difficulties in recent years, but they couldn't possibly be guilty of murder. Nancy was such a bright and educated woman—she'd never have done such a thing. Trey was so disabled that at times he was confined to a wheelchair; on his bad days, he couldn't even stand up.

"I just don't believe he did this," Denver anesthesiologist Dr. Laurie Haberstroh said following the arrest. "Trey was a gentle and interesting man, a good man. There's absolute disbelief on the part of the doctors who've known him. At the same time, chronic, horrible, intractable pain can change people. It can change your perceptions and brain chemistry. Trey was a salt-of-the-earth type of person. If he can do something like this, anyone can."

Said Dr. Ron Stevens, a founding partner of Colorado Anesthesia Consultants, from his home in Cheyenne, Wyoming:

"I was amazed after learning about the murder and how it had happened and that he and his wife were being accused of doing this. I thought, Wow, Trey, you're an anesthesiologist and you did this with a hammer? Really—a hammer? Why not use anesthesiology? We do these kinds of lethal injections every day. We take people up to the edge of death, but then bring them back. A *hammer*?"

28

Late on that Monday evening from Tucson, David Olmsted called the Pitkin County Jail, where the Stylers were being held, and asked for permission to speak with one of them. He made this request of Don Bird, an acquaintance of his who ran the jail's operations. Bird went to get Nancy.

When she was on the line, Olmsted told her that he was going to do most of the talking and she should just listen. Snitches were everywhere in the jail and she had to be aware that they'd be watching her and listening to everything she said.

His first question: how was she coping behind bars?

Not very well, she said, sounding shaky and afraid—just about what the private investigator had anticipated.

He gave her the standard advice he'd been giving many others in her position over the decades:

"Just hang in there. People are going to be working on the outside to help you and Trey. Be nice and don't give anyone a hard time. Make sure you don't speak to any inmates. All right?"

"Yes."

"Are you physically okay?"

"Yes."

"Does Trey have his medication?"

"Yes."

Nancy's usual personality was animated and outgoing, but Olmsted could hear and feel her deflation through the phone. Wanting to say something positive, he told her that if one were going to be incarcerated, this was the best jail in America to be locked up in. It had a well-deserved reputation for not being hard on inmates and for taking reasonable care of them. Nancy didn't seem much assured, but what could anyone expect? She'd never been arrested before, never been in trouble in her life. For years she'd been in the medical profession and a highly respected horticulturist in Denver, a worldwide expert in her field. She'd traveled the globe working with water lilies and was celebrated in the botanist community. She'd lived in one of Denver's finest suburbs and had opened her home, with its spectacular gardens out back, to one and all. She'd been married to a highly successful doctor who'd headed the anesthesiology department of one of Denver's leading hospitals. Jail was never a possibility for Nancy Styler.

"I'll be back in a couple of days," Olmsted told her, "and I'll come see you."

"Okay."

"Probably Friday."

"Okay."

"Hang in there."

Roughly a month later, Olmsted would write a letter to the *Aspen Times*, calling out one of its columnists, Doug Allen, for leaping to conclusions about the murder and who'd committed it. Olmsted was upset that the writer was presuming to know the evidence, which the public was not yet privy to, and presuming to understand what the defense teams would do with that evidence. He warned Allen, despite all the publicity the case had already generated for the accused, not to rush to judgment.

"The next morning," Olmsted wrote about the Stylers on the day after their arrest, "their jail photographs were splayed across local and national newspapers as well as broadcast outlets. The accompanying stories quickly attributed the crime to a dispute over rent. By the end of the first week, national media representatives had swarmed Aspen looking for anyone who would talk to them, about anything and anybody. It wasn't necessary that you have any real information to be interviewed. Rumor, apocryphal reminiscences, and speculation were welcome..."

On Tuesday, March 4, the Stylers appeared in Pitkin County District Court for the first time, clad in bright orange jumpsuits and with metal clamps around their ankles. They were, Olmsted continued, "accompanied by hastily appointed attorneys begging for some information about the charges. But by the end of that first appearance, the only information the attorneys learned was that their clients would be held without bond while the district attorney decided if and how to charge them."

During this appearance, Trey apologized to Judge Gail Nichols for not being able to show his respect and stand when Her Honor entered the courtroom. As with all his subsequent court dates, he made this one in a wheelchair, instantly raising a myriad of questions about how anyone in his physical condition could have killed another adult—at least without having some help.

As Olmsted pointed out, local, regional, and national media were on hand for the Stylers' initial hearing, which took place inside a courthouse and a courtroom that had become part of Aspen's history and lore. While murder was uncommonly rare in the small community, the few cases that had been brought to this courthouse were well known, if not notorious.

From 1961 to 1975, the Parisian-born singer/actress Claudine Longet was married to crooner Andy Williams, before taking up with an Olympic skier and local favorite, Vladimir "Spider" Sabich. In 1976, Longet was arrested and charged with shooting Sabich to death in their Aspen home. At her trial, she contended that the gun had accidentally gone off while Spider was showing her how to fire it. The prosecution believed that she'd murdered Spider, but the Aspen cops had made a pair of legal missteps, which her defense exploited—seizing her diary and taking a blood sample from her without a warrant.

The sample revealed cocaine in her blood and the diary contradicted her later claim that her affair with Sabich had not soured and provided her with a motive to kill him. But because the evidence was obtained without a warrant, it was inadmissible. She was convicted of "criminally negligent homicide" and sentenced to thirty days in jail, plus a small fine. If that sentence wasn't light enough, in an extraordinary legal move the judge allowed Longet to choose which days she wanted to serve, so that she could spend the most time with her children. She mostly chose the weekends. She later went on vacation with her defense attorney, Ron Austin, who had a spouse at the time. The two eventually got married and still live in Aspen. Following the trial, Spider's family began civil proceedings against Longet, but the case was settled out of court, with the provision that Longet could never write or talk about her story. The actual truth behind the killing, whatever it was, would remain sealed for all time. Nearly four decades later, the shadow of this case would fall on the murder of Nancy Pfister.

In 1977, the year after the Sabich case, serial killer Ted Bundy was picked up in Pitkin County and held in Aspen for a preliminary hearing. While acting as his own attorney, he wasn't forced to wear handcuffs or shackles. During a recess, the judge permitted him to go into the law library to do research (the library was later converted into the courtroom where the Stylers made their first appearance on March 4, 2014). Crawling behind one of the bookcases, Bundy opened a second-story window and leaped out, severely spraining his ankle on impact with the ground. He limped south of town and hid in the mountains, where he broke into a hunting cabin and made off with clothing, food, and a rifle. Five days later, he stole a car near the Aspen Golf Course, was arrested, and booked all over again. The town's police department and justice system had never quite lived down Claudine Longet's thirty days in jail or Bundy's escape.

Now a third high-profile crime had come to the Pitkin County District Courthouse. What sort of repercussions would it have on the community and its all-important image?

Indignation

29

Aspen has some of the atmosphere and many of the benefits of a much larger city, but for all its glamour and glitz it's still a very small town, made up of people connected by shared acquaintances and common experience. The enclosed and intensely intimate nature of the place can be obscured or even hidden until something unpredictable and wrenching occurs—like the murder of a well-known native daughter.

Bob Braudis was just one person struggling with the news of a body found in a closet at 1833 West Buttermilk Road. Like many others, he'd had his own up and down moments with Nancy, but was deeply attached to her, to her family, and to the Pfisters' role in Aspen's history. When he was sheriff, Nancy had come by his office to chat about the past or about mutual friends like Hunter Thompson and Thomas Benton. The walls of the Pitkin County Sheriff's Office, located inside the courthouse on Main Street, were lined with Benton posters of the election campaigns of former sheriffs. They were strikingly artistic and imaginative, starting with the rolled-up fist at the center of the one representing Hunter Thompson when he unsuccessfully ran for the office in 1970. The posters alone hinted that law and order was not quite the same in Aspen as in many other locales. The past was honored here, even some of the wilder parts of it and even some of the outlaws.

As much as anyone, Nancy Pfister and Bob Braudis represented the Aspen of the 1970s and '80s. Both had lived through the recent changes in the community and the massive influx of big money. Nancy had loudly complained about the arrival of the *nouveaux riches* and their "starter castles." She'd opposed her own father when he'd wanted to develop Maroon Creek into a golf and tennis club, and she'd cheered when Aspen's mayor had cut down billboards in order to keep the town pristine. She and Braudis had clung to pieces of the past well after others had moved on, as if those fragments of time might one day magically reappear. Both had been surrounded by a tangible air of nostalgia.

At 7:50 p.m. on February 26, Patty Stranahan had received a text from Braudis telling her about a possible suicide at the Pfister home. Within a few days, after it had been established that this was a homicide, Braudis would be interviewed by the police. He gave them a wide-ranging account of the woman who'd been such a part of Aspen for so many years—a woman who'd suddenly vanished from his life.

"The memorial service is going to be a circus," he told the detectives. "People who crossed the street to avoid Nancy for years will be her best friend when the memorial service goes down . . . I will miss Nancy. She sought my approval, like a father figure. She was definitely not someone that I could hang out with full-time . . .

"Nancy always bumped heads with [Aspen lawyer] Andy Hecht . . . A spoiled rich girl hated to have anyone control her. And the parents, knowing that Nancy was a wild child, injected Andy Hecht into her financial life . . . One e-mail I was copied in on was Nancy had her monthly income shrunk and her response was, 'Ask Andy if *he* could live on $2000/month . . .' Something was going on that I had no knowledge of, but I didn't want to . . . Over the years I didn't care about her financial situation because no matter how much she whined and bitched, she was doing better than all three of us put together ever will, but I don't think she knew that . . .

"There's a saying, 'Leave your children enough money that they can do something, but don't leave them too much that they can do nothing.' If I were a con man, Nancy would be a ripe target, naïve, impressionable, Holly Golightly, Zen Buddhist, all that good stuff."

. . .

As former Denver cop and current Aspen PI David Olmsted was quick to point out, major metropolitan police departments have chains of command and established protocols for dealing with homicides and the relatives of victims. Officers are trained to follow those procedures as a matter of course, but in a small town where murders are rare, nothing is quite as rigid—especially when it involved the grisly death of a member of one of the community's most revered families.

When news about Nancy's death first reached Braudis on the evening of the twenty-sixth, he didn't just talk about it with Sheriff DiSalvo and Patty Stranahan. He also made contact with Christina Pfister, who now lived in Denver. Both she and Suzanne were about to be extremely upset, not just over the killing of their sister, but over how they were informed of her demise. They felt that the authorities hadn't told them as quickly or as professionally as they should have. When Suzanne was interviewed by the police, she openly showed them her outrage—someone in her position in Aspen shouldn't have been treated this way and "she ran them out the door," according to Olmsted, who had access to the interview transcript. He felt that the police should have been the ones in charge.

"This is not," he said, "the way to handle a potentially important witness."

For Christina, it was "especially cruel and painful without being necessary," she told detectives, not to get an official call from law enforcement about Nancy, but to hear it from Bob Braudis, who was no longer working for the sheriff's department. When news of the homicide broke statewide and then nationally, Christina started hearing from people all over the world—she got sixty calls in the space of ten hours—who'd known her sister. While she was trying to cope with the situation, she still hadn't received a formal notification about the murder.

By the time the authorities questioned her about both the homicide and some potential law enforcement leaks in the case, Christina was steaming.

"I am very, very angry," she said to CBI Agent John Zamora, "because I believe Bob Braudis has told everyone from California to South America [about Nancy's death]. Every single person told me that this is where they heard it from."

Bob's words were "very painful for a family member" to hear and Braudis, according to Christina, had given her "the entire autopsy report... I'm beyond stunned... Why does Bob have an entire autopsy report? Is he on the sheriff department?"

The indignation Christina and Suzanne demonstrated at the very start of the case was not just a tangent of the tragedy. It revealed how prickly it could be to deal with the relatives of a prominent murder victim, who were very sensitive about the way Nancy had lived and about how she may have died. It revealed how important it was to protect and preserve the family name. All of this added to the pressure on the police to find the killer quickly, to make an arrest, to quiet Aspen's concerns, and to put the incident behind them. This wasn't the sort of thing that happened in their town, and it had to be controlled and contained.

The sisters' attitude gave a taste of the highly unusual legal developments to come.

30

While interviewing Christina, Agent Zamora agreed with her that someone no longer in law enforcement, like Bob Braudis, should not have acted this way at the beginning of a homicide investigation. He even characterized the behavior as outrageous.

As the two of them spoke by telephone on the day after Nancy's body was discovered, they ventured into painful territory and into some of what the Pfister family had always wanted to keep quiet. Their conversation became part of the official record of the case and Christina did something that no one else did, giving an inside view of the dynamics of two generations of Pfisters. Her insights stood in direct contrast to a glossy *Aspen* magazine article about Nancy's death that would appear a few months later, which strenuously avoided the longstanding conflicts within the Pfister clan.

This is not to say that Christina was unfairly critical of either Nancy or Suzanne. Her discussion with Zamora unfolded in the midst of grief and shock. She was trying to be as open and as honest—and as kind—as she could about some of the most difficult parts (and difficult people) in her life. Nancy's murder had loosened something inside many of those who'd known her, and not everything could remain buried.

Christina told Zamora what people in Aspen were already aware of—she and Suzanne were not close "and that is an understatement... We don't speak... I moved out of Aspen for a reason. I'm just not an Aspen girl... I live in Denver very quietly in a seven-hundred-square-foot condo... I'm the

Pfister that lives under the radar. I have never wanted to be a Pfister. I adored my parents [but] I don't flash that name around."

Her father was "big and easy to love," but her mother could be challenging. In the last years of Betty's life, Christina had come back to Aspen to be with her and to try to establish a deeper bond with someone whom many described as emotionally reserved. Since Betty's passing, Christina had also tried to get closer to Nancy and to help her with her finances, advising her on investments.

Christina told Zamora that she hoped to "be the woman that would be there when she [Nancy] decided to get sober."

Nancy had a "borderline personality disorder" and she "could twist up at any time... I wouldn't expose myself or my children to that. So I loved her from a distance... I was starting to have a love affair with her that would have really meant something, but it would have taken me a long time. I don't know that I ever would have trusted her."

Before his death, Art had offered to build houses on the Buttermilk Mountain lots he'd provided for his three daughters. Nancy and Suzanne had taken this option, but Christina didn't want it. She'd used her inherited resources to pay for medical expenses and to take care of her son. She seemed to cope better from Denver. When Nancy was murdered, she and Suzanne were fighting over land rights.

Christina said that over the past winter Nancy had been dating or living with a man in Australia and she'd felt that it wasn't a good relationship for her sister. The man, she told Zamora, should be looked at for a possible connection to the homicide. (An old friend of Nancy's would soon come forward to the police and say that another man, a former West Coast boyfriend of hers, should also be investigated, but these leads weren't seriously followed.)

Nancy had hired Kathy to be a "sober companion," Christina told Zamora, but Kathy had started drinking as much as Nancy. When questioned about her sister's sexual preferences and her intimacy with Kathy, Christina replied that Nancy wasn't gay, "just lazy." Nancy had a "horrific temper" and the reason she drank and drugged so much was to control her personality disorder.

The more Christina spoke with Zamora, the guiltier she sounded for betraying Nancy and her family, but it was too late to give in to denial. She admitted to the agent that she was "afraid for my life as a child." At thirteen, she'd put herself in a boarding school, skipping the seventh and eighth grades, in order to get away from Nancy, who "had the capacity to be... a little scary... She had every capability without being violent."

Christina now pulled back and acted as if she'd bring the interview to an end, but she wasn't finished. The love she felt for Nancy and the heartbreak around that love was entangled with the effort to tell the truth about her and to try to understand why she'd been killed.

"I saw three different pictures..." she told Zamora, when laying out possible scenarios for her sister's demise. "One is that Nancy went off on somebody... that was bigger and scarier than her... The second one is she just went and picked up... somebody that's crazy... and she got a bigger deal than she thought... She was always bringing new people into her life on a regular basis... I'm sure one hundred people have told you that and she just didn't have an edit chip."

Christina paused before revealing the third scenario and pulled back again, as if she could reveal more, but was choosing not to.

"In no way," she said, "do I want her image to be smeared."

These few words would become the operative sentence of the case going forward. Looking honestly at the dead woman's life was a dilemma not just for everyone she'd left behind, but for everyone investigating the homicide. It would evolve into a major issue for the legal system charged with prosecuting her murder.

31

Under questioning by the police, Bob Braudis came across as having a very knowing air about the crime. He was in regular communication with Joe DiSalvo and indicated to the detectives that he was aware of things that other people weren't—in part because of his decades in local law enforcement, his closeness to the victim, and his friendship with the current head of the Pitkin County Sheriff's Office. What he shared about the evidence was stunning and centered on the timeline of the murder, but for extremely murky reasons, no one focused on this information for a long time, or perhaps ever. When the press and the public finally learned what Braudis knew, it was too late to make any difference.

"I know stuff," he told his interviewers. "My theory, based on what I've been told, is that the murder or murderers found Nancy dead to the world asleep. I think she was in the habit of taking a sleeping aid, two sleeping aids, one called Soma, one maybe Xanax, washing it down with a bottle of champagne, probably way more often than we know... She might have been sound asleep... If Kathy Carpenter had the motivation and found Nancy dead to the world, she could have been the one... It's going to take one of the Stylers to tell the story...

"She [Nancy Pfister] was very sociable, outgoing... perhaps famous for picking up people, trusted everybody... My mind started racing. My first hunch is the renters because there'd been increasing hostility in the e-mails I was copied on... I didn't know if they were capable of this...

"We met with the [Pfister] sisters and boy, that was interesting. There's like a hate/hate going on. Pretty bizarre. We had to keep them physically separated. They detested Nancy… I talked to Nancy about this… Why do your sisters hate you? Nancy's theory was they were jealous… Of the three sisters, Nancy was the prettiest. I will attest to that. Of the three sisters, Nancy was the craziest… I will attest to that… Nancy had no love or respect for them… and they seemed to be even worse regarding her."

"Do you think the sisters," Braudis was asked, "would be involved with this—with killing their sister?"

"I would not ever think that."

What about Kathy?

"She could be a part of this…" he said. "I do believe Kathy was verbally abused by Nancy… Nancy's expectations were way over what anyone else would expect of a bank employee… She would ask people to do her bidding, way more than most normal people… It comes from that spoiled brat, entitlement all the way… because she was charming, good looking, rich… That didn't work for me… A lot of other people walked away… Kathy was one of the few remaining people in Nancy's life who would do that grunt work for her… I assume she was compensated… Hey, some people will compensate themselves… They'll put up with it and dip into the cookie jar."

In the first week of March, the police interviewed Suzanne, who wasn't nearly as introspective about Nancy as Christina had been, or as revealing about the Pfister family. Her attitude was more dismissive, or more resigned, as if she'd always known that something bad could happen to Nancy, but had long since given up trying to play a positive role in her life.

"I've only seen my sister several times in the last year," she said. "I'd drive by and try not to look… She had a grow [marijuana] business at one time… I'm not interested in what's going on over there… I'd kind of whiz by… Kathy Carpenter was sort of a hanger-on of Nancy's, a sucking-up relationship with my sister that I never understood, maybe a sexual relationship… I don't know what the deal is with those two…

"Kathy didn't have any money. My sister had a little money. My sister's an alcoholic. Kathy was a little sycophant… I've been sober for twenty-five years . . . My sister gets with these sucking-up, octopus people . . . Sometimes, Nancy took advantage of them . . . My sister was just a lost soul . . . I was estranged from my sisters for a long time . . .

"I heard so much stuff about it [the killing] that night . . . from people at bars. People were calling me and telling me things. I was so mad at Joey [DiSalvo] . . . I heard that she was wrapped up, that there was a bag on her head, that she was locked in a closet . . . Joey told me to keep my mouth shut, but the information was out there . . .

"I'm a little worried there's somebody else out there . . . Am I safe? Are my kids safe? It's a little town and I can't stand all these predators running up to me to talk about this . . . I locked my door for the first time in twenty-two years. All my girlfriends are staying with me in shifts . . . Nancy had a temper. She could make people mad . . . She could piss people off . . . She certainly pushed my buttons . . . and because she's dead, people aren't going to tell the truth maybe."

32

On Thursday, March 6, David Olmsted left the Pamela Phillips defense team in Tucson to fly back to Denver. That night he boarded a small plane taking him on the last leg of his trip from DIA to Aspen. As he waited in line in Denver with his boarding pass, two women standing next to him were talking about the Nancy Pfister case. Neither he nor anyone else outside of the Pitkin County Sheriff's Office or the CBI had yet seen the arrest warrants or other evidence, and Joe DiSalvo had publicly made a show of being tight-lipped about the ongoing investigation. Olmsted couldn't help picking up the women's conversation, especially after one of them sat next to him on the aisle and the other was in the row in front of him.

"They were saying," the PI recalls, "that Nancy had been beaten to death while asleep in her bed. Then she was dragged into a closet and covered up with sheets."

He wasn't sure what to make of the women's information, but listened carefully to every word. By the time he got back to Aspen, both of the Stylers were being represented by publicly appointed counsel, as they could not afford private legal help. Trey's attorneys were Tina Fang, the chief trial lawyer in the Glenwood Springs Office of the Public Defender, and Deputy Public Defender Sara Steele, who worked in Aspen. Nancy's attorneys were Garth McCarty of Glenwood Springs and Beth Krulewitch of Aspen. Olmsted didn't normally work on court-appointed cases because, as he puts it, "the pay is abysmal." He wasn't on the list of PIs to be hired for this one, but Krulewitch wanted his help and pulled a few strings. Although he was ambivalent about working with a lawyer he didn't know—on a high-profile murder case that could involve the death penalty—he decided to take the job and became the lead investigator for Nancy Styler.

Since he was now an official part of the case, he soon read the arrest warrants and affidavits. To his surprise, as he later wrote in the *Aspen Times*, "The women I'd overheard [on the plane] were remarkably prescient about the details of the murder, details which at that time only law enforcement and the prosecutors should have known."

Yet the women somehow knew how Nancy had died and that she'd been found under a pile of sheets and blankets in her upstairs bedroom closet.

"At a subsequent hearing," Olmsted wrote in the *Times*, "the Stylers again appeared in district court and their attorneys addressed several issues, including the apparent leaking of information... Sheriff Joe DiSalvo announced that afternoon that his office would have no further statements about the investigation...

"I have known DiSalvo for many years, as a friend as well as a diligent and fair advocate for the rule of law. No one representing the Stylers has suggested anything shady about his handling of this case. No one has attempted to soil his reputation. No one has accused him of unethical or illegal behavior...

"[But] presumably innocent people are on trial in the marketplace of public opinion and may someday be in a court of law... It is the responsibility of law enforcement and prosecutors to perform their jobs with impartiality and fairness and with ultimate dedication to the truth..."

After officially joining the case, Olmsted visited Nancy Styler in jail and spent ninety minutes explaining to her how things worked following an arrest and what to expect going forward. She was much more relaxed than during their first phone conversation, but she was also direct, telling him they needed to fix this situation.

He advised her that when it came to the criminal justice system, developments tended to happen slowly and she should prepare herself for that.

After looking at all the evidence, Olmsted felt that the charges against his client in particular were extremely thin. As far as he could tell, the only reason she'd been arrested was because the police felt that Trey could not have committed the crime alone.

Because of this, Olmsted wanted to push the case along quickly and had begun speaking about this legal strategy with Nancy's two attorneys, but McCarty and Krulewitch didn't share his desire to move as fast. The search warrants, the affidavits, and the police interviews had produced thousands of pages of legal documents and the lawyers felt that they needed considerable time to digest all of the information in order to prepare an adequate defense.

Olmsted wasn't certain that he could speed up the attorneys, but assured Nancy Styler that he'd assist her counsel in trying to set bond for both Nancy and Trey, so they could be released from jail before a preliminary hearing or a trial.

While Nancy was learning her way around the lockup, Trey's actions inside the facility indicated that he was so disabled he could no longer walk, literally crawling across his cell on his hands and knees—but at other times, according to some officers, when he thought he wasn't being observed, he walked around normally. The jail staff had decided to transport him to all of his court appearances in a wheelchair so they wouldn't risk injuring him or incapacitating him any further.

Olmsted told Nancy that he didn't want to speak with her on the jail's telephone system and didn't want her talking with others on that line. Leaks about the evidence may have been coming from the sheriff's department, the DA, the CBI or elsewhere, and Nancy Styler's defense team couldn't take any chances by conversing over the Pitkin County phones. Anything she said might be intercepted or recorded and any negative emotions she expressed toward the victim could harm her case.

Before coming back from Australia, Nancy Pfister had not only asked several local people to help her get the Stylers out of her house, including Bob Braudis, but had also been in contact with her friend Joe DiSalvo about the conflict with her tenants. As Olmsted explained to his new client, the odds were already tilted against both of the Stylers. Be patient, the PI cautioned

Nancy, watch everything you say to the authorities, and trust no one within the walls of the jail.

She wasn't the best at following orders.

When describing Nancy Pfister to the police in one of her interviews before her arrest, she didn't seem able to stop talking about her, as if the dead woman had unleashed something very deep and very competitive within her.

"We were going to try and help her," she told the detectives. "Maybe if she had a purpose in life when she got back... She'd talked about putting in a lap pool. She talked about building a world-class spa, but that was before she was going to use her money for the Hollywood movie and before she was going to buy a condo in Mexico. These were all these things she was going to do with her money that she was getting from her mother, but she was waiting till probate was done on November 18...

"It's a sad situation. It's second-generation wealth that has nothing to do with their life, no purpose. I was saying to my husband last night, there's not a soul in this town who can say anything nice about her... I thought to myself, *I don't like anything about her.* I was respected, I was in medicine. I've never had anyone disrespect me that way. She got my husband in her room and said, 'Rub my back, rub my shoulder.' She asked me to look at a pimple by her groin. She walks around naked all the time, in front of my husband, anyone... My husband's a doctor. We've seen it all. It's not that great, either. She thought it was... I told my husband, this is a reality show and there's going to be this crazy lady who does all this stuff...

"One night when she had me in there and she wanted me to massage her shoulders and I thought, *I'd like to wring her neck because she's such a drunk and making me so crazy*... That woman got me more upset than anyone I ever encountered with her lies."

If she and Trey were innocent of the crime, she was asked, what was her theory of how Pfister had died?

If she had to guess, she told the detectives, she couldn't rule out Suzanne because her older sister was "the one she had the most venom for."

33

The murder of an Aspen "Golden Girl" had made headlines in the *New York Post*, *People* magazine, and the papers in London. But locally, the news hit hardest.

Teresa Wyatt learned of her friend's death online. Because of how the information was presented on Facebook, she thought that Nancy had died in a plane crash on her way back from Australia. When she grasped that this wasn't true and that Nancy had been murdered inside her own home, Teresa felt what many people do when coming face-to-face with a personal tragedy:

It can't be! She just sent me an e-mail! Is someone playing a joke on us? She had all sorts of global adventures, but got killed in her own bed in Aspen?

As the news of the homicide sunk in over the next few days, Teresa tried to absorb the very limited facts of the case and the arrest of the Stylers. Looking at pictures of Trey in a wheelchair, she immediately visualized the steps that carried one into the Pfister house and the flight of stairs leading up to Nancy's bedroom. This was not a home that any disabled person could navigate or would ever choose to live in. Why was Trey now using a wheelchair? He obviously couldn't have gotten around Nancy's residence like that. Was he faking his illness or greatly exaggerating it to fool the authorities?

She thought how Nancy-like it had been for her friend to change her plans on a whim and return to Aspen in late February, instead of staying away until late May, as she'd originally intended. Nancy was known for altering plane reservations at the last moment, no matter the expense. Whenever she made up her mind to go, nothing stopped her. It probably cost her more to change her flight home than it would have to hire a lawyer to evict the Stylers. It didn't make sense. Was Nancy worried about something other than the rental dispute? Something about Gabe or other problems?

In the aftermath of the murder, Teresa e-mailed Kathy Carpenter and expressed her sympathy, saying that she couldn't imagine what it had been like to discover Nancy in the closet. She never heard back from Kathy, who'd stopped going to work and communicating with almost everyone.

Teresa wasn't the only one struggling with the supposed motive behind the homicide. Juliana Pfister also refused to accept that her mother had been killed over a landlord-tenant conflict.

"How could someone," she told ABC News, "just be so angry that they got kicked out of a house? There's got to be something more... I have no idea how someone could do something like that and especially to her... My mom could never hurt anything or hurt anyone and that is one thing that everyone that knew her knew. She cared about a lot of people and helped the wrong people this time."

Arriving in Aspen following the crime, Juliana was interviewed by the police and was very casual with them. Freely using the F word, she displayed the manner of a young person of means who'd been largely protected from life's harsher realities. In the wake of her mother's death, she found a comparison for what she was experiencing in the world of entertainment.

The murder, she said, "feels like a David Lynch film... Like *Blue Velvet*... I never trusted Kathy Carpenter, but I do know that she really cared about my mom... I think my mom exposed a whole new world that she never was a part of, maybe more interesting people... The way that I'm looking at the case... if they [the Stylers] were framed, that would be the smartest person in the world to frame them to find that kind of evidence so close to where they are... or they're just clearly very guilty."

On March 10, a week after the Stylers' arrest, Nancy Pfister was cremated. Her memorial service was scheduled for four days later at the Hotel Jerome.

Columnist Paul Andersen was one of the first to eulogize the victim in the *Aspen Times.* Like many others, he walked a tightrope between telling the truth about the deceased woman—and being kind and respectful:

"Nancy was unapologetic about who she was. Her cavalier ways were accepted by friends, some who celebrated her eccentricities, others who struggled to cope with them. She was a ward of the community from which she derived enough love to fuel herself with the raw energy that exploded in shrieking laughter. Bright meteors fall, sooner or later, to the inevitable pull of gravity... Suddenly, they're gone. The glow vanishes. Earth absorbs them. Their fire goes out."

Nancy's death, the *Aspen Times* wrote, "will leave a hole in the fabric of the Aspen community."

The memorial, held in the Jerome ballroom, drew a standing-room-only crowd estimated at four hundred. The event featured a rock band—some mourners found this inappropriate, but others felt that it perfectly reflected what Nancy would have wanted—which played well into the night. Prosecco was served and each attendee received a crystal, wrapped in a small gift bag, and hundreds of Tibetan prayer flags were draped across the hotel ceiling. Naked trees were set up throughout the room so that people could attach personal notes of remembrance to them.

Teresa Wyatt and Daniel Treme were at the memorial and made an effort to speak with Bob Braudis and Joe DiSalvo, both of whom lived downtown within walking distance of the Jerome. Teresa was careful when speaking with DiSalvo, understanding that he was in the middle of an unfolding murder investigation. She was even more cautious when taking to the clearly grief-stricken Braudis, certain that if she said the wrong word, he'd start crying.

The memorial's speakers reviewed Nancy's life after graduating from high school: she'd departed Aspen to study at the Pratt Institute in New York, before moving on and traveling to Africa, India, and Nepal. She'd loved gardening, permaculture, and had her father's gift of dowsing for water.

George Stranahan went first.

"Nancy was the senior adventurer of the world," he told the assembled. "She was a travel adventurer, a relationship adventurer, a social-cause adventurer—a life adventurer. Adventure is always about surprise and discovery, and these are what fed her spirit. To be with Nancy was to be swept along into her adventures, to discover and to be surprised. Let us honor that spirit, remember the stories and celebrate that she chose us for the adventures."

"She carried a bright light within her," Juliana told the crowd. "Sometimes, it was so bright it was hard to understand. It was like she wasn't even really from this world. It was so embracing and otherworldly... She loved being a connection for people. I know a lot of people who are married and she introduced them. She had a really big heart."

"People say there are Seven Wonders of the World," said Christina Pfister, "but I believe Nancy was the eighth. She was a force of nature... The greatest gift that Nancy gave to us is her daughter—beautiful, elegant and poised... I would travel the world and, inevitably, when I would say to people, 'I'm from Aspen,' they would say, 'Oh, then you must know Nancy Pfister.' And then some fabulous or hysterical story would ensue. She was one of the most gregarious and vivacious women, following in her father's footsteps of never knowing a stranger."

"If somebody moved to Aspen," Braudis told the memorial, "Nancy was a natural at figuring out who they should be introduced to. I know many of those introductions that have lasted twenty, thirty years as friendships... She always found something to rejoice about and life in general was something she rejoiced in."

Said Hunter Thompson's widow, Anita: "She was the kind of person that this community might take for granted, because her friendship was just always there for you. There are so many people that will miss that."

Added historian Douglas Brinkley, who'd befriended Nancy while working on a biography of Hunter Thompson: "She was an integral member of Hunter's extended family. She was an effervescent and warm person who loved Aspen and was most proud of being a mother."

The tone was celebratory and highly positive, but not everybody was pleased with the memorial.

"The event was a total whitewash," says Shane Todd, a manager at Aspen's Sky Hotel who'd lived in the town off and on for decades. "They did everything they could to cover up who she really was and how she really lived."

Following the memorial, Nancy's friends placed a tribute to her near a ski run on Aspen Mountain, alongside similar ones dedicated to Elvis, Marilyn Monroe, and Jerry Garcia. The shrine, set in a circular clearing in a grove, included the laminated program from Nancy's service and a crystal in a small yellow bag.

A letter about the deceased woman, written by John Cunningham, soon appeared in the *Aspen Times.* Three decades earlier, he'd met Nancy at the Oberoi Hotel in New Delhi, India. During a gathering of his associates, "a young girl entered the lobby . . . barefooted with her blond hair flowing. She wore blue jeans and a cute little hat and walked into the lobby curious to see what was going on . . . She joined in the meeting and some of her comments found their way into the project. She helped to bond my group of experts and never realized that she had done it."

Nancy and Cunningham became friends and she'd spontaneously show up in his life again and again, always "full of exciting ideas and dreams—and ready to go on any adventure at a moment's notice."

She invited him to Aspen for an education conference, dedicated to making science less threatening for girls. One thing led to another and Cunningham went to the Burning Man festival in the Nevada desert and wound up buying the world's largest solar-powered art machine. He created an art foundation called eatART.org, based in Vancouver, British Columbia. EatART, which stands for "energy awareness through art," now has 2,000 members.

"This has all happened because of Nancy," he wrote, "and she had no idea that it was because of her that it happened."

With Pfister's death, Cunningham's organization decided to change the name of the art machine from "Daisy" to "Nancy."

"I Know *She* Didn't do it"

34

After March 3, the authorities had the Stylers behind bars, the couple had been appointed attorneys, and the police were no longer interviewing them. The two detectives charged with interrogating Kathy Carpenter about the murder, CBI Agent John Zamora and DA Investigator Lisa Miller, clearly believed that she was the weakest link of the three main suspects. Maybe she hadn't killed Pfister herself, but knew who had. Maybe she hadn't covered up the crime, but was aware of how it had been done. Maybe if they spoke with her long enough, she'd eventually reveal the secrets behind the crime—or break down altogether.

She'd already been caught in a couple of inconsistencies. On the evening of February 26, she'd told Deputy Ryan Turner and Joe DiSalvo, but not Peace Officer Brad Gibson, that she'd seen the Stylers at the Pfister residence around 5:30 (when they were on their way to Glenwood Springs). She'd told Turner that she hadn't been drinking, but he said he smelled alcohol on her breath. She'd told the authorities that when she'd first looked in the closet she'd seen Nancy Pfister's blond hair, when all the available evidence made this an impossibility. And she was about to admit that not long after finding the body, she'd taken $6,000 in cash and two pieces of jewelry from Pfister's safe deposit box. Did that make her guilty of *something*?

The police began questioning her on the night of February 27 and, following her failure to pass a polygraph exam the next day, Zamora started pushing harder—telling her that she'd "bombed" this test. Perhaps she was ready to do what she hadn't done in their previous discussions and change or expand or alter her story in some way.

"I think you have this kind heart, trying to help," the agent told Kathy. "Then all of a sudden, holy crap, some bad stuff happened... If you know what happened and we show you know what happened and you don't tell me, that's just like you killed her. That's the same charge, I don't want to charge you with that... I'm concerned that the Stylers might have got you involved in something... He [Trey] pointed to you. He said, 'Tell Kathy I love her... I'm sorry for what happened to her.'"

The agent described a scenario in which Kathy and the Stylers were all at the crime scene and Pfister was dead. One of them protested that Nancy couldn't "go out this way" and felt compelled to bury the body in sheets.

"That would be you..." Zamora said to Carpenter. "I believe that you know what happened and I'm going to be able to prove that, because that's my job and I have them in jail and you have to worry greatly what they tell me."

"They're liars!" Kathy blurted out.

"You have knowledge," Zamora pressed. "Everything is crashing down on you... You need to come clean... You failed the polygraph..."

Among all of Kathy's inconsistencies, one was most significant. In the twenty hours of interviews the detectives conducted with Carpenter, they returned to it again and again: what happened right before Kathy made the 911 call on the evening of February 26?

"When you opened the closet door and you saw her," Zamora asked, "what exactly did you see?"

"I'm having flashbacks," Kathy said.

Until now, she'd been flat and emotionless.

"I opened the door," she said, crying. "She was covered. I just saw the head. I knew the blond hair and the length of the hair... I know she was wrapped... I saw the head and blood... blood on the head..."

Zamora told Kathy that he'd studied every crime scene photograph and every image taken of the body of Nancy Pfister after the police had arrived at her home. He'd spoken to every deputy who'd come to the house, gone upstairs, and looked in the closet. They'd all said the same thing: no part of the victim was showing.

"You would have seen *no* hair," Zamora said to Kathy.

She started to whimper.

"No, no, no," she muttered.

"You *know* what else happened," Zamora insisted. "She was covered with a sheet, very respectfully, with dignity. Covered with a sheet. So the time that you would have seen the hair is *before* she was covered with the sheet."

Kathy didn't respond.

"There was no hair sticking out," Zamora said.

"It wasn't out!" she wailed.

"You said you saw the hair. We also listened to the 911 tape and there were discrepancies. You said you saw a lot of blood and her hair and guess what? That didn't happen. There was no hair to see. She was fully covered with the plastic bags. You may have seen her hair *before* she got covered with the plastic bags..."

Kathy kept silent, conceding nothing.

Yet she was able to tell the detectives precisely where the injuries were on Pfister's head. According to Lisa Miller, these descriptions were "spot on." How could Carpenter have known the location of the wounds if she hadn't seen them prior to Pfister being wrapped up? Or had she unwrapped the bundle after finding it in the closet?

Zamora and Miller brought out pictures of Nancy lying on the closet floor. They studied them in front of Carpenter, poring over every detail and once again pointing out that no hair was visible in any of the images.

Staring at the photos, Kathy reached up and twisted a lock of her own hair, in a feeble attempt to demonstrate what she'd said she'd seen. They offered her a crime scene photo of the covered body, which she initially recoiled from, but then she took it and studied it, holding it up to her face, reaching out and touching the area where Nancy's head would later be discovered. She gazed at the spot, saying nothing.

Once more they asked about her involvement in the murder.

She vaguely replied that she'd told a few people, "I was a suspect."

Why was she a suspect?

Because she was the last person known to be with Nancy, on Sunday night, and the one to find her on Wednesday evening.

Zamora brought up the $6,000 and the two rings Kathy had taken from the Alpine Bank safe deposit box soon after she'd found the body. She hadn't mentioned this to the police in her first interrogation, but only confessed to it later.

Did Kathy know that Nancy Pfister had repeatedly inquired of lawyer John Beatty why the Stylers hadn't paid her the second installment of $6,000 they owed her when she'd left for Australia? Wasn't it obvious that Kathy had gotten this money from the couple, but never passed it along to Pfister? Wasn't that at the heart of the conflict between the Stylers and Pfister?

"What?" Zamora asked her, "were you going to do with the money?"

"I was going to give it to Juliana and the ring for her..."

"I've got a big problem with your son," Zamora said, referring to the statements Michael had made to the police about the cash and the jewelry.

He'd told Zamora that Kathy had taken the money to pay for his plane flight home and his tuition fee of $825. He'd also claimed to have advised his mother to give the rings to the Pfister sisters. Kathy herself told the detectives that she didn't want the jewelry to go to lawyer Andy Hecht because Nancy Pfister had never liked him. Carpenter said that Nancy Pfister had told her that if anything happened to her in her travels, the jewelry should go to Juliana.

"He lied," Zamora said about her son. "We've got some kind of cover-up in a murder case. He's protecting you so much that *he* might go to jail."

Carpenter sat quietly in front of them, looking dazed or drugged, disheveled, but still wearing the eyelashes Nancy Styler had applied to her. She didn't seem to know what to say, not even when they threatened to arrest her son.

Zamora and Miller zeroed in on the timeline leading up to the murder, asking Kathy to go over it with them once again.

"Nancy gave them an ultimatum to get out by the twenty-second," she said. "They dragged their feet, which I found very odd... Trey said to me, 'What's she gonna do if we're still here?'"

Kathy told the detectives that she'd replied to him in a singsong manner, as if she were scolding a bad boy, "Treyyyyyy..."

She looked at the investigators and continued speaking about the Stylers. "There was always something that I didn't trust about them... Trey had asked me if Nancy had a lot of money... I said, 'You know, she's a Pfister. Her house is paid for.' He said, 'She must have a lot of money in your bank. Does she get the VIP treatment from your bank?' I said, 'Treyyyyy... She's treated just like every other customer' and I would not disclose any of her personal information."

If Nancy Styler really despised Pfister, why did she make everything comfortable in the house for when she got home?

Kathy fumbled for an answer.

"You're telling us," Zamora said, "that she hated Nancy... This is a deep hate... But then they hate her so much they want to put stuff back in order for her?"

Kathy shrugged.

Why didn't she tell someone in a position of authority after hearing Nancy Styler talking about putting cyanide in a piece of chocolate for Pfister?

"I feel guilty," Kathy said, "that I didn't go to the police when they made these comments."

She finally confessed something to the detectives: she hadn't called the cops because she thought the Stylers were joking.

35

That was the only thing she confessed to, as hour after hour passed and Zamora and Miller could get nothing new out of Carpenter. When they became exasperated, they took turns leaving the room, before coming back for another round of questioning. Zamora tried everything: posing as her friend, her psychologist, and her religious counselor—attempting to make her feel guilty or innocent or guilty again. He went soft with her and then hard, alternately becoming passive and aggressive. Nothing caused her to change her story: she didn't know more than she'd already told them or what had happened to Nancy Pfister.

Lisa Miller acted increasingly impatient, if not hostile, but that didn't work, either. Kathy refused to bend and her demeanor returned to maddeningly flat and dull. This didn't change until she began talking about her seven-year relationship with the dead woman. She began to relax and to speak with more animation, bringing her friend back to life in a way that no one else had.

At times Nancy Pfister's behavior, with both women and men, was at the edge of extreme and there was no easy or clear psychological explanation for this. People who knew her best or had heard her talking in a confessional (or drunken) mode had picked up hints of murkier things in her past. Sometimes, it takes a murder to push the most uncomfortable issues to the surface, issues that can play out in a courtroom in most unforeseen ways—or never be allowed to play out at all.

What Kathy now hinted at with the detectives might have carried pieces of the truth—or could have been a total fabrication. It may have explained some of Nancy's choices after she became an adult. Or Kathy might have only been remembering the ramblings of someone who'd been drinking heavily with a companion and feeding her lies or false memories in the hope of generating sympathy or affection. Nancy Pfister had leaned on women for emotional support and constantly craved the affection of men, just as she'd constantly wanted to exploit them for money.

With nearly everyone, she'd veered away from reaching into the depths of her background, except perhaps with Kathy. Both women needed each other and needed the friendship, no matter how volatile it was.

Kathy recalled Nancy telling her that she didn't have anyone but her and that she loved Carpenter "as a sister... We really clicked. Not only did I really like her, but I really did feel sorry for her... Some of the stories she shared with me of the past... Her mother trying to take her daughter away, possibly molested [by a family member] ... She really confided in me... She shared everything with me, her feelings... I was all she had."

Remembering, Kathy fought off tears, as if she'd already said things better left unsaid, but then she spoke again:

"We had fights a couple of times when we were drinking... A shouting match: 'You stupid bitch!' When we were drinking a lot—you know you get two drunks... She could really push your buttons sometimes... If you ever stood up to her, she'd go off and call the police...

"I asked her if she was having an affair with this married guy we know and she called the police... It triggered her... like getting called on something... Just do as she says, and I'm more passive. She's the aggressor in the friendship/relationship. She'd boss me around, but in a fair way... I knew that there was a beautiful, great side to her... but when she'd get drunk she'd get in your face, but she'd always apologize... She could call me at midnight, 'Kathy, I'm at the bar drunk. Can you get me and take me home?'... Or, 'Go get the dog, bring him home in the morning...' I did, but it gets tiring."

The same drama she'd played out with the Stylers in the winter of 2014 had been enacted with others years before.

"She rented her house to two guys," Kathy said. "That turned out to be a nightmare. When she rented the house there are all these rules—they were to rent the two bedrooms downstairs, no guests. She had me as her house manager... She didn't have a contract, I always told her, 'Nancy, I would do background checks, credit checks, get a driver's license.' But she said she had 'good juju'... I had them evicted before she came home. That was very stressful...

"She's really a lovable person. She just has a cantankerous side to her as well... I try to see the good in people. I'm not perfect."

Zamora and Miller refocused on the evening of February 26 and asked what had really happened up on West Buttermilk Road.

"When I got to the house after work," Kathy said, "it was around five forty-five... The door was unlocked. I went in and called for Nancy. I looked around... I'd tried calling her [on the phone] several times. It went right to voice mail."

Earlier in the day, Nancy Styler had communicated with Kathy, telling her that Pfister's medicine bottles holding her collection of pills were in her bedroom—a critical detail that would come into question later on.

"When I went there," Kathy said to the detectives, "the pills were gone... She always had to have her pills. Ambien—big plastic bags of pills. I noticed they were gone when I went into the house... That's not like her... That's so bizarre...

"I looked around. I opened up the washer to see if her dirty sheets were in there... No sheets... I looked in the dryer. I had washed her robe on Sunday night... That was still in the dryer."

She walked back upstairs, looking for more of Nancy's possessions.

"I didn't see her pearls... I went into the bedroom. They had put everything back in her bedroom... The one thing that was odd was that her bed was made and Nancy never made her bed. Never... There was a strange smell in the bedroom... I looked in her bathroom. It looked like the way we left it... I looked to see if she took her purse and credit cards... I didn't see her purse so I thought maybe she went somewhere... I opened up the nightstand drawer. All the drugs were gone."

She moved toward the master closet, but the key she'd put in the lock for Pfister's return from Australia was gone. Nancy Styler, she told the detectives, had earlier in the week said that she'd needed to "put stuff in the closet" and had asked Kathy to bring the key and let her in, which she'd done. But now the key was gone.

Kathy called her mother, then Patty Stranahan, and then put Gabe in her car and drove into Aspen. Retrieving the second key from her condo, she rode back up West Buttermilk Road and walked into the master bedroom, pulling open the closet door.

"I saw her on the floor!" she told Zamora and Miller, crying again. "I saw blood on the headboard—that was before I saw her... I wet my finger and touched the stain. Oh God, what is that? Is it blood?... I didn't see blood on the mattress...

"It was a body... I ran out of there so fast... I was afraid they would come back and get me... because they were so angry with her and they talked about killing her... I jumped in my car and I flew out of there... Half way down the hill I called 911..."

She was sobbing so hard that Zamora tried to comfort her.

"Take a breath," he said. "Okay?"

His words seemed to help and she was able to go on.

"I didn't go in there [the closet]," she said. "I saw a head. Maybe there was a little blood on her. I don't know... I couldn't stare at it... her hair... I had to run fast... I didn't know if someone was in there and they were going to get me... I saw Nancy Pfister. I saw the blond hair..."

She said that when the deputies began arriving at the house that evening, "I asked them to call my mom to come... I sat in the police car. I felt faint. I couldn't breathe... They gave me something to calm me down... An ambulance came..."

Letting her narrative hang in the air for a few moments, Zamora replied, "I talked to Trey Styler and he said they were concerned about you. He thought that you and Nancy [Pfister] got in a huge fight and maybe Nancy had killed you or you had killed her. He said you were mad because Nancy was treating you like a slave... He does have a temper. I know that and I've seen it..."

Then he added, "Trey said to tell you he loves you and he's sorry it happened this way."

Kathy had retreated into her glazed state.

"You know what happened..." Zamora said, more forcefully now. "You got sucked into this... Maybe you're the one that killed her... and you just snapped... Trey says that he was worried that you were the one that was dead... He's pointing at you... So if there was any loyalty there, that's gone...

"You absolutely know what happened... I really don't want to have to come back and arrest you on a warrant... You have to tell me the truth, and who's involved. Do not be afraid of them... You're more scared of them than going to jail... When it comes down to the hard questions [on the polygraph]... you failed... What were you thinking when those questions were asked?"

"I felt," she said, "that I should have gone to the police when they initially made those threats... I feel like I should have done something... I feel in my heart that they did it, but I don't know for a fact..."

"Do you think... that somehow you gave them the means to kill her? For instance, did they get the closet key from you?... Or they got something else from you and you allowed that? You might have set it up or there was a master scheme for money... How much money did she recently come into?"

"Six hundred something... Nancy told them that she was asking them for help as to how to invest it..."

Zamora paused to bring Rosa Perez into the room. She'd recently administered Carpenter the polygraph test that she'd badly failed. Now Perez began to speculate about why Kathy could not pass the exam.

"You wanted her dead..." she told Carpenter. "It worked out perfectly. These Stylers got so pissed off they were going to do it. Even though they told you they were going to kill her, you chose to not do anything because you would be just as happy to have her out of your life. She sounded like a pain in the ass. You were doing her grocery shopping. You're doing everything for her... You use the word 'demand' almost every other word when you described that woman...

"I'm not saying you hit her with an object... But you knew the Stylers were going to so you chose to kind of stand back and let this happen because it benefited you... That's why you feel guilty about her death."

Perez's pointed accusations generated no more of a response or an admission from Kathy than anything else had. Zamora and Miller were out of options, except for one.

Based on all of their interviews with the suspect, the detectives reached the same speculative conclusion, which could be pared down to a single sentence:

"It is apparent that Kathy Carpenter saw the body of Nancy Pfister after she was killed, but prior to being placed in the plastic bag."

That was enough for them.

On March 14, following their exhaustive interrogation of Kathy and seventy-two hours of surveillance on her employee housing unit at the Christiana Lodge, the police took her into custody. Clad in her pajamas at the time of her arrest, she looked disoriented, having been on Xanax lately in an effort to get some sleep. On the night of Kathy's arrest, Nancy Pfister's memorial was unfolding at the Hotel Jerome, a couple of blocks away from the jail. Locked in her cell, Kathy heard a band playing tributes to Nancy and thought that, of all people, she should have been at the event, celebrating the life and grieving the death of her friend.

Like the Stylers, she was charged with first-degree murder and conspiracy to commit first-degree murder. As this news was broadcast throughout the region, along with some highly unflattering mug shots of Kathy, a new wave of shock moved in and around Aspen. Despite her problems with alcohol over the years and having spent several nights sobering up in the custody of the Aspen Police Department, Kathy had maintained a reasonably good image in town and some people were eager to give her the benefit of the doubt.

"I know *she* didn't do it," said more than one customer at Alpine Bank. "She couldn't have killed Nancy."

As reporters searched through Kathy's background, they soon uncovered the flare-up between her and Pfister in August 2012, after a night of drinking in Glenwood Springs.

A woman named Pam Fisher came to Kathy's defense in a letter to the *Aspen Times*:

"It seems like striving to bring a guilty verdict against her [Carpenter] when the papers go digging two years into the past to say that Nancy Pfister was afraid of Kathy Carpenter."

Had anyone reading her letter to the editor, Fisher inquired, ever drunk too much with a friend and gotten into a disagreement? Had anyone ever made a poor choice with alcohol, before rectifying this and becoming friends again with the other person?

The arrest photos of Kathy, Fisher wrote, "are terrible and for a woman who has worked here for many years and whose reputation was one of a dedicated employee, a caring and compassionate woman, this creates a pretty ugly picture for one who may indeed be innocent."

With three people now behind bars for the murder, the Pitkin County Sheriff's Office announced that the case was still under investigation and they were continuing to work on new leads and to interview more witnesses.

In the meantime, David Olmsted and the lawyers for the Stylers were going over the evidence and had begun putting together their legal strategies.

36

Olmsted was the kind of thorough private investigator who'd awaken at three in the morning to get a drink of water and start to question himself about what he'd overlooked in a criminal case. Had he missed something in the arrest affidavits, the search warrants or the police interviews that could help his client? Had he asked the right follow-up questions when talking with potential witnesses? Which of them should he go back to and speak with again to help his client, Nancy Styler?

During his career as a PI in Aspen, one of his tactics had been to communicate freely and openly with the deputies in the sheriff's office, a small-town maneuver that helped him get closer to law enforcement and to understand more of their thinking about a criminal matter. (Olmsted went out of his way to say nice things about those who worked for the Pitkin County Sheriff's Office, but some of them saw the PI as part of an adversarial legal process and weren't always so complimentary toward him.) The court-appointed lawyers he was working for in the Pfister case, Garth McCarty and Beth Krulewitch, didn't necessarily think that Olmsted *should* talk with the deputies, and that wasn't their only disagreement. On nearly every front, the attorneys were more cautious than he was. They didn't want to hold press conferences to speak about their client, didn't want to push for a preliminary hearing as hard as Olmsted wanted them to, and weren't as driven to explore alternative explanations for the murder—explanations that excluded the Stylers or Kathy Carpenter from having committed it.

The lawyers were feeling their way through a delicate set of circumstances, and were inevitably going to butt heads with Olmsted.

The PI hadn't signed on for a nine-to-five job or taken the gig just to get a plea bargain for Nancy Styler. Over and over again when talking with reporters, he reiterated that he wanted to know the full truth behind the homicide, no matter what it was, but working with Garth and Beth, he wasn't sure that his point of view was appreciated. Because of his urban background first growing up in New York state and later as a cop in Denver, he carried an attitude that some big-city people and metropolitan police officers have toward rural cops or small-town lawyers who have far less experience dealing with major crimes. He openly said that when it came to investigating complicated homicides, the Pitkin County officials were in over their heads.

For a decade, he'd been in law enforcement in the Denver suburb of Northglenn, serving on the Organized Crime Strike Force, and had regularly looked into conspiracies or murders or other felonies. He felt strongly that the Nancy Styler defense team, to cite one example, should study the police reports and witness interviews not randomly, but in the exact order in which they were collected. Information and narratives changed as the reports were gathered and this could alter how you read the documents and formed your thinking about a case. He had many ideas that he wanted to implement, but he was working with lawyers he didn't know well and nothing was going to be simple or easy.

Near the end of March, Suzanne Pfister gave a victim's impact statement to the authorities about the murder. Such comments could later be used at bond hearings or at the sentencing of those convicted of a crime. With three people in custody for the death of her sibling and with Nancy's memorial fading into the past, Suzanne was no longer concerned with eulogizing a family member in public, but seemed more focused on protecting herself, her relatives, and her position in Aspen.

"My sister was killed in a totally violent manner," she wrote. "The people who killed her should go to prison for the rest of their lives . . . I have never locked my door before. I lived next door to my sister and now I jump every time the dog barks. I have installed cameras outside and motion-activated lights. I live in fear. I am a prisoner in my beautiful home since this is a very small town."

And then she added, as if to emphasize what the murder had cost her: "I can't bear all the very sweet and well-meaning condolences I am subjected to if I go into town, so I don't go . . . Every time there is a hearing, it heats up again."

It was a deeply revealing set of remarks, which would resonate throughout the legal proceedings to come. Suzanne had made a point of saying that she was *upset* when receiving the sympathy of those who'd known Nancy—while in another forum Juliana had talked about being annoyed because some people kept referring to her mother as a "socialite" instead of calling her a "philanthropist." If they were this sensitive about the outpouring of condolences and the use of a word or two, one could only imagine what they might be facing when the Stylers and Kathy Carpenter went on trial for murder and who knows what kind of stories about Nancy Pfister emerged in the courtroom. This testimony would not just be heard in their hometown, but would likely attract regional and national attention.

In many homicide cases, the defense doesn't like to put the victim on trial; it's a risky strategy that can backfire—but there are exceptions. As David Olmsted was the first to underline, Nancy Pfister had been "a very busy girl whose lifestyle invited problems." She was well known for picking up men she barely knew or had just met, and taking them home. She was just as well known for her drinking and drug use. As part of Nancy Styler's defense, Olmsted had already lined up a potential witness or two or three whom Nancy had made jealous with her flirtations and other behaviors with both women and men. Whether or not these actions had done anything to get her killed was an open question. But her background and parts of her family's background were sure to be exposed in court, along with certain details of the Pfisters' financial dealings.

Given Aspen's unconventional relationship with the drug culture, and given Nancy's past, the town itself might be put on trial.

One thing was undeniable: the work that Olmsted had begun doing on behalf of his client and his commitment to learning more about Nancy Pfister's last days weren't going to make Suzanne, Christina, or Juliana any happier.

37

Like everyone else in town, Olmsted knew of the longstanding conflict between the three sisters and wondered if these raw-edged relationships had played any role in Nancy's demise. Delving into their family history wasn't going to be a popular strategy in Aspen, but Olmsted wasn't deterred.

From the start of the case, he contended that the Stylers had paid Nancy Pfister the initial $12,000 they'd owed her (the known facts appear to bear this out, with the final $6,000 ending up under Kathy Carpenter's control). The rent money or lack of it may have been a serious aggravation to Pfister, but in Olmsted's view the motive behind the killing might not have involved a mere few thousand dollars.

"Trey and Nancy," he says, "were people who'd had lots of money in their lives. They weren't going to murder someone over this small amount. I've seen all the evidence, read all the police reports and the interviews with the witnesses, and it's very thin against all three of the defendants, but especially against Nancy Styler.

"I know what Kathy Carpenter told the police about the Stylers right before they were arrested. She spoke about the rental issue, but she didn't give them a smoking gun. People have jumped to a lot of conclusions based on inaccurate information and the initial press coverage of the case. Things aren't always as simple as we want them to be. You don't kill someone because of a minor rental disagreement."

If rent was the only issue, as Olmsted and Teresa Wyatt pointed out,

Pfister could have had her attorney, John Beatty, evict the Stylers for probably the same amount of money it cost her to fly back from Australia.

A much larger money issue was in play, the PI suggested, but the police were so pressured to make arrests and solve the case, no one had bothered to investigate it. Nancy Pfister might not have dropped her plans to keep traveling throughout the winter of 2014 and return to Aspen that May just because of her conflict with the Stylers. Had she flown back to Colorado on February 22 for another reason? There were witnesses or potential witnesses, Olmsted hinted, who were aware of this reason and could have informed the police of its significance—if this scenario had been explored.

On February 6, Pfister had sent out an e-mail from Australia asking that someone contact Kathy Carpenter about renting her house, saying that she hoped to return to Colorado three or four months from now. At that moment, Olmsted conjectured, she clearly had no intention of cutting short her travels abroad. When questioned about this, the PI would tell more than one person to look in the direction of something that happened just over a week later, on February 14. That Valentine's Day, two new corporations were formed in Aspen—both of them named after the ranch owned by the late Art and Betty Pfister. One was called "Lazy Chair Lot 2 LLC" and the other "Lazy Chair Lot 3 LLC." The agent for both LLCs was Aspen lawyer Millard J. Zimet, but the owner or owners weren't listed in either the transaction records or the incorporation documents on file at the Colorado Secretary of State's office in Denver, because the law doesn't require the disclosure of such persons.

On February 22, eight days after the creation of these entities, Nancy flew home. Did she change her plans, Olmsted asked, because of the Stylers or because of her concerns about the new LLCs and their role in the imminent sale of land from her mother's estate? Was she upset because she wasn't being consulted on these transactions; or because none of the money from the sales was going to her; or because she felt the properties were undervalued; or because she didn't want the family assets to be sold in this manner; or because she didn't like the participation in these deals of some people, starting with her longtime nemesis, lawyer Andy Hecht?

After coming home, according to the report of Pitkin County Coroner

Dr. Steve Ayers, Nancy was killed by multiple blows to the head sometime between February 24 and February 26, an estimated thirty-six to forty-eight–hour window for the crime. When a family member involved in the transfer of land from an estate dies right before a closing, it's not uncommon for the transaction to be postponed, at least temporarily. That didn't happen in this case—and in fact the deals were then completed with great speed.

On midafternoon February 28, two weeks after the LLCs came into being and two days after Kathy had found Nancy's body in the closet, Lazy Chair Lot 3 LLC bought property from Betty Pfister's estate for $1.8 million. The beneficiaries of the sale were the Juliana Elizabeth Pfister Trust, the Daniel Patrick Kelso Trust and the Arthur James Douglas Kelso Trust, for Suzanne's children, and the Chasen Arthur Smith Trust and the Tyler Reed Smith Trust, for Christina's. None of the three Pfister sisters—Nancy, Suzanne, or Christina—was named in the sale. This sale echoed an earlier one from June 2008, when Betty Pfister was still alive and had sold $1,944,600 worth of property to the same configuration of trusts.

"Skipping one generation of children to give assets to the next generation is a common practice in avoiding tax liability," says a local lawyer. "If you want to be an attorney in Aspen and make a lot of money, become an estate planner."

Also on February 28, 2014, with attorney Andy Hecht acting as the trustee for Betty's estate, Lazy Chair Lot 3 purchased a second piece of property for $200,000. That same afternoon, with Hecht again acting as the personal representative for Betty's estate, Lazy Chair Lot 2 LLC bought a third piece of property for $2.5 million. All of the February 28 deals, worth a total of $4.5 million, were done in cash and none of the Pfister sisters was cited in official documents as beneficiaries of the transactions.

"If I'd been doing the police interviews following the murder," says Olmsted, "I'd have wanted to know everything that Suzanne Pfister, Christina Pfister, Juliana Pfister, and Andy Hecht knew about these deals. To my knowledge, they were never questioned about any of this in any depth by the police after Nancy was found dead. I think that the sale of $4.5 million worth of property right before or after someone gets killed—someone who may have stood to lose money or other assets from these sales—is at least as important as a dispute about a few thousand dollars in rent money. I also think that Nancy was worried enough about this to come home from halfway around the world to examine these deals, if not do something more about them. It's very difficult for me to understand why *none* of this has been investigated."

He then speculated, "Let's say that Nancy realized that these sales were going to happen and she wasn't going to benefit from them. Let's say that she came back from Australia to intervene in these transactions or to keep them from happening. Someone may have been very, very concerned about this. There's a lot more money at stake here than in a couple thousand dollars. The Stylers and Kathy Carpenter may have killed Nancy, but there are other, equally plausible explanations."

Behind Olmsted's words was the notion that it wasn't only the dead woman's sexual or drug exploits that were about to be examined in open court during the preliminary hearing or at an eventual trial. Whether or not it had anything to do with Nancy's death, the private conflict over money within this old-guard Aspen family was about to be made public and broadcast everywhere.

38

Once Olmsted had scoured the police interviews, search warrants, and arrest affidavits for all three defendants, he was struck by one thing above all. The trio was charged not only with first-degree murder, but with conspiracy to commit first-degree murder. As a police officer and then a private investigator, he'd seen many cases where conspiracies were alleged and in most of them he'd come across something resembling a specific agreement between the parties to carry out a specific crime. In none of the charging documents could Olmsted find anything like this between the Stylers and Kathy Carpenter. In his view, there was simply no evidence showing a conspiracy among the three to kill Nancy Pfister.

The Stylers had been arrested based on statements made by Kathy about their conflict over the rent with their landlady; on the "Owner's Closet" key found on the sidewalk near their motel room; and on the bloody hammer, Nancy Pfister's prescription bottles, and Trey's expired car registration. The latter three had all been found in a garbage bag in downtown Basalt, very near the Aspenalt, on February 28, two days after the discovery of the body. Just as CBI tests revealed that the "red flakes" on the hammer matched the DNA profile of Nancy Pfister, the DNA on the garbage bag did not exclude Trey or any of his paternal male relatives from being the sources. No DNA or any other physical evidence linked Nancy Styler to the crime, not yet, anyway, although some of it was still being tested in the CBI lab.

The DNA from Trey, Olmsted asserted, might be explained by the fact that he'd lived in the Pfister home for more than three months. He could have innocently picked up the hammer or some plastic bags or the medicine bottles while staying in Nancy's house. Putting aside the question of Trey's genetic material, Olmsted continued to maintain that any evidence against Nancy Styler and Kathy Carpenter for either murder or conspiracy was "razor thin."

Based on this opinion, he kept encouraging his client's attorneys, Beth Krulewitch and Garth McCarty, to ask for a preliminary hearing sooner rather than later. He wanted the hearing to happen before all the forensic evidence came back from the CBI because, as he once put it, "things could not get much better for Nancy Styler, but they could get worse." If this hearing were held in April or May, his client might not be bound over for trial because there was nothing directly tying her to the murder. Yet even if Judge Nichols did bind her over, her lawyers might be able to convince the judge to set bond and Nancy would be released from jail pending a trial.

Again, Krulewitch and McCarty saw things differently. Within weeks of the Stylers' arrests, the Pitkin County Sheriff's Office and DA's office produced nearly 8,000 pages of discovery on the murder, a file that would soon grow to 13,000 pages. The attorneys felt they needed considerable time to go through all the material, but Olmsted quickly read most of the pages and believed that the great bulk of them were extraneous to Nancy Styler's defense. In his view, her legal team could be prepared for court in a month, if not less. Krulewitch and McCarty had some scheduling conflicts that went against this plan, but apart from that, they were more hesitant. When Olmsted told them to ask the DA for a bill of particulars detailing the conspiracy charge for all three defendants, he met resistance. It was a fundamental struggle between a private investigator, who'd worked primarily with lawyers he knew well, clashing with attorneys he'd never been paired with before. The harder he pushed, the more they told him to be patient and the more restless he became.

"I'm not suggesting that Beth and Garth didn't care about the case as much as I did," says Olmsted. "Our ways of doing things were just incompatible. And I gradually began to realize that I'm too old to change mine."

He didn't know if he could assist Nancy Styler to the degree that he desired and wondered if her legal team would be better served if he left the case.

The only defense lawyer as aggressive as Olmsted was the well-named Tina Fang, the public defender representing Trey Styler. Widely regarded as the most qualified and toughest PD in the region, she saw the evidence in much the same way that Olmsted did—razor thin—even against her client.

On March 14, 2014, at one of the early hearings in the Pitkin County District Courthouse, she spoke with Sheriff DiSalvo and let him know with absolute certainty that a huge courtroom battle was coming, on a scale that the Ninth Judicial District and the local DA's office hadn't seen for a very long time. The prosecutors could be assured that Fang was going to do everything in her power to exonerate the former doctor she was now charged with defending. Trey was going to get free legal representation from Fang—and the kind that money can't buy. When she showed the strength of her commitment to DiSalvo, it left him unsettled.

"I understood perfectly what she was saying that day," he recalled months later. "The two sides in this case were going to go balls to the wall. It would be a fair fight, but it would be a very hard fight and a difficult one for us to win. The whole process could take maybe two years and cost the legal system millions of dollars. When Fang threw this challenge up in my face, she was dead serious and I was worried."

On April 9, the DA's office asked the court to unseal the arrest affidavits. Through Denver attorney and First Amendment specialist Steven Zansberg, nine media groups joined this request. If Judge Nichols ruled in favor of the DA and Zansberg, the public and press would have the opportunity to see at least some of the evidence and to develop a better understanding of why the police had arrested the Stylers and then Kathy Carpenter. For the past six weeks, much of Aspen, Denver's medical community, and people elsewhere had been conjecturing about the events leading to Nancy Pfister's death. Yet no one outside of law enforcement or the defense attorneys had heard anything more than a few details about the case.

The defense teams for both the Stylers and Carpenter opposed the DA's motion, saying that the affidavits contained false information, or information that in time would be shown to be false, and their release would prejudice a future jury pool against their clients. The judge sided with the defense and the affidavits remained sealed, along with the 13,000 pages of discovery and the many hours of police video recordings. In her ruling, Judge Nichols wrote that until the defense had had the opportunity to "put the information in context or show that the information is inaccurate, [it] would result in more persons within [Pitkin] County forming an opinion of the defendants' guilt...

"Defendants assert that the privacy of the witnesses and the defendants will be wrongfully invaded if the Court's files are unsealed because the press will harass them. Once the preliminary hearing is completed... the privacy of these witnesses may be invaded."

The upshot of Nichols's ruling was that the upcoming preliminary hearing, in which the prosecution would present some of its case against the defendants, was now more important than ever. The judge had originally set the hearing for late April, but then rescheduled it for June 9. At that time, the prosecution would lay out its murder scenario—describing what each of the defendants had done, when they'd done it, and how three people had conspired to commit murder and then carried out the act. Because the press and public had so far been denied any access to the evidence, anticipation for June 9 began building on every side.

By mid-spring, David Olmsted had been saying for weeks that he doubted that the information in the arrest or search warrants could get past the threshold of a preliminary hearing—at least for Nancy Styler—let alone support proof beyond a reasonable doubt at a first-degree murder trial. He believed that bond should have already been set for all the defendants and they should have been released until the ninth of June. Law enforcement, of course, strongly disagreed.

All these legal maneuverings brought more protests from the defense that the other side had been leaking information. They alleged that Bob Braudis had talked with people about things he could only have gotten from the Pitkin County Sheriff's Office. Trey's lawyer, Tina Fang, implied that within a day or two of the discovery of the body, Braudis had given information to a Pfister relative, perhaps one of Nancy's sisters. The leak included that the victim had been murdered by blunt-force trauma, had been dead for twenty-four to forty-eight hours when found, and had been wrapped in carpet (which turned out not to be true). The relative had apparently asked Braudis if Nancy's death had been "painful, long-lasting or torturous."

"From whatever conversations I had," Braudis was quoted as saying in response to the leaks, "I was led to believe Nancy never felt a thing, and I was enforcing that with [the relative]. I didn't know much for sure then, and I still don't."

The defense teams compelled Judge Nichols to rule on the alleged law-enforcement leaks, and while she condemned them, she said that this "information does not suggest in any way who committed the murder and therefore is not prejudicial to any defendant."

The matter was closed and the next hearing was set for several weeks later, on April 23. Nothing that had happened to date had given any sense of how the crime had unfolded—it remained a jigsaw puzzle in which none of the pieces seemed to fit. And nothing had dampened the rampant gossip about the death of Nancy Pfister and her place in one of the most colorful chapters in the life and lore of Aspen, Colorado.

While everyone waited for the legal process to move forward, people up and down the Roaring Fork Valley couldn't stop talking about the murder, especially in the places the victim used to frequent.

Fear and Loathing in Woody Creek

39

A Monday evening in April 2014 and the Woody Creek Tavern, just north of Aspen, is jamming. Outside the establishment an ugly black warthog perches above the front entrance and inside every table is full and every waitress is carrying at least two plates above her elbows. Beers are moving from hand to hand, from glass to mouth. Floor space is extremely tight and virtually every inch of the walls is covered with snapshots of those who've dropped in, from the very famous to the downright obscure. Glowing Christmas lights are strung here and there, while a silver disco ball rotates overhead. The leopard-skin-pattern carpet is worn and the leopard-skin cushions in the booths are lumpy. The décor is intentionally funky—in direct and self-conscious opposition to the polished, lavishly elegant interiors that one finds in Aspen itself. Everything and everyone in the Woody Creek Tavern is making a statement: "We're different from Aspen. We're authentic." The waitresses are brisk and full of attitude, particularly when serving tourists. Then they become all but dismissive.

A Hunter Thompson poster hangs on the wall depicting the author holding a shovel and declaring, "There is some shit we will not eat."

Defiance and paranoia were mother's milk to Dr. Gonzo. The savages were always knocking at the door, trying to barge in and ruin the party. Some of the people in his circle may have come from great wealth or accumulated great wealth themselves, but they tried to remain rebellious and subversive for as long as they could. For a certain percentage, that meant getting high and staying high until you were dead or had committed suicide. For others, it meant attempting to hold on to the "Golden Age of Aspen" of the 1960s and '70s, long after both Aspen and America had moved on.

Next to the tavern is a sandwich shop, selling Dr. Hunter S. Thompson T-shirts and other HST memorabilia. If you look closely enough, you might see a ghost holding court over in the corner, floating inside a haze of smoke. It's three o'clock in the afternoon and he just rolled out of bed a few minutes earlier, washed off the shotgun residue on his hands from the night before, and made his way down to the tavern to kick-start his day. He's wearing a cap and smoking a Dunhill, tucked into his trademark Venturi Tar-Gard cigarette holder, while drinking a Corona, a Heineken, or a Bailey's Irish Cream. As he drinks and smokes, he's talking, talking, and talking to anyone who will listen. He talks now much more than he writes.

One thing everybody in Aspen talks about is Aspen: its history, its future, its character, its fate. Greater Denver has more than 2,600,000 people and one daily newspaper, the *Denver Post*, which is a shadow of its former self. Aspen has fewer than 7,000 people and two daily newspapers devoted to covering... Aspen. The town has a glossy periodical called *Aspen* magazine—made of a paper stock with a sheen and thickness rarely seen anymore.

One thing everybody in Woody Creek talks about is Hunter Thompson, the last true bad boy of American literature, the final author to enter the realm of mythology well before he died. He followed step for step in the road cut by Ernest Hemingway, who liked to brag to journalists visiting him in Havana in the late 1940s that he held the house record for drinking oversized daiquiris at the La Floridita bar: sixteen of them, back to back. After achieving worldwide success through the rigorous discipline of his craft, Hemingway created an image and a personality that overshadowed nearly everyone else's, in part by imitating some of his own fictional creations. He tried to become the figures he'd first imagined. Like other literary stars of his generation, he was distracted or derailed by liquor: his own end came in Ketchum, Idaho, in July 1961, at age sixty-one, when he walked down into his basement and shot himself to death.

Thompson aped Hemingway, but threw drugs into the mix of literature and fame. His first book, *Hell's Angels: The Strange and Terrible Saga of the Outlaw Motorcycle Gangs* (1967), was a more or less straightforward, first-rate piece of journalism about renegades on wheels. After the author had ridden with them for a year in California, the Angels severely beat him because they felt he was exploiting them through his writing and they wanted a share of his eventual book profits. He fled the West Coast, in part to escape the thugs, and settled just outside of Aspen, in the stunning hills of Woody Creek. Natural beauty encased him, as well as peace and quiet—as if that were what he was seeking. He called his home Owl Farm and never was there a farm quite like this. He liked to stay up all night, run around outside naked, and play "shotgun golf," pulling a twelve-gauge firearm from his golf bag, aiming it into the darkness or at a distant sound in the woods or at an annoying passerby, and squeezing the trigger.

After he was established in Woody Creek and had made an unsuccessful attempt at running for the Pitkin County sheriff's office in 1970—on the "Freak Power" ticket—a series of rock stars and movie icons began finding their way out to his farm. For some people living in or visiting Aspen at that time, who are now in their sixties or seventies, that period stands as the Golden Age of the Roaring Fork Valley. Everything since that time had been a long, slow slide into vulgarity and uberwealth.

"Back then," says Michael Cleverly, a friend of Nancy Pfister and an artist who for years lived in a log cabin a mile or so up the road from Thompson's home, "we had very rich people around here, but they still knew how to mind their manners. They sat down to dinner with their gardeners and were polite to everyone. They drank with the workers in the same bars. The town hadn't yet become the snootiest fucking place on earth. The ski bums who come here now are as stuck up as the rich pricks themselves. Today the wealthy have moved in and taken over every local institution, except for the Aspen Historical Society. They don't care about it because they think that nothing was here before they arrived. The young people who come to Aspen now haven't read anything Hunter ever wrote. They just want to do the drugs he did."

In recent times, Aspen had become home not just to fifty billionaires, but the kind of place where certain hotels demanded that you cancel your reservations two weeks in advance of the date of your arrival. If you didn't, because of circumstances utterly beyond your control, they charged you the full amount for your stay, plus a 25 percent tax on top of that, and insulted you for questioning this policy. The aura of self-importance was staggering.

At Owl Farm in the 1970s, Thompson tried to create an environment that ran counter to the money and materialism growing in Aspen, while doing some of his best work. He wrote the infamous drug-saga, *Fear and Loathing in Las Vegas: A Savage Journey to the Heart of the American Dream* (1972), and then *Fear and Loathing on the Campaign Trail '72* (1973). He accomplished what only a handful of American writers have ever done, inventing a style all his own and then labeling it—Gonzo Journalism—but the second half of his life was devoted far more to gonzo than to journalism. He drank and took drugs at a more prodigious level than perhaps any author in American history and the higher he got, the less he produced.

"His writing," observed Jay Cowan in his *Hunter S. Thompson: An Insider's View of Deranged, Depraved, Drugged Out Brilliance*, "was growing so self-centered it was becoming a trap . . . He was fast becoming a prisoner of his own game, enjoined by myth, laziness, self-absorption, show business, and addiction. He had pursued the rock star dream and was suffering the rock star syndrome."

No one knows how many stimulants (cigarettes, marijuana, cocaine, booze, and whatever else was at hand) Thompson consumed each day, but Cowan claimed that his alcohol intake alone included one to two quarts of whiskey every twenty-four hours. He also estimated that Thompson did more than $3 million worth of coke in his lifetime, leading to the constant need to make money in ways unworthy of his gifts. His drug intake and behavior were so alarming that one night he sent John Belushi, no slacker when it came to substance abuse and a man who proudly claimed to be made of "Albanian Oak," running scared into the Woody Creek darkness. Not long afterward, the comedian turned up dead in L.A. from an overdose.

Thompson's inner circle held court in his kitchen, where the celebs and the not-so-well-known launched barbecues at midnight and stumbled toward bed around dawn. When Jack Nicholson showed up at Owl Farm, he took a backseat to Hunter, as did other major stars, many of them looking upon the author with an avuncular, protective air.

This was the world that Nancy Pfister entered into as a young woman and became a charter member of (she dated Nicholson, whom she referred to as her "Godfather," and had a brief engagement to Michael Douglas). She and Thompson were so close that after she gave birth to her daughter, Dr. Gonzo himself, according to local legend, served as one of Juliana's babysitters.

Nancy's mother fiercely disapproved of this behavior, but Nancy did it anyway. Betty was so worried about her daughter's drug and drinking habits, her lack of parenting skills, and her carousing at Owl Farm that she insisted George and Patty Stranahan take in Juliana and raise her themselves. It was a longstanding battle and only one of the many things that mother and daughter fought over.

Despite Betty's worries about Nancy, she could hold her own with Hunter's friends—the rock 'n' roll lifestyle fit her as perfectly as it did Thompson himself. At first her nickname around Aspen was "Nancy Pants." In time, it evolved into "Nancy No-Pants."

"She used to bring the one-night stands she picked up at Hunter's over to my place," recalls Michael Cleverly. "It was much closer than driving them up to her home. From the day the party started at Hunter's in the early 1970s until the last day of her life, Nancy never changed one iota. She never backed away from the fun.

"Believe me, she could be exasperating. She could come into my house and turn it upside down, but she couldn't do that so easily at Hunter's, where *he* was the center of attention. One night she went off about something in his kitchen and stomped out the door. I turned to him and said, 'Why do we put up with her?'

" 'We've known her for too long now,' " he told me. " 'It's too late to change.' "

Despite all her partying, Cleverly says, "Nancy was a tough cookie, not a dithering little heiress. That underlying toughness was a real contrast to her normally bubbly personality. If you didn't realize she had this other side, it could come as a shock. If she had a problem with you, she'd definitely let you know it."

Like Ernest Hemingway, Hunter Thompson committed suicide, in his home in 2005, at age sixty-seven. As part of saying good-bye to the author, actor Johnny Depp (who portrayed Thompson in *Fear and Loathing in Las Vegas*) placed his ashes inside a cannon perched atop a 153-foot-high tower and shot them deep into the sky, scattering the remains to the winds above the Roaring Fork Valley and letting some people know that the party, if not over, might be starting to wind down.

40

This is a very tight-knit community and local people always feel that their hold on Aspen is precarious," says a native who's been in and around the village for nearly sixty years.

On this Monday evening at the Woody Creek Tavern, he's having dinner in a rear booth and reflecting on the passing of Hunter Thompson and the murder of Nancy Pfister. He grew up interacting with two generations of Pfisters: Art and Betty, along with their three daughters.

He points to the Hunter Thompson poster on the wall.

"That poster," the man says, "means that many people who come here have type-A personalities and a lot of money and they always want to change Aspen. They have big ideas for improving the town. This is usually seen as a threat to those already here. We try to protect our way of life against the outside world. We try to preserve what we have."

The summer 2014 issue of *Aspen* magazine, which would be published in about two months, would feature an article on the demise of Nancy Pfister. Bordered by warm family photos and pictures of the victim enjoying herself in distant corners of the world, the story would skate over the intense sibling conflict inside her family, the strife over raising Juliana, and the drugs and alcohol that underlay Nancy's existence. The words describing her were as shiny as the ads for pricey accessories one could buy at Gucci or Dior just off Aspen's Main Street. The unspoken message of the article was clear: what goes on in Aspen stays in Aspen. How we deal with our troubles is our business and no one else's. We protect our own, while striving to keep things as neat and clean and as profitable as we possibly can.

At the time the article was published, no one could quite have imagined how this attitude would play out in the legal resolution surrounding the Nancy Pfister homicide.

"The thing you need to understand about Nancy," the man in the back booth was saying, "was that she was the black sheep of her family. The one who made everyone else nervous. Like many people here, and especially like many who used to congregate at this tavern around Hunter, she no doubt thought of herself as an outcast. She came from a very rich family, but Art and Betty were always more interested in pursuing their work and their social lives than in bringing up kids. Nancy was emotionally scarred by that and it shaped her youth. Aspen adopted her as a waif, an abandoned child of the community. People took care of her when she was young because she had nowhere else to go.

"As she got older, she often came across as flighty and flitting around, like a lost child or a lost soul. The town was protective of her and she was accepted here, especially here in this Woody Creek world. She was at home here, where she hung out with Hunter and Bob Braudis and all the rest."

He takes a swig of beer and wipes at his chin.

"Bob was very close to her," he says. "He was fond of troubled people, but he left the untroubled alone. He has a good heart and watched Nancy like all the rest of us did, hoping for the best. Over the years, Nancy's mother said some very harsh things about her and her sex life. This was after Nancy got a reputation for sleeping around and earned the nickname 'Nancy No-Pants.' When people used that term with Betty, she always said that her daughter wasn't a whore, because she never did it for money.

"When Nancy had Juliana, she became somewhat the same kind of mother Betty had been to her. Sometimes, Nancy took Juliana with her when she traveled so her mother wouldn't place her with someone else. Juliana grew up without a father and she was kind of like a flower child. We all knew about this and we all tried to be protective of both Nancy and her daughter. Especially Bob."

As if on cue, the tavern's front door swings opens and in swaggers ex-sheriff Braudis, all six feet seven inches of him, wide-shouldered and towering in his trademark sport coat, his hair grayish-white and his face creviced and cratered by time, like a geological phenomenon. He approaches a table near the front and people jump up to give him a hug and a chair. He sits down and looks around, taking everything in, picking up the vibe and getting a pulse on the action, forever the lawman. Something about him appears a bit haunted now, a bit at sea, as if he's here but not quite here, living in a time that has passed, yet he remains the most dramatic-looking character in the room.

"Just as people in Aspen were very protective of Nancy in life," says the man in the booth, "they're being protective of her in death. It's part of our mentality. Let's keep our secrets inside the city limits and away from the press. Don't let outsiders know too much. Nancy's dead now so let's leave all of this alone. No good can come from dwelling on her murder or from digging up the uncomfortable things that surrounded her life. Let's hold the best memory of her we can and move on for her sake and for Juliana's."

He abruptly stops, as if he's said everything about this subject he's going to say—even if he knows more. It's obvious that he's been speaking with caution, perhaps revealing more than he intended to, but his sudden silence raises new questions. Are there intimate clues about how the three sisters were raised and why they grew up so hostile to one another, clues that no one wants to utter or touch?

"Protect our way of life," the man has said more than once this evening, a handful of words that would become increasingly prophetic as the Pfister case played out in court. "We want to protect our way of life."

After a considerable pause, he takes another sip of beer and says, "I've got to tell you that I'm very puzzled by her death. Everyone says that the people who were renting her house were involved, but I can't figure out why anyone would have killed her over a rental dispute. It will be quite interesting to see how her case unfolds inside the legal system. Based on what I know right now, when this goes to trial, it will be ripe for reasonable doubt."

41

A Tuesday afternoon, just a few miles from Woody Creek Tavern, and the lush rolling hills are lit with April moisture. Pulling up in front of Michael Cleverly's log cabin, you see a brightly colored totem pole featuring snake and turtle carvings, which suggests that the interior of his home might be unconventional. Then there's the sign in the front window: "Cleverly disguised as an adult." Then there's his reputation for irreverent commentary. If irreverence were money, he'd be the richest man in the Roaring Fork Valley.

In torn blue jeans and a worn cap and with an accent that reveals New England, Cleverly greets you with genuine friendliness and welcomes you into his crowded living space. Tribal masks stare down from the walls and shark's teeth hang in the window. Above the couch a prominent Hunter Thompson poster states the fundamental credo of HST himself: "It never got weird enough for me."

Next to a black wood stove sits a classic reddish Gretsch guitar, which Cleverly occasionally plays Carlos Santana licks on. He got the instrument from Jimmy Ibbotson of the Nitty Gritty Dirt Band, who lives just up the road. Cleverly once built a deck for Ibbotson and received the Gretsch in return and never gave it back, even though Jimmy said he wanted it back and claimed it was his, but Cleverly said no. Or something like that.

A shortish man of sixty-seven, with a scratchy Vermont voice, Cleverly conjures up pieces of Richard Dreyfus. In his youth, he'd been a ski instructor in the Green Mountain State and, once again, he'd originally visited

Aspen for the slopes. When he returned home, he couldn't help noticing that the freezing rain and ice of a northeastern winter were a lot less fun than the sunshine, dry air, and champagne powder of the Colorado Rockies. He decided to move west and to pay his bills he "pounded nails" as a carpenter, while pursuing painting, writing, a little music, and eventually carving totem poles. Hunter Thompson was hunkered down at Owl Farm and Cleverly became a regular at the author's kitchen table—whether he wanted to or not.

"Hunter would call me at three a.m.," he recollects, "and ask me to come over. I'd tell him, 'It's three in the morning.' He'd say, 'Fuck you! If you don't come over now, you can't ever come over again!' I'd tell him, 'Fuck you, Hunter!' and hang up.' The next night he'd call again at three in the morning."

He pauses, as if remembering the kitchen, and adds philosophically, "After he died, I didn't have a sense of loss for all the drugs we did, but I did miss the sense of escape they provided. I never gave up a bad habit because it was the smart thing to do. I just got tired of doing it."

Cleverly's cats are roaming around the cabin and the sofa is so worn that when you sink down into it, you don't ever want to get up. Beyond the windows blue mountain jays dart past and are lost in the green hills and cobalt sky. A pack of emus graze around the next bend at the ranch of singer John Hall, of Hall and Oates. With very little prompting, Cleverly will tell you that he's lived in Woody Creek for the past four decades and all through the "Golden Years of Aspen," when many well-known musicians and actors moved into the area—before everything went to hell.

Nearly all of his neighbors, he says, have become fed up with what Aspen's turned into since being overrun by the super-rich. One of those is billionaire William Koch, of the Koch Brothers oil and gas empire. In the next few weeks, Koch will put his nearby 32,614-square-foot home and fifty-five acres on the market for $89.9 million, almost doubling the next highest listing in the area. The house has fifteen bedrooms, eight bathrooms, five half-baths, and eleven three-quarter baths.

"In the 1970s," Cleverly says, "along with the rich people, we also had pinko, hippie, commies running Aspen and things were going pretty well.

These were good, smart people with a sense of Aspen's history, who wanted to do the right things for the community. They did such a good job that they made Aspen the most attractive place around for the rich. For a while, that was all right, but then it changed. The goddamn bartenders in town look down their noses at you now if you don't order the most expensive drinks on the menu. Who the fuck do they think they are? They don't know anything about what made Aspen what it once was."

He pauses to scratch one of his cats. "I've had enough of this. I'm packing up and leaving."

The next morning, in fact, he's departing the cabin for good and moving over to Hotchkiss, Colorado, population 923.

"I don't have high expectations for Hotchkiss," he says, "and they'll probably be met. I don't think it's 2014 over there yet, but an earlier time in human history."

In the great American tradition, he's leaving Aspen and heading west, ninety-seven miles farther west, determined to get away from too many people, too much elitism, and the ever bigger money that for him has made Aspen unendurable.

There is some shit Cleverly won't eat. Hunter's death and then Nancy Pfister's murder and other, more personal things signaled the end of his time in Woody Creek.

"Nancy was Dorian Gray," he says. "By that, I mean she never changed. In the early 1970s, I met her at Aspen's Fourth of July Rodeo. She was a lovely young girl then and became a lovely middle-aged girl, worldly and effervescent."

He laughs and says, "If you were that goddamn rich, you might be happy 24/7 too. Nancy never let things like responsibility weigh her down. We were all like that in the seventies, but the rest of us grew up and grew old. She managed to avoid that entire process.

"She brought you into her vortex and that vortex was all about partying. If you were sitting in Aspen having lunch with the mayor and the sheriff and Nancy swept in, everything changed. If you'd been discussing politics or the Middle East, you started talking about something entirely different. She was a force of nature and a weather event that you just weathered. She had a lot of inner joy and cheerfulness, and when you thought about her afterwards, you didn't think about her interrupting your conversations. You thought about her smile and her happiness."

Cleverly got to know all the members of her family and was especially fond of Betty. He admired the older Pfister couple because they were self-made people who didn't put on airs or call a lot of attention to themselves or live in an ostentatious house. Suzanne Pfister had married a "drinking buddy" of his named Doug Kelso, a house painter, and they had two sons. Before Nancy had left for Australia in the fall of 2013, she'd invited Cleverly to her going-away party, where Trey and Nancy Styler were also guests. At the time, he didn't think much about missing this gathering, not realizing that he'd never see Nancy again.

"I thought it was a little odd for her to throw this party," he says, "because she was always going away somewhere. For Nancy, going away was not a big deal. She just liked to have parties."

While she was gone, he heard that she was having problems with her new tenants, but knew little more than that. He assumed that they were young ski bums who couldn't raise enough money at the start of each month. From Australia, Nancy had asked Cleverly to move into her home, rent free, if he'd get rid of her renters. He gave some thought to her offer, but declined.

"Living in her house would have been good while she was out of the country," he says, "but not so good when she was there. She was allergic to cats and I was keeping my cats."

When he first learned that Nancy was dead, he was told that she'd committed suicide, but didn't believe it.

"Nancy was a major narcissist," he says, "and those people don't tend to do themselves in. On the other hand, we don't have a lot of murders around here."

When he heard that Kathy Carpenter was under suspicion, he tried to fit her into the picture.

"Kathy picked up Nancy's mail in Woody Creek," he says. "She was a glorified gopher for Nancy, who didn't feel bound to lift a finger for herself. She let others handle the unpleasant details of life."

Cleverly had friends formerly and currently in law enforcement, starting with Bob Braudis, and he spoke regularly with them about the murder. Everyone was shocked not just by the homicide itself, but by its brutality.

"We just don't have that kind of violence in Aspen," he says. "When people find out what happened to Nancy and how brutal it was, there will be a lynch mob."

By early March, he'd said good-bye to Nancy and by late April, he was ready to say good-bye to both Aspen and the Roaring Fork Valley.

Walking outside his cabin on a glorious spring afternoon, he stands next to a totem pole in his front yard, looking out over the exploding green above Woody Creek. Emerald hillsides, laced with red cliffs, surround Aspen, making one think of the beauty of Ireland at its peak. Standing beside Cleverly, one feels his poignancy at leaving this landscape behind, the home he could never find on the East Coast of his birth or anywhere else. As he talks about relocating to Hotchkiss, he interrupts himself with small bursts of laughter at the futility of trying to resist change.

"I love Aspen as you love a woman," he says, gazing out over the exquisite scenery. "And this is the worst divorce ever for me. But I've got to go. I just can't love this place anymore."

Lady Justice Wasn't Blind

42

At the April 23 hearing for all three defendants, the police officers checking the public in through a metal detector at the Pitkin County District Courthouse were surprisingly open and friendly compared to the gruffness of their big-city counterparts. They liked to joke about the terrible things they'd do to you if your cell phone went off while court is in session. They wore blue jeans or stylish khakis and greenish shirts, emphasizing the theme of environmental awareness that rules in Aspen. They actually looked amused to have some company on the job—the town only sees a murder case that draws in spectators and reporters about every dozen years.

The redbrick courthouse on Main Street is in keeping with Aspen's image as a place that honors its past and is rooted in its history. The building is surrounded by a black wrought-iron railing that in springtime sprouts wild yellow roses. Lady Justice herself, covered in bright silver paint, stands atop the front entrance, welcoming you into the elegant building. One block away are Gucci and Dior boutiques. Few local people shop in these high-end stores, but wealthy tourists frequent them during the Christmas season and the major summer festivals, including June's Food and Wine Classic. It's still worth it, high-end retailers believe, just to have an Aspen address. They've succeeded in driving up the rents for other local businesses and driving some of them out of business.

Lady Justice holds a sword in one hand and scales in the other, but unlike at many other venues, she doesn't wear the traditional blindfold, signaling her impartiality. She looks down upon the scene with eyes wide open. Everything in Aspen, including law and order, feels slightly different.

"Nancy Pfister," says Teresa Wyatt, "felt that she could get away with anything in Pitkin County, and so did the rest of us. As long as we didn't venture too far out of town, we all felt that we had a get-out-of-jail card, because we were friends with the sheriff. One time I got stopped in my car and the officer wrote me out a ticket. I told him that I knew Sheriff Joey DiSalvo and he tore it up."

Courthouses today are mostly composed of cement and steel—the essence of bland and impersonal. To reach the second-floor courtroom for the Pfister hearings, one ascended a winding, graceful, wooden staircase covered in green carpet. The walls held light green wainscoting and the waiting area outside the courtroom was trimmed in oak, while the surrounding office names were stenciled in gold lettering and overhead hung pale white chandeliers. Inside the courtroom was more carved oak, with brown leather chairs for the jury and red leather for the attorneys. Rows of law books climbed halfway to the ceiling and were accessible by a rolling wooden ladder, a Victorian touch. All of it evoked Aspen's nineteenth-century heyday as a mining town.

For this morning's hearing, seven heavily armed guards stand in the courtroom surveying everyone who wanders in: local spectators, journalists from around Colorado, TV producers from New York, David Olmsted, Kathy Carpenter's mother, Chris . . .

Of the three defendants, Trey Styler arrives in court first, a guard bringing him in in a wheelchair. While being pushed to one of the small defense tables, he tilts his chin downward, making eye contact with no one. He has on a bright orange jumpsuit, setting off the pallor of his skin, his white hair thinning into emerging baldness. His ankles are bound in chains and he looks exceedingly frail and angry or ashamed of himself, or both. The guard deposits him at the table next to his lawyer, Tina Fang, who wears black pants, black cowboy boots, a black jacket, and a feisty attitude. She will prove to be the most forceful voice in court today, easily overshadowing the judge.

Nancy Styler comes in next, wearing an outfit labeled "Eagle County Jail." Soon after her arrest, she'd been separated from her husband and transported nearly a hundred miles away to another correctional facility in Eagle, Colorado. Her hair, so blond and shimmering in the past when she'd stood in her backyard in Greenwood Village in front of her giant water lilies, has been reduced to a series of tight, light brown braids (women behind bars tend to braid or cornrow each other's hair to fill up the time). Her cheeks have sunk and the bones in her face have become more prominent, jutting out at harsh or tragic angles. A guard escorts her to a second defense table located right in front of Trey. When she gets there, she glances over her shoulder at her husband, smiling and whispering, "Happy birthday." Yesterday, April 22, he'd turned sixty-six, but his body language said at least eighty. While he looks defeated, slumped over in his wheelchair, his wife sits up straight and tries to show some dignity.

The last defendant is Kathy Carpenter, but there's no third defense table set up for her inside the stuffed courtroom. The area in front of the judge is so limited that Kathy and her head lawyer, Greg Greer, take a seat in the jury box and stare down on the other players. Kathy is being held at yet a third jail, in Glenwood Springs, and for this hearing she's conspicuous in old-fashioned black-and-white stripes, making her appear even stockier. Her eyes are skittish, her hair in disarray.

Observing Kathy, a female in the gallery says under her breath, "Why wouldn't you at least comb your hair or tie it back when you're coming into court? She looks wild."

With three people accused of murder and conspiracy to commit murder, the situation was as complicated as the courtroom was cramped. How would the case play out if they were all bound over for trial? This wasn't just a legal question, but one of logistics as well. How could the various attorneys consult with their defendants in private, when the other defendants were only a few feet away? Would the Stylers join forces in a hostile strategy designed to make Kathy look guilty of murder? Would Carpenter accuse them of collaborating to kill her friend? Would she confess to *something* short of murder and be given immunity so she could testify against the couple? Would the trio work together to contend that all of them were innocent and other people had caused Nancy's death? How might these pieces and questions coalesce in the interest of justice?

At the moment, courtroom observers knew virtually nothing at all. The aging male defendant seemed confined to living at least part of his life in a wheelchair and looked too physically disabled to have committed the murder alone. His aging wife had told people that she'd wanted to kill Pfister *after* she'd been found dead—didn't that argue for her innocence because what guilty person would have said this under these circumstances? And the third defendant had repeatedly told the police, during twenty hours of questioning, that she'd seen things on the corpse she couldn't have seen, *if* the rest of her story was true. For now, everything about the case was guesswork.

Two months after Nancy Pfister had been found bludgeoned to death in her closet, the key legal documents remained under seal (by contrast, when William Anderson Anaya was charged with two counts of first-degree murder in nearby Eagle County in July 2014, his arrest affidavits were released within a few days). But this wasn't Eagle County. This was Aspen and nothing predictable was going to happen.

Judge Nichols took her seat behind the bench, with the assembled portraits of previous Pitkin County District judges gazing down at her from the walls. Most of them had beards and none was female. With court in session, the lawyers rose from their chairs and did what they do best: they argued. Tina Fang asked the judge for a closed hearing so they could discuss the leaks in the case, allegedly coming from law enforcement. The judge resisted this, gently and respectfully, as if she herself did not like to argue. Nichols had a reputation for asking attorneys to submit their legal opinions to her in writing so she could peruse them in private and in silence, and did not have to listen to squabbling in open court.

With three defendants and eight lawyers involved in the case—six defense attorneys and two prosecutors—one could only imagine the bickering to come inside this tiny space.

The prosecutors opposed a hearing about the potential leaks and again asked the judge to release the warrants and affidavits.

Fang protested, accusing the DA's side of feeding information to the *National Enquirer.*

Thus far, she said, "The media has been denied nothing."

She then requested that the judge "sever" the three defendants so that each of them could have a separate preliminary hearing and, if necessary, a separate trial. Nichols replied that she'd take this under advisement, but by now Fang had taken over the courtroom. She wanted the defense to have access to all of the forensic evidence collected and currently being tested by the CBI—before the judge set a firm date for the preliminary hearing. Judge Nichols did not make a ruling on her request and the hearing suddenly ended, with no new revelations.

The preliminary hearing was still set for June 9, when the DA's theory of the murder would finally be unveiled. Or would it?

43

Nearly four weeks later, on May 17, each of the defendants was additionally charged with being accessories to—with aiding and abetting—the homicide after the fact. The new felony charges alleged that they'd helped cover up the crime or helped the perpetrator get away from the Pfister residence or both. This move by the DA's office indicated that the prosecutors felt their case against the trio was only getting stronger. If there were any doubts that all three would now be bound over for trial and that a huge legal struggle was coming with their eventual trial (or trials), they seemed to have vanished.

Yet David Olmsted was still questioning everything about the case and how it had been framed. He knew things about the timeline surrounding the crime that no one outside the legal system knew—things that he hadn't chosen to share with any civilians.

"The way Nancy died," he said, after learning about the new counts, "you'd have expected to see a lot of blood, but that's not true. She died without a struggle. You'd have expected blood on the carpet of her bedroom floor from this kind of blunt force trauma, but it isn't there. This opens up all kinds of new questions and possibilities."

Despite the strength of his convictions, three months into the case Olmsted felt so much ongoing conflict with his defense team of Garth McCarty and Beth Krulewitch that he was close to quitting. In his view, they still weren't being forceful enough in dealing with the legal system, the media, or in exploring other murder scenarios, which could help exonerate their client, Nancy Styler. Olmsted argued that when the preliminary hearing began on June 9 and the case file was unsealed perhaps that same week, the newly released information would portray the Stylers in a very negative light. Incriminating physical evidence might point to Trey and Nancy's comments about wanting Pfister dead and would clearly make her look bad, if not guilty. Her lawyers needed to have a strategy to provide some context and a time frame for her remarks, but...

The PI was also at odds with the DA's office and the Pitkin County Sheriff's Office. He believed that they'd arrested the Stylers too quickly, without looking into other credible leads or expanding their investigation far enough. After conducting his own legwork on the murder, he wanted to share his ideas about alternative suspects with the authorities, but the lawyers he was working with didn't like this idea, either.

"They've wanted me to play a limited and very restrained role," he said of McCarty and Krulewitch as the preliminary hearing approached, "but that isn't my style. I didn't come into the case with a closed mind. I want to know what happened to Nancy Pfister. People can think anything they want to think about the murder, but I want them to know what the facts are.

"Everyone in town knew Nancy and felt the shock of her death and that made the crime very personal. People in Aspen didn't know who'd done this or why or if they too might be in danger. There was a lot of pressure on the police and the DA to find the killer or killers quickly and to make an arrest. So that's what they did, whether they got the guilty party or not. Once law enforcement has made a commitment to a particular scenario, it's very tough to change their minds."

With the filing of the new charges, all of the defendants asked to have their cases severed. Kathy's lawyers, Greg Greer and Kathleen Lord, believed that Carpenter's defense would be highly antagonistic to the Stylers'—and that the couple would try to exonerate themselves by helping to convict Kathy.

"This is not at all surprising," Greer and Lord wrote of the Stylers, "given their longtime marriage and what discovery tends to show is genuine affection and concern for one another."

The couple's attorneys have "already assumed a strident prosecutorial role toward Ms. Carpenter" and have "assumed a quasi-law enforcement role vis-à-vis Ms. Carpenter by interrogating and obtaining statements from her before she was arrested and before she was appointed counsel."

In addition to battling Deputy DAs Andrea Bryan and Scott Turner in the courtroom, Greer and Lord contended that Kathy would be fighting the four other attorneys representing the Stylers:

"Ms. Carpenter should not be confronted in court at every hearing with six prosecutors, four of whom are not constrained by a prosecutor's ethical duty not to convict the innocent."

The smallness of the courtroom itself might also deny Carpenter due process and an effective assistance of counsel. In order to establish the hostility between the Stylers and Carpenter, Greer and Lord alleged that at a prior hearing Trey had asked his lawyer—within hearing range of one of the deputies—about the legal penalty for leaning over and spitting on Kathy.

The prosecution, not surprisingly, argued against severance. With the preliminary hearing near, the message from the DA's office was one of growing confidence and eagerness to move things forward.

"We have never agreed to sever the preliminary hearings in this case, and this court has not severed Ms. Carpenter's case," said Andrea Bryan. "They are joined, they are charged with conspiring with the other two defendants, and we need to be able to present the exact same evidence for her as we would for the other two defendants... We have defendants here charged with conspiring with one another. The evidence is inextricably intertwined. It is simply impossible for the [DA's office] to separate out all of the evidence."

Judge Gail Nichols denied the motion to sever the defendants, at least for the duration of the preliminary hearing, ruling that two or more defendants can be charged jointly "if they are alleged to have participated in the same act or series of acts arising from the same criminal episode... Without knowing what the defenses are, it is impossible to determine if the defenses are antagonistic... The prosecution has charged all three, however, with conspiring to commit murder, and there is some evidence to support that conspiracy charge."

Judge Nichols then did something unexpected and guaranteed to anger one or more of the defendants. While no one knew it at the time, it was a decision that would alter the entire unfolding of the case. She pushed back the preliminary hearing once again—despite an impassioned plea from Greg Greer.

"Your Honor," he said, referring to the arrest affidavit for his client, "eighty days ago a member of the Pitkin County Sheriff's Office brought you some papers and you signed those and that resulted in Ms. Carpenter sitting here for eighty days. Those papers deserve a hearing in court... so you can see really, really what and if there is probable cause in this case. That's the day in court. It's such a tired old phrase, but it's real."

The delay had come because Deputy DA Andrea Bryan had wanted her lead investigator, Lisa Miller, to attend the hearing and Miller was going to be on vacation the week of June 9. Like John Zamora, Miller had played an important role in the interviews with Kathy Carpenter, leading to her arrest.

"At this point," Bryan said, "we believe she [Miller] is a critical and crucial witness... The people believe that we have a right to put forth the best evidence that we can."

Greer countered by saying that Carpenter's investigator had canceled her own vacation so that she could be in court for the hearing.

"Ms. Carpenter's not just missing a vacation," he said. "[She] has lived in this valley for most of her adult life. She worked at the same job at Alpine Bank for twenty years. She used to live right down the street and walked past this courthouse every day, and now she's unemployed and homeless based on the papers you signed...

"Don't you want to see if there's really probable cause in those papers and give her her day? We're asking to come into court Monday and start that hearing."

When the judge ruled against Greer, Kathy was escorted out of the courtroom in tears.

The key legal documents in the case, Judge Nichols also ruled, would not be unsealed until after the preliminary hearing, now scheduled to start on June 25.

The hearing had been delayed another sixteen days.

"If that June ninth hearing had been held," Joe DiSalvo said two months later, looking back over the case, "everything might have happened differently."

He paused and said it again. "Everything."

44

In mid-June, after DA investigator Lisa Miller had returned from her vacation, she heard from Deputy DA Andrea Bryan, who'd just spoken to Tina Fang, Trey's lawyer.

As a result of this call from Fang to Bryan, on Tuesday, June 17, eight days before the start of the preliminary hearing, Judge Nichols scheduled an emergency court hearing. To the shock of everyone who'd gathered in the courtroom awaiting the next development, *all* of the charges were now dropped against Nancy Styler. After 106 days in jail, she was set free, with no explanation from the Ninth Judicial District Attorney's Office. The office said only that new evidence, which it did not disclose, had led to the dismissal.

"With the new information received," District Attorney Sherry Caloia said in a statement, "and a lack of other evidence refuting the new information, the district attorney could not prove that Ms. Styler was involved in the crimes... There is insufficient evidence to prove the defendant's guilt beyond a reasonable doubt, and the [DA's lawyers] do not believe there is a reasonable likelihood of success on the merits at trial."

The office did "receive additional evidence in the cases against Nancy and William Styler and Katherine Carpenter late last week and early this week which led to the filing of this motion."

David Olmsted's contention from almost the beginning of the case—that the evidence against his client was extremely thin—appeared to have been borne out. It was possible that if Nancy Styler's defense team had listened to the private investigator and pushed for a preliminary hearing back in April or May, she might have been released earlier from the Eagle County Jail.

Or not—as the case was still anything but resolved.

For the emergency hearing that freed Nancy Styler, Juliana Pfister was in the courtroom, while Suzanne and Christina listened in via a conference call.

"I do think," Juliana told Judge Nichols, "she [Nancy Styler] had something to do with it, but she just has to be released."

"I don't know all of the facts," Nichols replied.

Juliana asked the judge how this decision squared with Nancy Styler previously being accused of the murder of her mother, and conspiring to commit that murder, and being an accessory to that murder after the fact.

Nichols responded that she hadn't set Nancy free "lightly" and that while the Pfister family members didn't have any legal standing to challenge the dismissal of the charges, she wanted them to be aware that this was happening today. The judge suggested that Juliana speak with the DA's office to learn more.

When Juliana asked if there would be a restraining order against Nancy Styler following her release, Nichols said that the order in place since her arrest would now be lifted.

After the hearing, DA Caloia, who'd been largely a non-presence throughout the case, came forward and said that she didn't regret that police and prosecutors had jailed Nancy Styler for three and a half months without bond, a sentiment repeated by Sheriff DiSalvo.

"I'm not saying she's innocent," Caloia said. "I'm saying we received new evidence, and based on what we already had, it made it quite clear we would not be able to establish any of the charges against her. Rather than take it through a preliminary hearing and hope we got better evidence, we decided to just do the motion to dismiss now."

The DA underlined that Styler was being released "with prejudice," meaning that she could *never* be charged with the crime later on.

Asked about the reasons behind this development, Caloia said only, "It will come to light."

Speaking for his client, Garth McCarty said, "We are very happy that

Nancy Styler has been exonerated and is free. This is an emotional time for her family, and we ask that you honor her privacy. We express our sympathies to the Pfister family and hope this brings some closure for them."

A statement from her defense team announced that Nancy Styler would not be granting interviews.

"This has been a long and difficult ordeal for Nancy and her family," it said. "Nancy is thrilled to be exonerated but knows this story is not over."

The court set another hearing for June 20, three days hence, which Andrea Bryan said would be "very different in nature" from Nancy Styler's. For now, the preliminary hearing was still scheduled to commence on June 25, but only Trey and Kathy were left as murder suspects.

The revelations, if in fact they were revelations, were about to begin.

Aspen Confidential

45

Friday, June 20, was the longest day of 2014 and the most spectacular of the fading Aspen spring. The cool rains had stopped, the snow on Buttermilk Mountain had melted, and no clouds had yet formed for the next storm. The high-country weather was clean and fresh, as it can only be at 8,000 feet above sea level, and the sunlight made everything glitter and glisten. The landscape looked as if it had just been washed. Money, beauty, and glamour came together in the Roaring Fork Valley today in a way that defined but a handful of locales on earth. Driving toward Aspen on Highway 82, with the airport on the right, one saw row after row of private jets lined up at Sardy Field. Nearby was the Maroon Creek golf course, sitting on pristine land once owned by Art Pfister. At the city limits, nothing was out of place, with no trash anywhere. One felt what one often felt here: that something new or extraordinary could happen because the rules were slightly different, because of all that wealth.

This was the feeling that had drawn the Stylers to town in the fall of 2013, determined to relaunch their lives in Aspen in their mid-sixties. It was the same feeling that had brought people to the community from all over the world, and the same feeling that some mentioned when they spoke of Nancy Pfister, the same feeling that had drawn Kathy to her friend seven years ago. She wasn't just flesh and blood, but a spirit that had defined Aspen for a certain period of time, a few decades earlier. In her presence, anything might occur. She'd never wanted to grow up or grow old or give in to convention and become as predictable as the rest of the adult world; she was always ready for the next person or the next adventure. There was no one quite like her left in Aspen—no one that touched by spontaneity, freedom, and indifference to opinion.

Today, June 20, on the eve of summer, the village reached one of its peaks of action and expense. Rooms that went for $160 a night in April cost three times that now. Parking was impossible to find on the street and the sidewalks were jammed with fashionable people from the town and far beyond. The Food and Wine Classic, perhaps the premier event of Aspen's warm months, was under way, while a five-kilometer race was about to commence. At 7:45 a.m. loudspeakers were churning out Robin Thicke's pop hit "Blurred Lines," the beat lacing the air and adding rhythm to the pavement. The Aspen Ideas Festival, costing $3,000 a day to attend, had begun and would feature quite possibly the next President of the United States: Hillary Clinton. In nearby Snowmass, Diana Krall was tuning up for a jazz concert, to be followed by three hundred classical performances at the world-renowned Aspen Music Festival.

The only things jarringly out of place this morning were the media trucks surrounding the courthouse, covering a hearing about the murder of a daughter of Aspen royalty.

"Nancy was somebody everyone in town knew," said a contemporary of the Pfister sisters who was at the courthouse for the legal proceeding. "People like her aren't supposed to die like that. It's like someone coming in and stealing a baby from a crib. Everybody in Aspen will be glad when this is all over. Our insular community will be even more reluctant to let outsiders in. We'll be more cautious now."

For the hearing, Judge Nichols had a scheduling conflict on her calendar. In a move that struck many as strange, she was being replaced on the bench this morning by Chief District Judge James Boyd of the Ninth Judicial District, who'd had absolutely nothing to do with the case until now.

By eight a.m., the courthouse was stirring with media and curious civilians, arriving for the event an hour ahead of the gavel. Just before nine, Trey, again dressed in his orange jumpsuit, was brought in via wheelchair and parked at the defense table next to Tina Fang. Chatting with his attorney, he appeared much livelier than in the past, making eye contact with a few spectators. He'd only be the center of attention for a few moments longer.

The courtroom door swung open and in a rush of movement that seemed choreographed, Suzanne Pfister swept in with her tall, handsome teenage son. She wore dark fitted jeans below a navy blue blazer, an overly long scarf that reached her knees, a dark, wide-brimmed straw hat, and oversized Jackie O sunglasses. Taking off her hat and revealing short, dark hair, she found a seat toward the back of the gallery. Everything about her—her walk, her posture, her aura—suggested how much she disdained the kind of attention she'd been getting since her sister's death and how deeply she wanted to separate herself from the hoi-polloi in the courtroom. She was clearly all the things that Nancy Pfister had never been, conjuring up distant memories of the grande dames named Pussy, Fabi, and Goodie who'd once ruled Aspen's social scene with an iron hand and a secret scroll.

With Suzanne seated and with only slightly less flourish, Juliana Pfister made her entrance, surrounded by an entourage of young hipsters. She was clad in a white, frilly blouse with cutouts over the arms and black fitted pants with black boots, her long, messy, blond hair secured to the side with a clip, completing her outfit with lots of jewelry. Juliana resembled a young and better-looking Courtney Love, but an air of fragility hung around her shoulders and posture. As she mingled by the front row of gallery seats, Suzanne approached her, the two briefly hugged, and the older woman unceremoniously returned to her seat. Sheriff DiSalvo came over and kissed Juliana on the cheek, as she lowered her head and wiped at tears. Both Suzanne and Juliana, by doing nothing in particular, conveyed a sense of privilege that had no doubt followed both of them around throughout their lives, whether they wanted it to or not.

Christina Pfister was not physically present, but connected to the proceeding via speaker phone from her Denver apartment.

Judge Boyd, who evoked Vladimir Lenin, came into the courtroom from a rear door, ascended the stairs up to the bench, and called things to order.

. . .

Standing over Trey, Tina Fang spoke first and came out strong again, saying that the prosecution's cases regarding both of the Stylers and Kathy Carpenter were "highly circumstantial and possibly not provable beyond a reasonable doubt against any of these three people." She went out of her way to declare that the media reports about the Stylers not giving Pfister her rent payments were false.

"They paid that money in full," the lawyer said, but other conditions, which Fang did not spell out, had led Pfister to think that she hadn't been paid. "I don't know why she believed that because it wasn't true, but she came to feel that way."

Fang let it be known to the judge and the prosecuting attorneys sitting next to her, Andrea Bryan and Scott Turner, that nothing was going to happen today, nothing at all, unless the DA's office made an unalterable pledge that Nancy Styler could never be prosecuted for anything in this case in the future. Without that promise, her client would not go forward.

Deputy DA Scott Turner stood and delivered that promise. He told the court that Trey Styler was pleading guilty to second-degree murder and that his office would recommend sentencing him to a Colorado Department of Corrections medical facility for twenty years.

Turner's stunning words rattled around the courtroom and did not quite take on an air of reality, at least not immediately. The charge, he'd said, was second-degree murder, not first. Trey wasn't going to be sent to a regular, full-scale, maximum prison for convicted killers, but a medical unit. He was likely to be sentenced to twenty years with a shot at parole that would possibly come much sooner than that. Nothing about this announcement had been anticipated and nothing quite made sense. What did Trey's plea mean and what had he actually confessed to?

With no explanation forthcoming, Turner sat down and the judge asked Trey about his acceptance of his legal fate.

Staying seated, he said simply, "I plead guilty, Your Honor," and then he fell silent, which clarified nothing.

Turner stood again and briefly explained the crime of second-degree murder. Judge Boyd added that the charge included elements of committing the act in the heat of passion—and knowingly causing the death of another person following a "serious and provoking act" by the intended victim.

"Do you understand those elements?" Boyd asked Styler.

"Yes, Your Honor," he replied.

Why, the judge pressed, was he pleading guilty?

"Because I am guilty, Your Honor," the ex-doctor said.

And with that, the case was over, or almost over, but the surreal feeling in the courtroom was getting thicker by the moment.

46

There would never be a preliminary hearing now, nor a trial. The prosecutors would never have to say in open court what they believed had happened to Nancy Pfister or how it had happened or why or even precisely when. Or who was involved or not involved. They'd never have to prove anything beyond a reasonable doubt about the three people they'd alleged were involved in first-degree murder, conspiracy to commit that murder, and being accessories to the murder after the fact. The legal system in Aspen, Pitkin County, and the Ninth Judicial District of Colorado was instantly and completely off the hook, but the questions were just beginning.

Who'd killed Nancy Pfister? Had the case really been solved or had Trey confessed so that his wife could be set free? Had his confession been accepted so easily by the authorities because they thought it was real? Or because Aspen, as the summer season began, could now get on with its Food and Wine Classic, its Ideas Festival, its jazz concerts and its Music Festival—and get away from all the unwanted publicity over the death of one of its wilder children?

Judge Boyd had not yet adjourned court. In the gallery, spectators were shaking their heads, reporters were glancing at one another, and the room was buzzing with astonishment or disbelief. No one had foreseen this outcome, and the ghost of Spider Sabich was filling the air. Claudine Longet had gotten thirty days, to be served at her leisure, for shooting and killing her lover. Trey might serve less than twenty years, as he was apparently taking full responsibility for the murder.

The judge asked the Pfisters if they wanted to speak. They all did and they all requested that he not do what the DA's office had recommended—give Trey two decades in prison—but impose the maximum sentence of thirty-two years for what Styler had pled guilty to.

Christina spoke first by phone and said that the aftermath of Nancy's death had been "harrowing" and "awful."

"I truly believe that we will never know all of the true facts," she told the court. "But as a Christian woman, it is not my job to be a judge and jury of these people. 'Vengeance is mine' is the Scripture that comes to mind. People always get their judgment in the end. Life is about living and I intend to get on with the living part of my life. I want closure for my niece."

Then she said, "A comfortable medical situation [for Styler] is obviously not in my best interest."

She wasn't finished until, like many others, she questioned Trey's claim to being disabled.

"I saw Mr. Styler walking around just fine before he was arrested," she said, "and I am not interested in him being comfortable... Mr. Styler is in fine shape to serve hard time... I think this is a ploy, and I would like him to have the maximum harshest sentence available to the court."

Suzanne was next, rising and warmly thanking everyone involved in law enforcement for investigating and prosecuting the case.

"The longer the time this man spends in jail," she said, "the happier I will feel."

Instantly, her tone changed and she began castigating the *Aspen Times* for invading her privacy by publishing her victim's statement in the paper. After asking the media to go away and let her family live in peace, she sat back down.

It was Juliana's turn. She stood alone in the courtroom, fighting off tears. She looked very young and very frail and very far removed from the kinds of things that would lead someone to beat another person to death with a hammer. Like her aunts, she seemed completely ill at ease within the realities being exposed in the courtroom.

Glancing over at Styler, she said that she didn't understand his plea or why the authorities had allowed him to make it.

"It doesn't make sense to me, and it upsets me," Juliana told the judge, adding that there is no such thing as "an eye for an eye. I don't think it's fair. What this man has taken from me is never going to come back. My mother's the victim and she can't be here to defend herself... I think maximum time would be in my best interest, but this means nothing."

It seemed that she had more to say, but chose not to, quietly taking her seat.

Scott Turner was next.

"We have to deal with the law and the facts we have," the prosecutor said. "We have to deal with what we know and not with what we think we know and with the uncertainty of going to trial and with what's best for the community and the Pfister family. And taking all this into consideration, we've reached this conclusion. This is as difficult a homicide case as any we've been involved with."

After crediting the work of Sheriff DiSalvo, who was sitting in the front row, and his department, Turner continued, "Juliana said this won't be justice in the right way. She's right about that. What is justice to the outside world is one concept. And justice to family members is another concept and justice in the walls of this courthouse is an entirely different concept. We as prosecutors are limited in what justice we can obtain inside these walls.

"Some might find this outcome distasteful and I understand that. Nothing can repay the Pfister family for what they've gone through and they may not consider this justice. The family's feelings are not of vengeance, but of closure and the desire to see this matter resolved. Mr. Styler provided us with information to bring closure and I hope there's a price to pay for this information and that it may give the Pfisters some understanding of why we do what we do...

"It is never an easy situation, when we're dealing with a case such as this, to dispose of the matter when the defendant is receiving anything less than a life sentence... Taking into account Mr. Styler's age and medical condition... we feel this [twenty-year prison term] will, in fact, be a life sentence for Mr. Styler."

Ending his address, Turner acknowledged that there "will never be a consensus among all of the parties" and that this sentence was a just one.

Judge Boyd looked down at the defendant and gave Trey the chance to speak before pronouncing his sentence.

Without a pause, Styler said quietly, "I have nothing to add to what's been said by the people's attorney and my own."

Denying the wishes of the Pfisters, the judge gave the defendant twenty years in a Department of Corrections prison with medical facilities. He knocked off another 115 days, which Trey had already served in the local jail.

Even if this amounted to a life sentence, Boyd said to Styler, "It's still shorter than the amount of time that you likely took away from Ms. Pfister by taking her away at the age that she was... This death adds a shadow to Aspen... That light within the community is gone, and you are the one who turned that light off. That loss will then ripple through the community perhaps forever."

Speaking on Styler's behalf, Tina Fang addressed the judge and reemphasized that the case against all three defendants had been weak and that without her client's confession the DA wouldn't have been able to get a conviction against anyone.

"The prosecution," she said, "presumed Mrs. Styler was involved solely because she is married to Dr. Styler, and such presumption was untrue. Dr. Styler is deeply saddened for the pain and suffering of the entire Pfister family, and also for his wife, who had nothing to do with this. He accepts sole responsibility for the death of Nancy Pfister. He hopes that the privacy of all involved, including the Pfister family, will be respected."

The judge adjourned the hearing, but almost no one left the gallery because the morning's drama was not yet finished. The legal proceedings soon resumed as Kathy Carpenter walked into the courtroom looking very different from her prior appearances. She wore a dress and her hair was combed and pulled back from her face, as if she were preparing to go to work later that day at Alpine Bank, which wanted nothing to do with her. Very quickly, the DA dismissed all the charges against her "without prejudice," meaning that the investigation into her possible role in the murder would remain open indefinitely. The authorities might also look into the jewelry and the $6,000 of Nancy Pfister's money that was in Kathy's possession when she was first questioned by the police.

Following the hearing, DA Caloia took issue with Fang's statements about the arrests of Nancy Styler and Kathy Carpenter, telling a group of reporters, "When you look at the [arrest affidavits] you will see that we did have circumstantial evidence against Mrs. Styler, Mr. Styler, and Kathy Carpenter."

Her office issued a statement that read, "We do believe that this is a good and just resolution to these cases and hope that Nancy Pfister's family can find peace in knowing what happened, knowing that Nancy Pfister's killer is in prison, and avoiding potentially years of litigation for which the result is always uncertain...

"In light of (William Styler's) confession and statement that he alone was responsible for the death and subsequent hiding of the body, we dismissed the case against his wife, Nancy Styler. With this new evidence, it became clear that we would not be able to establish that Mrs. Styler played any role in the death of Nancy Pfister. After careful review of the evidence against Ms. Carpenter and in light of the statements of William Styler, we realized that the evidence we have to prove her involvement is also inadequate to proceed to trial. Therefore, we dismissed the charges against Katherine Carpenter today."

When court adjourned, David Olmsted was quick to point out that Trey's confession was in the works before all the forensic evidence had come back from the CBI. As the PI had been saying for months—while pushing for Nancy Styler's lawyers to set a preliminary hearing date as soon as possible—there was nothing connecting his client to the murder or to a conspiracy to commit the murder. That might have changed when the state lab completed its exams, so it was always in Nancy Styler's best interest to have the case resolved sooner rather than later.

47

Outside the courthouse, Joe DiSalvo spoke to the press, but only added to the confusion, saying that the evidence his office and the CBI had collected last February and March was strong enough to lead to three arrests.

"Just because Mr. Styler told us it's true doesn't mean it's true," he said to the *Aspen Times* about Trey's confession. "We need to corroborate the things he said; that's what a good investigator would do. Believing a man who just admitted to a homicide is not the prudent thing to do... Believe me, this is no Club Fed [Styler will be sent to]. This is still in the state Department of Corrections. Medical services will be available. It doesn't mean it's going to be a light or easy ride for him. This will be hard time; this will be real time."

Raising issues that many others in the courtroom this morning had been pondering, DiSalvo went on, "I don't believe now... that [Nancy Styler] was there [when the murder happened]. I do believe she knew after the fact... When you're sitting in a two-hundred-square-foot hotel room... I find it hard to believe, I find it impossible, that she didn't know."

Regarding Kathy Carpenter, he said, "If you are maliciously arrested, that would be a case for an apology. I can say that in this case, the probable cause went through two levels of judicial review—the district attorney and then the district court judge. If this had been a warrantless arrest where we yanked her off the street and it turned out to be a bad arrest, I'd be the first to apologize. But that wasn't the case."

His office had done "a righteous investigation," yet he acknowledged that had the case gone to trial with three defendants, it would have been at least a two-year ordeal for everyone: the Pfister family, Aspen, and himself.

"I think it's a good resolution," he said, "and I learned early on in my law enforcement career not to get too invested in these things because it will tear you up inside. I'm asking members of the community to take it day by day. Today we have a guilty plea with a sentence of a person who I truly believe killed Nancy. Whether or not there were accomplices, the investigation will continue to bear that out."

Although no one mentioned it in the immediate aftermath of the June 20 proceedings, financial considerations were in play around Trey's confession. Without a trial, the Pitkin County Sheriff's Office would still have to ask the county commissioners for about $175,000 for work on the case in the near future. They'd already racked up $85,000 in overtime costs for the sheriff's office staff and $35,000 more for the deputies in the Pitkin County Jail. A trial would have cost exponentially more. Among other things, Trey's willingness to take complete responsibility for the crime was a great bargain for the local judicial system.

With the case resolved, other law enforcement officials stood outside in the courthouse shade and answered questions, as tourists and onlookers from the Food and Wine Classic came by and listened in.

Were William Styler's actions premeditated?

"Well," DA Caloia responded, "you could certainly come to that conclusion. As I said, that plea was a negotiated plea, and oftentimes there is a dispute as to the facts that would support that... The charges [against Kathy Carpenter] could be reinstated if we get more evidence. And I'm not saying that it will be. I'm saying that there's a possibility out there. She [Carpenter] said very clearly that she saw the head and blood and stuff in two interviews."

If Kathy didn't look at the body, Caloia said, "How did she know who it was? It's very puzzling to us."

While the authorities spoke to one pack of journalists, Greg Greer and Kathleen Lord held their own press conference, centered on the just-exonerated Carpenter. They played parts of Kathy's 911 call on February 26 and displayed some crime-scene photos. Before the murder, Greer said, piling on to what Christina Pfister had just told Judge Boyd, William Styler had been spotted at the Woody Creek post office moving boxes to his car. He was "standing up, not using a wheelchair."

Greer went especially hard after CBI agent Kirby Quinn Lewis, who'd headed the agency's off-site investigations, and DA investigator Lisa Miller. Throughout the twenty hours of police interviews with Carpenter, Greer insisted, Kathy never changed her initial story, yet law enforcement concluded that "after listening to this 911 call, Kathy Carpenter is guilty." The transcript of the call, prepared by Lewis, had been attached to the arrest affidavit that had led to her being jailed for ninety-six days without bond. Greer went carefully back through the call and whether Kathy had said that she'd seen blood on Pfister's *forehead* or on the *headboard* of Nancy's bed.

"She said 'headboard,'" Greer told the media. "Believe me, I've listened to this a hundred times. That was their sole basis for focusing on her and really saying that she saw things she couldn't have seen with the story she was telling."

Despite Greer's best attempts to rehabilitate his client, in another part of the courthouse the DA's office was having none of it.

"The statements made by Kathy Carpenter," said Caloia in her press release, "were things that she said over and over again in her investigation. So the mis-transcription is there, but it was a very minor piece to this whole matter."

Greer and Lord made a point of saying to the media that the relationship between Pfister and Carpenter had been "platonic." And Kathy had only taken the $6,000 in cash and the jewelry from the safe deposit box on February 27 in order to give them to Juliana Pfister.

"That is not theft," Lord said, because "she turned the full amount over to the police... I'm very, very disappointed in the criminal justice system in this case."

"Kathy," Greer said, "is an unemployed homeless person now because she called 911... The government has an enormous amount of power and with one wrong fact they can do a lot to you. If Kirby gets a word wrong, he should be accountable for that and we should make him accountable for that... They rode this forehead transcript and decided that makes Kathy guilty. And they think [Carpenter's] 911 call is a fake."

"She honestly thought," Lord said, "that if you had nothing to hide you can speak freely with the police and she didn't know that wasn't true."

"Because she called 911," Greer insisted one final time, "her life has been turned upside down... and we're going to help her in any way we can. Right now, she's just enjoying her first hours of being out of jail."

In the wake of the confession, many people were unforgiving toward all the suspects and felt that the full truth had not yet come out. Within hours of Trey's sentencing, the Facebook group "Friends of Aspen" was bubbling with protest:

> **Betsy Roberts:** "They let the two women off... What a farce, another one... sounds like Claudine's case years ago..."
>
> **Patricia A. Dickson:** "And how pitiful Styler is in his wheelchair... but strong enough to kill and... Did he really move Nancy to the closet by himself? Finding it difficult to believe that his wife knew nothing/saw nothing/heard nothing and was in no way a part of anything... I know it's time to live forward, but nagging questions remain."
>
> **Marsha Stovall:** "It all stinks, if Art and Betty were alive all hell would be breaking loose."
>
> **Betsy Roberts:** "Apparently they did not want to spend the money or time needed in court..."
>
> **Ivan Lustig:** "A dark day for Aspen justice. Many of the richest hedge fund billionaires are serving time in 'prison hospitals.' Nancy deserved better than this. Why do doctors, lawyers, and financial criminals always go free or get a break?"
>
> **Marsha Stovall:** "It just saddens me. I was there for her birth and so many things. She was not Ms. Innocent but did not deserve this."
>
> **Dick Stephenson:** "The DA should be recalled!!!"

Sometime later, after the events of June 20 had had time to settle in, Teresa Wyatt posted on Facebook: "Can't stop thinking about it all. Flipping a mattress. It was NOT a light mattress. I slept in that bed. Nancy couldn't sleep and spent all the money she could on peace. Only one who got out free and clear is N Styler..."

48

As the press conferences unfolded around the courthouse on June 20, something much quieter was happening a block or so away. Near downtown, David Olmsted sat at a picnic table in the radiant mountain sunlight and talked about what had just transpired. Earlier that morning, he'd slipped into the courtroom and had been listening in the back, absorbing the case's shockingly abrupt ending. A resolution had been reached, but no one outside of the Ninth District legal officials and the defense attorneys and their investigators had glimpsed the 13,000 pages of discovery the murder had generated. No one who'd seen the massive criminal file was willing to talk about any of it with civilians—except for Olmsted. He knew things about the case, or he thought he knew things, that no one not directly involved in it could have known, and they were things that had not yet been revealed.

Was he surprised at the swift outcome?

"I wasn't that surprised," he said, shielding his eyes from the sun, his voice still carrying a trace of the eastern United States where he grew up. "Aspen doesn't like the kind of publicity that comes with Nancy Pfister. The community is very sensitive to this." He then opined, "You had a sheriff department and a DA's office that wanted to believe the story Trey was telling. They didn't want to disprove what he was saying, so he had a very good audience. I've personally never heard of a second-degree murder case being called a 'crime of passion,' so that alone is unusual. I've said for a long time that I didn't think the DA could have gotten this evidence past a preliminary hearing and they knew this, so they decided to take the deal with Trey."

He looked across the picnic table and said, "They needed somebody to be guilty."

Olmsted reached down and adjusted his pink wristband, indicating that he or someone he knew was a breast cancer survivor. The light was growing more intense by the moment, as the sun moved toward its apex in the sky, and at a mile and half above sea level, it was nearly blinding. Olmsted honed in on the fact that in court this morning Scott Turner had indicated that Trey had confessed to killing Pfister on the morning of February 24. More than anything, this was what the PI wanted to talk about.

"I don't believe," Olmsted said, "that this could have happened on February 24, not the way that the DA's office said it did. The window for this crime is on the twenty-fifth and the twenty-sixth."

When asked to explain why he felt this way, he hesitated and tried to slide away from the subject.

Was it possible, he was asked, that the murder had occurred very early on Monday morning, the twenty-fourth, when police officer Joshua Bennett had stopped Trey at 12:15 a.m. for speeding across the Midland Bridge in Basalt in his Jaguar sedan? He was out late at night by himself and was perhaps hurrying back to the motel and his wife. Could he have been returning to the Aspenalt after killing Pfister?

"No." Olmsted shook his head. "No one thinks she died on Sunday night because she had contact with several people on Monday. That isn't when it happened."

For weeks leading up to the scheduled preliminary hearing, Olmsted had stated that the murder's timeline was critically important, but he wouldn't say why. The coroner's report had placed the crime within a twenty-four to forty-eight–hour period before Kathy opened the closet on the evening of February 26; forty-eight hours would only reach back to Monday evening—not Monday morning, when Trey said he'd killed Pfister. When pressed to talk about this now, Olmsted didn't look comfortable offering anything more.

Because he'd worked for Nancy Styler's defense team, he remained in a gray area when speaking about evidence—and he would stay in that area for as long as the case file remained sealed. At the moment, there was no indication that the file would ever be opened to the press and public. Everyone outside the legal system was left to speculate on the murder, when no one in that realm had seen any of the evidence.

"One thing is certain," the PI said. "When Kathy Carpenter called 911, what she described seeing in the closet she couldn't see. It's as simple as that. She couldn't have seen the blood or hair that she described seeing."

Shielding his eyes again, he went on, "Everything about this case is contrived. The DA kept Nancy Styler and Kathy Carpenter in jail for four months" based on evidence that he speculated might not have held up at a preliminary hearing. "That's unconscionable. If Trey hadn't confessed, they'd still be sitting [in] jail. In thirty-some years of doing this kind of work as both a police officer and a private investigator, I've never seen evidence this thin against suspects laid out in arrest affidavits."

He brought up again, as he had more than once in the past, that the first cop who spoke to Kathy Carpenter on the night she found the body, Deputy Ryan Turner, said that she smelled of alcohol.

"Back in March," he said, "I spent five hours interviewing Dr. Styler and it's very difficult to believe that he's so stupid that he'd put his own car registration in a bag with the hammer and leave these things a short distance from his motel room. He can't find someplace else to put them between Pfister's house and the motel? It's arguable that they were framed."

Is that what he really thought?

"The evidence isn't there. The police would have been much better served if they'd gotten their investigation together and made a less urgent decision about all this."

If the evidence wasn't there, why were the authorities so willing to accept Trey's confession? The PI hinted at what had now been avoided.

According to Olmstead, the authorities were likely concerned "that if the case had gone to trial, the Pfister family would have been a part of it and I don't think they wanted that to happen. Nancy Pfister's character and lifestyle invited trouble and the defense would have put her character on trial. There were other motives in this case besides the rental dispute. Suzanne lived next to Nancy and didn't get along with her and told people that if anything ever happened to her, they should look at her sister."

Olmsted implied that Nancy had told people that she was coming home because of a legal issue with Suzanne and she was worried about this.

"Suzanne," he said, "was upset by something someone said in the *Aspen Times* after her sister died. Juliana was upset because people called her mother a 'socialite' instead of a 'philanthropist.' How upset would they have been if the case had gone to trial and all these other things about their family had come out?"

He stopped and then bluntly added, "If I were the cops, I'd want to know more about Suzanne Pfister in the days after her sister came home from Australia and more about who benefited from the land transfers. What does my gut say about the murder? I'm still not sure. Trey could have done this alone, the way he said he did, but it didn't happen on Monday morning. If you want to believe he did it by himself, that's all right, but people need to have their facts straight about the murder and to understand what those facts mean."

Which facts in particular?

He didn't answer.

How could one get at the facts if they were kept in sealed files, possibly forever?

He shook his head.

"I've seen a lot of cases with bizarre aspects," he said, "but I've never seen as many bizarre aspects in one case as in this one. The victim and the suspects are all bizarre. The investigation is bizarre. The outcome is bizarre. I'd never seen arrest warrants as empty as these. I've just never seen anything like this."

49

With Nancy Styler and Kathy Carpenter both out of jail, Suzanne Pfister filed motions for restraining orders against the two women.

"I have had confrontations with her [Carpenter] in the past," Suzanne Pfister wrote in the order. "She knows where I live, [and] I am afraid for myself and my son."

"She has been released," she wrote of Nancy Styler, "and I am afraid for myself and my son . . . I also want to protect my public privacy, which has been invaded by the press for months."

A Glenwood Springs judge granted Suzanne one temporary restraining order, preventing Carpenter from coming within a hundred yards of her and her teenage son.

Several days after Nancy Styler had been set free, the *Aspen Daily News* reported that she'd gone to an undisclosed location, where she was surrounded by family and friends. Before long, she'd be on the national media circuit, with the major networks vying with one another to give her the opportunity to tell her story. David Olmsted said that following Trey's confession she was not at all happy with her husband taking the fall for the murder. Soon afterward, Trey wrote her a letter, saying that he knew she was innocent of the murder and that he was innocent too. He tried to send the same letter to the media, asking his jailers to distribute it to reporters, but that didn't happen.

"I think the letter didn't go out to the papers," says Olmsted, "for the same reason that people in authority" may have wanted Trey's confession to matter. It seemed like "nobody wanted what he had to say to get out there. There isn't anybody who didn't want this to go away."

Trey was soon shipped out of Aspen and put into the state prison system. Colorado has two lockups that offer infirmaries for inmates: the Denver Reception and Diagnostic Center, where Styler was now sent, and the Colorado Territorial Correctional Facility in Cañon City. In Denver he underwent rigorous physical and mental assessments, based on his risk level for escape and on whether he was prone to be a victim or a predator inside the prison. Both of these institutions had clinics with the resources to manage long-term and chronic illnesses, and one would eventually become his new home. His first parole hearing would come up in October 2028, with a shot at parole on January 15, 2029, less than fifteen years from the time of his confession.

With the case resolved, Kathy's attorneys continued fighting to clear her name and to stop the release of her portion of the investigative materials. Because she'd been exonerated, they argued, all the information the police had gathered about her should be sealed forever. (Trey and Nancy were hoping for the same legal fate with their files.)

The press disagreed, led by Denver attorney Steven Zansberg who represented the *Aspen Daily News*, Aspen Public Radio, the *Aspen Times*, and other media groups. In his motion to Judge Nichols, he wrote that because of the extensive media coverage devoted to Carpenter's arrest and subsequent criminal proceedings, "including an hour-long press conference conducted by her attorneys following the dismissal of the charges against her, there is no basis upon which the court can find [that] the statutory requirements for sealing have been, or can be, met."

The DA's office filed a motion in support of Zansberg: "Mr. Styler has pleaded guilty and has been sentenced and the remaining cases against the other two defendants have been dismissed. There are no pending trials involving the death of Nancy Pfister. Thus, this court's sole justification for sealing or redacting portions of Mr. Styler's file prior to the previously scheduled hearing, i.e., to 'protect the defendants' right to a fair trial by an impartial jury in Pitkin County,' no longer exists."

Deputy DA Andrea Bryan also contended that by keeping the files sealed, the defense attorneys had been able to "cherry-pick parts of the sealed files" and to create a "one-sided and incomplete version" of events leading to the arrests. On the day Trey was sentenced, Carpenter's lawyers had, after all, played for journalists only a part of Kathy's 911 call. They'd also displayed crime-scene photos and talked about details of the case contained in the sealed affidavits. Now Greer and Lord were asking that "the public be denied access to the arrest warrant affidavits to protect Ms. Carpenter's 'privacy,' yet [they] have themselves very publicly discussed, in detail, facts of the case."

As the two sides battled over the files, Kathy's legal team filed a civil action seeking to seal all of her arrests records, including those from the CBI, Garfield County Sheriff's Office, and the Aspen, Basalt, and Snowmass Village police departments. The DA opposed this maneuver as well.

Then Doug Allen, a columnist for the *Aspen Times*, heatedly weighed in on Judge Nichols's ongoing refusal to open the files to the public. In his view, the cover-up of the crime and the murder investigation itself were now essentially complete.

"If a district-level judge," Allen wrote in an opinion column, "can indefinitely seal information regarding a case that is over, our right to freedom of information is virtually nonexistent. It's a terribly dangerous precedent to set, and in my opinion is a total abuse of her power as a judge. Nichols works for us... and in that capacity, she has completely failed in her duties to adjudicate this case while also balancing the community's right to know what the hell went down on West Buttermilk Road this past February. Based on her handling of this case, particularly the public disclosure aspects, she should resign."

In the midst of this dispute, DA Caloia announced that her office would not pursue a theft charge against Kathy for being in possession of Nancy Pfister's jewelry and the $6,000 in cash.

"This decision," Caloia said in a press release, "may be reviewed in the future should the district attorney's office be presented with additional evidence."

By all appearances, the local legal system was doing everything in its power to put the Pfister case to rest forever. And if the defense attorneys had their way, the press and the public would never know what the police investigation had uncovered about Trey Styler, Nancy Styler, Kathy Carpenter, and Nancy Pfister.

Six weeks after Trey's confession, nothing had yet been decided about Carpenter's files. On August 11, Judge Nichols held a hearing to determine what should be done with Kathy's search warrant and arrest affidavit (by now, in separate actions, both of these documents for the Stylers had been released, giving the interested parties a glimpse into the evidence). Media representatives argued that Kathy's information needed to be made public, while her lawyers contended just as vigorously that this should never happen. She'd been released from jail and cleared in the murder, and she wasn't going to be investigated further for putting some items that didn't belong to her in a safe deposit box. Case closed. Carpenter ought to be free to live and work in the Roaring Fork Valley—rumor had it that she was currently holed up in Carbondale—without any more negative publicity.

Kathleen Lord cited Colorado statutes which recognize "that one accused of a crime that is never proven by the prosecution has a statutory right to have arrest records related to the dismissed charges sealed and to have their reputation and right to privacy safeguarded by requiring the court to seal unproven and unreliable allegations."

The judge, to the dismay of reporters covering the case and to some of the public, sided with Lord: at least parts of Kathy's file would be sealed going forward—a death blow for anyone outside the Ninth Judicial District trying to penetrate the secrets of the case.

50

The day after this ruling, August 12, in a maneuver as mystifying as everything else surrounding the murder, Judge Nichols decided to release nearly the entire case file, including the 13,000 transcribed pages of discovery and police interviews, plus the videos, audio recordings, and photographs kept away from all civilians since last February 26. Some of Carpenter's file would remain untouchable, but her 911 call and her twenty hours of speaking with detectives were now available. The darkness around the investigation, if not the murder itself, was lifting at last.

In late July, Joe DiSalvo had sat in his courthouse office, with a Tom Benson poster and an electric guitar hanging on the wall, and said that until he'd witnessed Trey's video-recorded confession, he hadn't believed that the man had committed the crime alone. *After* studying it, the sheriff had come to accept that Trey had killed Nancy by himself. Yet DiSalvo said that he thought that both women had had some knowledge of the murder, either before or after the homicide.

DiSalvo seemed very relieved that the case was over.

"When Tina Fang came to us in mid-June and told us that she wanted to make a plea bargain," he said, laughing, "I was so surprised that I wondered if she was drunk. Back in March, she'd told me that we were in for a very long and hard fight and there was a very real chance that we'd lose. When she wanted to make a plea, it was a compliment to us. It gave us a way to bring the case to a conclusion without going to court for the next two years.

"Trey Styler must have seen his confession as the best plan for everyone.

We'd heard that in the past few years, his wife had really been wearing the pants in that family. She may have been very angry with him. You have to wonder that if he got out of jail, she might have kicked his ass for getting her involved in all this. Maybe he was afraid of her and just decided to stay locked up."

With total conviction, DiSalvo stated that as part of Styler's plea bargain, his confession would never be revealed to the public—so the only actual account of the murder on the record would be buried forever. This was highly curious, but as DiSalvo had put it with a broad smile, "It works for me. And it works for our community and for the Pfister family."

Then the judge did exactly what the sheriff said she'd never do, revealing both the roots of the confession and the investigation leading up to it.

On Monday morning, June 16, nine days before the preliminary hearing was set to begin, Trey had made contact with the authorities through Tina Fang, telling them that he wanted to talk. As DiSalvo himself had pointed out, one could only wonder what might have happened if the preliminary hearing had started on June 9, instead of being pushed back sixteen days to allow DA investigator Lisa Miller to go on vacation.

That Monday the deputies transported Styler, in orange prison clothes and via a wheelchair, from the Pitkin County Jail into an interrogation room used by the sheriff's department. For the duration of the coming interview, he stayed in the wheelchair. Deputy Brad Gibson and Lisa Miller questioned him as he poured out a narrative, both videotaped and later typed up and running to 185 pages, his new story contradicting things he'd said in previous interrogations. Tina Fang was also in the room, but not the most forceful presence today. That distinction belonged to Miller. Tall and broad-shouldered, she wore a gray pantsuit that made her appear even larger. She had a swath of brown hair, a no-nonsense twang in her voice, and a girlish smile that she did not use in these circumstances.

She quickly let Styler know that this was not her first face-to-face sit down with someone taking credit for a murder (as well as someone who'd had months to study the police reports, reading and absorbing what the evidence looked like). Because of her twenty years of experience in dealing with criminals, she explained, she needed "to feel very comfortable that you're telling me the truth."

"I intend to tell you the truth," he replied.

"The complete truth?"

"Yes."

Miller read him his Miranda rights and he began by asking them to abide by the terms of the deal they'd made with him regarding the release of his wife from jail. If he took full responsibility for the murder, they'd agreed to set Nancy Styler free (which happened on the following day, June 17). Trey added, rather oddly, that he had no hard feelings against them and then he locked his hands together in front of him and started to lay out his latest version of the crime.

"I'll tell you what you haven't been led to believe prior to this," he said. "There may be things that seem inconsistent to you. There are times during these things when I was not thinking clearly. I'm not sure what the appropriate legal or medical terminology would be, and I'm a doctor. If my answers don't appear to make sense to you, I'll do my best to explain."

For the next two hours, Gibson and Miller let him ramble. Both were clearly unwilling to take at face value Styler's account of how he'd killed Nancy Pfister and covered up the murder with no involvement from anyone else. Ever since his arrest, he'd made a dramatic show of his disability in the lower half of his body. He'd crawled across the floor of his cell, consistently used a wheelchair in the courtroom, and made it appear as though he could barely stand up. Under these circumstances, how could he lift anything heavy or negotiate the stairs of the Pfister residence?

Over those two hours, he kept approaching the murder, then backing up and looping around, coming nearer the decisive moment, but veering off again, as if he were remembering or inventing things as he went along. Miller regularly tried to refocus him and move him forward through the timeline between when Pfister came back from Australia on the evening of Saturday, February 22, and when Kathy found her body on Wednesday evening, the twenty-sixth. While Miller did this, Trey more than once let it be known that he had the intelligence and the vocabulary of a once-prominent physician.

One couldn't help feeling—and sensing that Miller felt it, too—that Styler considered himself the smartest person in the room. He clearly thought that as a doctor he still had some moral authority.

"My scorecard," he told them, "is that I've saved a whole hell of a lot more lives than I've taken."

Miller looked unimpressed, if not disgusted.

She guided him back to the timeline, the linchpin in his credibility.

On Monday morning, February 24, at around eight o'clock, Trey said, he'd left his wife sleeping at the Aspenalt Lodge and gone to look for a storage unit in Basalt. He needed to empty out the loaded rental truck he'd parked at Pfister's home, so that they could load it up again with more of their possessions and clear out of West Buttermilk Road as soon as possible. But the storage business didn't open until 10:30. With nothing to do, he didn't want to return to the Aspenalt and risk waking his wife. Ever since yesterday afternoon, when Kathy had given him the new list of demands from Pfister written on an envelope, he couldn't stop thinking about them or the crushing effect they'd had on his spouse. The amount of money Pfister said that the Stylers still owed her—$14,000—galled him, but was probably even more humiliating for Nancy. Her stress level was as high as he'd ever seen it, even before this happened. Now it was higher still. Why couldn't Pfister just let them get their belongings and leave? Why did she have to grind more threats into them, when they were moving out as fast as they could?

With time on his hands, he decided to drive up West Buttermilk Road in the Jaguar and speak with Pfister. He also wanted to see if his rental truck was still blocked in by the car that had been there the day before. If it wasn't, they could resume the move. As he drove down the long gravel road toward the residence, he saw that the car was still there; it would be difficult to do anything today. Maybe he and Pfister could resolve things this morning without more conflict. Maybe it was a stroke of luck that the storage locker business in Basalt hadn't opened until 10:30, giving him and his landlady a chance to work things out.

The last time he'd seen her had been four months earlier, back in November, when he'd taken Nancy to the airport for her trip to Australia. Even though the couple had had a few early squabbles with Pfister, Trey had enjoyed some good times in this house, no longer drinking because of his medical condition, but occasionally smoking marijuana on the recommendation of a physician. Photographs of Trey taken at the November 16 going-away party Pfister had thrown for herself reveal a far happier and more robust-looking man than the one who'd shown up in court after his arrest. In the pictures, he's relaxed and appears much closer to his actual age of sixty-five.

As he recalled some of this in front of the investigators, Miller tried to nudge him away from November 2013 and back to Monday morning, February 24, 2014.

51

Trey backtracked again, this time focusing on one day earlier, Sunday, February 23, when he'd gotten the envelope from Kathy on Sunday afternoon during the exchange of their cars.

"As you may well know," he told the investigators, "Ms. Pfister is an alcoholic. Her habit was to begin drinking champagne about noon. She'd not be making sense altogether. Sometimes, she'd contradict herself. Sometimes, she'd just make things up. It's very possible that, being intoxicated, she may have believed these things when she said them... She had a tendency to be melodramatic when she was intoxicated."

Styler reached into the pocket of his jumpsuit and pulled out his dentures, slipping them into his mouth, before resuming his story and returning to Monday morning.

When he reached Pfister's home around nine a.m., he said, he found a sign on the entrance in Kathy's handwriting, saying that Nancy was sleeping and "Do Not Disturb." He said that the door was unlocked (although Kathy had earlier told the police that she'd locked it before going to work at the bank that morning). As Trey pushed his shoulder against the door, it opened wide. He stuck in his head and called out Pfister's name, hearing nothing in return. He walked inside and called it again, awaiting a response, but getting none. Gabe bounded down the stairs to greet him and he petted the big dog, before locking him in one of the rooms so he wouldn't be a distraction.

Trey had just mounted a few steps to get into the house. Now he went up the stairs to the master bedroom, calling Nancy's name once more, but hearing nothing in return. Her bedroom door was slightly ajar so he nudged it wider and saw her sleeping on her bed. Everyone who knew Nancy knew something about her sleep routine: she went to bed with ear plugs and an eye mask, often taking an Ambien or a Soma and washing it down with a glass of champagne.

He called her name again, but she didn't stir.

Breaking his narrative flow, Trey told Miller and Gibson that all he'd wanted to do this morning was to speak with Pfister and try to end their differences. She still had their spa equipment, including a $20,000 "facial machine," five industrial sewing machines, and other expensive supplies crucial to any business they hoped to start in the future. If she'd just let them get their possessions out of the house without any more trouble or demands . . . they'd be gone in a day or two at most.

Standing over her bed and watching Nancy breathe, Trey said that something happened, something he wasn't able to articulate very well. Or maybe he just couldn't recreate the emotion or the reality of that moment, which had occurred almost four months ago. Or maybe he was too upset to try to recreate it. Or maybe he wasn't telling the truth, but fabricating a tale on the spot in order to protect his wife and relieve her stress and get her out of jail. Or maybe he was doing his best to talk about one of the most difficult things criminals can speak of. A number of people who've carried out extreme violence appear not to have been present when a murder occurred. They seem to be absent during the act itself and then to come back to themselves a short while later, after a great release of energy and feeling, a purging of rage. And even they can't believe what they've done and don't really know why they did it—because the need to do it has finally been removed. Sometimes, they feel regretful, but the victim is still dead.

Standing over the sleeping Nancy Pfister, Trey felt something like the collective fury of the last fifteen years of bitterness at the legal system; of anger at the medical colleagues whom he felt betrayed by; of the burden of living with constant pain; of not being able to support his family in anything like the lifestyle to which he and his wife had so long been accustomed; of their long, slow descent into poverty on the threshold of old age. In that moment, he told the detectives, all it took to solve their problems was a single action.

He and his wife had been beaten down enough by Pfister. They'd suffered enough from her demands and her disregard for their struggles. They'd tried to accommodate her as best they could, but nothing had softened her. Nancy Styler had told Trey that they weren't going to pay Pfister the $14,000 she'd asked for before releasing their equipment—they weren't going to pay her anything.

After Pfister had left for Australia, Trey tried to explain to the investigators, "Things went sour for reasons I still don't understand completely... She [Pfister] had made statements and allegations that were untrue... We had been left in nowhere land, as the Beatles would say it."

He told the detectives how supportive his wife had been throughout the years of his disability and how important it was for him to be able to relieve her own suicidal thoughts, which she was now having.

While trying to generate some sympathy or understanding from his interrogators, he did what he'd done with many others in the past and said that he'd been "robbed of my assets by my employer."

Miller cut him off and attempted to steer him back to Monday morning. Trey refocused and slid back into his story of February 24.

Staring at Pfister, deep in sleep, he felt in a "kind of a daze" and as if he'd stopped using his "rational mind."

He paused again and crossed his arms against his chest, in something like a self-protective gesture, before plunging forward in a clinical tone.

Looking at the prone figure, he saw that Nancy was helpless and "the threat could be removed immediately."

Because of his familiarity with the house, he walked back downstairs and picked up an old hammer from a toolbox in the garage. He returned to the master bedroom and bent over the sleeping woman. Pfister was lying on her left side and facing him, but her eyes were covered. An "irresistible impulse" came over him—an impulse to end their troubles and get rid of his wife's stress, the one thing he wanted to be able to do for her.

Trey "struck her in the head... I hit the back of her skull. To be honest,

I was surprised that the hammer penetrated as deeply as it did... I thought the skull was a stronger bone than that..."

She didn't move or make a sound.

"I wasn't sure that it would [be] immediately fatal," he said, "and this may seem hard to believe, but there was a part of me that said, 'Okay, I've committed to this course of action and...' I did not want her to become conscious and aware of what was going on. She had not reacted at all to the first blow and, in retrospect, it may have been unlikely that she would have regained consciousness at all.

"But to ensure that, I hit her again in the front of the head, knowing that the frontal lobes are important for consciousness, and I believe that I hit her again after that... Making sure that she could not regain consciousness and be aware of what was happening or suffer in any significant way with what is happening... I was already remorseful for having done what I'd done. There's a part of me that doesn't want to believe and the question was, *Now what? Ah shit, what the hell have I done?*"

She was bleeding from the skull and his first thought was to "contain the blood." He went back downstairs for some large plastic trash bags of the kind they'd been using to move out and returned to the master bedroom. He slipped a bag over her head to hold the blood, which wasn't spurting, but just gradually oozing out.

The thought came to him, he told the investigators, to call the police and inform them of what he'd done, but instead he grabbed a cover off the bed and laid it down on the carpeted floor. He took her right arm, which was easy to do because she was lying on her left side, and pulled her nude body off the mattress and onto the cover. She was in a "supine position—that's a medical term," he explained, but she was too big to fit completely into one trash bag. He remembered seeing an extension cord downstairs under the sink in the guest bathroom so he went back down the stairs to look for it. After retrieving the cord, he wrapped it around her, putting her knees up against her chest and making her small enough to slip into a garbage bag. Once she was tied up and inside the bag, he dragged the cover and the body across the bedroom floor, ten to fifteen feet to the closet door.

"I'm admittedly not the strongest person in the world," he said to Gibson and Miller," but I did that... I was in a pathological state, but as I was doing it, I was trying to deny it."

The key, the one with the oval tag reading "Owner's Closet" attached to it, was in the closet lock, so he opened it. He manipulated her into the closet, but didn't remember putting a towel over her body, yet he must have done so because he knew from seeing the evidence that a towel was present.

He locked the closet door, put the key in his pocket, and went back to the bed, summoning all his strength and flipping over the queen-sized mattress to hide the bloodstains.

"In retrospect," he said to the duo, "this wasn't the most thought-out action. Totally inadequate."

Admitting this, he made a sound like laughter and said, "If I was really trying to hide all the evidence, I should have done something more thorough."

The detectives kept silent, as they had throughout most of his description of the crime.

Pfister had a strong reputation as a free spirit, Trey said, and she loved to make last-minute decisions about catching the next flight out of town, so he decided to use this as part of the cover-up. He wanted to "try to create the impression that she had voluntarily left the house, which she had been known to do spontaneously, unexpectedly, and from the stories that we heard, she had disappeared for days or weeks at a time..."

Getting another plastic bag, he rounded up her cell phone, her prescription bottles, an airline boarding pass, a coat, a hat, and the pearl necklace from her mother.

"They were sort of her signature," he said of the necklace. "She never went out without her pearls on."

To have left them in her bedroom "would be inconsistent with the concept I was trying to achieve."

Spotting a computer case in the room that belonged to him, he picked it up. Dropping the bloody hammer in the bag with the pearls and Pfister's other items, he went back downstairs and left the house, wondering if he should have done something else with the body, like getting it out of her home and into the nearby woods, but he felt that he wasn't strong enough for that. He'd put the bag containing the hammer and the dead woman's effects in the trunk.

"Part of me," he said, "didn't want to deal with the fact that I'd done this at all... Let me use a metaphor now. My medical condition has caused me to have pain pretty consistently for the last ten years. You have techniques where you can put the pain in a place and ignore it. I did the same thing with this event... I compartmentalized it—put it aside so I could continue with my regular self." He paused for a moment and added, "The little boy that lives in all of us still wanted it to disappear and not have happened."

52

Leaving Pfister's house, he drove back to the Aspenalt, where Nancy had gotten up and was dressed for the day. Telling his wife nothing about where he'd been or what he'd done (according to his story for Miller and Gibson), he now returned with Nancy to Pfister's home to see if the car that had been blocking their rental truck had been moved. It hadn't, so there was no reason for them to go inside the residence. They retraced their steps to Basalt, ate fast food, and prepared to visit a rental property outside of town on the Frying Pan River. At four p.m., they arrived at the address twenty minutes early, to the annoyance of the owner, looking around and chatting for about an hour. During the conversation, Trey felt sick and excused himself to go to the bathroom, where he vomited.

"I assume this has something to do," he told the investigators, "as an emotional reaction to the events of the day."

He quietly rejoined the others, determined not to let his wife see that he'd been ill or was upset. His goal, as he'd reminded the detectives throughout his confession, was not to increase her stress or distress in any way.

If she'd known what he'd done that Monday morning, "She'd have thought much less of me and still doesn't believe I'm capable of such a thing."

On Tuesday, Nancy Styler called a lawyer to ask about their rights as renters and also phoned the sheriff's department to ask for a civil standby to come to the Pfister house and keep the peace while they continued moving out.

During this time, Trey told the investigators, he wrote an e-mail to Pfister, "even though I knew she wouldn't get it." Throughout Tuesday, the Stylers and three hired helpers worked to get their possessions out of the residence, with Nancy buying lunch for the men at Subway. That morning Nancy Pfister's friend Patrick Carney had come by and gone upstairs to look for her in the master bedroom, but when he didn't find her, he soon left.

Or—as Nancy Styler later told the police—Patrick Carney was already in the house when the couple arrived there that morning, which Carney denied. Either way, according to Trey, his wife made several comments about a strange odor.

"I didn't know for sure," he said to Gibson and Miller, "if she was smelling the body."

For his part, Trey never mentioned to anyone this odor or the smell of the waste that Gabe had left in the house on Monday and Tuesday. In his youth, Styler told the investigators, he'd injured his nose and "no longer had a sense of smell."

The rest of Tuesday, he said, was uneventful and on Wednesday they finished moving and unloaded the last of their belongings at the storage unit in Basalt. Around noon, Nancy Styler called Kathy to see if she'd go up to the house and get Gabe. The couple then drove to Glenwood Springs, where Trey turned in the rental truck and Nancy had a 6:30 p.m. appointment for eyelash extensions. On the way back to the Aspenalt, Nancy called Kathy again, but she didn't answer. By now, Carpenter had gone into the closet, found the body, and dialed 911. Nancy Styler phoned Susan Wasko, who said that her boyfriend had just seen police activity around the Pfister residence.

According to Trey, rather than return to the house on West Buttermilk Road for their left-behind trash bags, as they'd originally planned, the couple stopped by Heather's restaurant in Basalt and briefly met with Merlin Broughton.

While Nancy went inside to speak with Broughton, Trey had enough time to slip away and dispose of the bag, which had been in the Jaguar's trunk the past two days, holding Pfister's' prescription bottles, the bloody hammer, the pearls, and his car registration. He gave no explanation for why his registration was with these other items, saying only that he dropped the bag into the municipal Dumpster near Alpine Bank.

His story ended there.

For hours Miller had been listening with great intensity and a skeptical expression, but she and Gibson had been largely quiet and unaggressive. She now leaned in closer to Trey and asked him to sign a form waiving all of his legal rights. One sentence in the document read, "I understand that in what I am doing, no promises or threats have been made to me and no pressure or coercion has been used against me."

He balked at signing and glanced at Tina Fang, sitting to his right. He again insisted that his confession was dependent on "my wife's dismissal and release . . . I wanted to make sure that this doesn't undo that in some fashion."

Before receiving such assurance from the detectives, he went off again on the legal system, saying that in the past he'd been misled and robbed by corrupt attorneys, but Miller shut him down. Her politeness was starting to fade.

Because Trey had tried to convince them that killing Pfister was not premeditated, but a spontaneous act—potentially making it something less than first-degree murder—he repeated that he'd had no intention of harming the woman until he had been leaning over her bed, watching her sleep.

"You're telling me that you made a snap decision?" Miller asked.

"I have a question," he responded vaguely and glancing away, "that it was a decision as I think of it."

"Where was the hammer?" she said.

"It was in a toolbox in the garage."

"You go to the garage—that pretty well goes to decision-making."

"Not really. Because whatever was made was while I was standing over the bed."

"Why not strangle her then, if you'd made the decision?"

"It didn't occur to me to do that. By doing what I did, I could make it instantaneous. Strangling her could have woken her up and she'd have been aware that she was being attacked. If would be easier on her if she did not wake up."

Miller came even closer and demanded that he look her in the eye when talking about killing another human being.

He did as he was told.

"You're not going to like me for this," she said. "In your profession, there are many other ways of killing someone."

"Yes, there are. In my work, I came to the conclusion that the greatest evil in the world is not death, but suffering..."

He paused and offered the closest thing he would give to an underlying motive for his actions.

"Even though I decided this was something I should do to spare my wife's suffering, I didn't want Nancy Pfister to suffer in the process. I wanted it to be immediate and to render her unconscious until she was dead... It may sound silly, but I still had compassion for someone I was about to murder. She had to die and die quickly and not suffer. This was the only way I could think of at the time... It sounds absurd, but—"

"Here's the absurd part," Miller shot back. "You sitting here minimizing it."

She came in closer and harder still, posing a question he wasn't prepared for.

"Why was your wife's phone," she asked, "hitting off the cell tower by Nancy Pfister's address?"

The implication of the question was that Nancy Styler's phone, and Nancy Styler herself, was with him in the house. The authorities had had difficulty tracking this phone because forensic testing had revealed a gap in the data of Nancy Styler's cell phone between January 30 and the day they were discussing: February 24, 2014.

Trey was groping for an answer. "It might have been in my bag."

"Your wife's phone had outgoing calls from this tower proximate to Pfister's address. I have concern about the phone issue."

"She was not there. She was asleep when I left. Her phone could have been there in my bag. I made no phone calls when there, but later that day we were both up near there."

. . .

In his first police interview on February 27, Trey had told CBI agent John Zamora that on the morning of the twenty-fourth he'd phoned Pfister to straighten things out between them so they could finish their move—making the call on his wife's cell. He said that he did this while Nancy was asleep at the motel and that he'd taken her cell with him so that no one would call her and wake her up. Since he couldn't reach Pfister, he'd left her a message, saying that he'd spoken with a lawyer and that he and his wife had the right to retrieve their possessions from the house without more resistance from her.

The essence of his call, he'd said to Zamora, was "don't give us any crap or you will get more crap than you ever wanted..."

Unexpectedly, Miller dropped this line of inquiry and went in another direction.

53

When was the last time, Miler asked, that Styler had seen Kathy Carpenter?

"Sunday afternoon," Trey said.

"She said she saw you on Monday at Buttermilk."

"That's not true. If she said that, she's lying."

"Why would she lie?"

"I thought I knew who Kathy Carpenter was and have no idea why she said this."

"What's her motive to say that you met on Monday?"

"She was mistaken."

"Mistaken? Or she owes you because you saved her and she's trying to save you now and cover you?"

Miller was referring to the incident back in January when Trey had given Kathy the medication epinephrine and taken her to a local emergency room when she was having acute respiratory distress—trouble breathing. She was in a panic state and later told people that the former doctor had saved her life.

"To the best of my knowledge," Trey said to Miller, "she was completely unaware of the events as of Monday, and as far as I know, she had no knowledge of anything having been done with respect to Nancy Pfister, until she discovered the body on Wednesday."

Had he been involved romantically with Carpenter?

No, because he was no longer capable of having sex.

Why did he ask Zamora during his initial police interview to tell Kathy that he loved her?

Again he fumbled for a response. "Kathy was much closer to my wife than to me..."

Once more he said that during this time his spouse was suicidal. Trey told them that he had a million-dollar life insurance policy on himself and had thought about ending his own life so that Nancy could get this money.

Miller asked about his wife's suggestion that the couple put cyanide in a piece of chocolate for Pfister.

He dismissed this as "facetious."

What about Trey's temper, which several people had told Miller about?

He joked that those who spoke about him in this way were only doing so out of their own self-interest.

"I've been referred to as typical Taurus," he said. "Somebody who takes a lot and then explodes."

Miller turned back to the details of the murder and Trey inquired if he could demonstrate where he'd stuck Pfister on the skull with the hammer—by reaching out toward Miller's head.

She recoiled and said, "I *do* mind you touching me!"

Agitated, she pointed out that if Trey needed a wheelchair to move around at the jail or today in the courthouse, how could he possibly have committed the crime alone?

He had no answer.

Miller counted out loud the number of times that he'd told them he'd gone up and down the stairs in Pfister's home on the morning of February 24: once to get to the master bedroom, again to go down to the garage to get the hammer, again to get the plastic bags that he put over the body, again to get the electrical cord to wrap around Nancy Pfister—and then he needed the strength to drag her into the closet by himself, cover her up, and flip over the mattress to hide the blood.

"And you want me," Miller said, "to believe you had no help in that room?"

"I'm telling you I had no help in that room."

Earlier this morning, Miller asked, when they'd taken a break from his confession, why hadn't Trey stood up and stretched his legs?

Because he couldn't, he replied. He'd deteriorated so much since last February that he could barely move now.

Why had he deteriorated so badly? she asked in a mocking tone. *Why?*

He offered no fuller explanation.

"I give you an opportunity," she angrily said, "to stretch your legs today... I know most people need to take a stretch and you tell me you can't stand up... You are giving me an accounting of a story where you were saying you were up and down stairs multiple times."

In his best formal tone, he replied, "Regrettably, it is true that I have a progressive neurological disease... I also have a spinal disease."

"But how can you tell me today you can't stand up?"

"Over the last week, I have been unable to bear weight reliably on my left leg..."

"So you were in a different place physically than you were even on the day of your first court appearance?"

He nodded, saying that his sense of balance was so fragile that he fell "a couple times a week."

"Mr. Styler, you were able to walk into this courthouse. You were able to walk into this interview room on that first interview that you did with Agent Zamora. You were able to walk then."

"Yes, but I was not shackled."

How, in his condition, could he have done all the physical acts he said he'd done on the morning of the murder?

"The adrenaline effect is the only way that I can explain that," he said.

54

Pfister had been naked when she was killed. Miller now asked Trey if he'd tied her up for sexual reasons, since she'd discovered numerous bondage scenes on his computer. He acknowledged having those images, but said that he'd done this simply to make her to fit into the bags, and he denied touching her at any time in an erotic manner. Miller requested that he stand up and demonstrate how he'd pulled Pfister's body into the closet after she was dead, but Tina Fang, who'd been silent throughout the confession, protested this demand on her client and the investigator dropped it.

How, Miller asked, had he been able to flip the bloody mattress by himself?

"I have learned," he said, "that I am capable in short bursts, or was at that time, at least, of more exertion than I'm normally capable of."

He again brought up adrenaline and how in emergency situations panicked mothers had lifted cars off of their children in order to save them.

With undisguised sarcasm, Miller replied, "I will do a lot of things in an interview room, but I'm not going to compare a mother saving a child with you murdering Nancy Pfister."

She mentioned the trunk of the Stylers' Jaguar, which had been used to move their possessions on Tuesday. Was the bag holding Pfister's belongings and the murder weapon still in there?

It was, Trey answered, but it wasn't visible and it would have been "very atypical" of his wife to have noticed anything unusual in the trunk.

Miller pointed out that when Trey was talking about things not connected to the murder, he made eye contact with her. But whenever he spoke of his wife, he closed his eyes or looked away.

"I'm not at all comfortable," he said, "with what I'm telling you. I'm deeply ashamed of it."

Was what he was telling them really the truth or was he "falling on the sword for his spouse?" Miller asked. "Falling on the sword for somebody that he loves?"

"That's why I'm down here today," he responded ambiguously.

"And I'm concerned," she insisted, "about how much you may be doing that."

"My wife had nothing to do with it. No knowledge of it. No knowledge that I did it... De-stressing her was the point of the exercise..."

"How much are you falling on the sword for the two women that you love?"

"Fortunately, that's not necessary. Neither one of them were involved in any way and I'm falling on the sword by giving information that in all probability [you] could not have discovered on your own."

But hadn't his wife made repeated comments about killing Nancy Pfister?

Such as, "I can't look at that woman. I'd have to kill her..."

Struggling to make eye contact with Trey, Miller said, "She had made some commentary along those lines, Mr. Styler."

He denied having heard such remarks, but conceded that "in a moment of emotion and exaggeration" Nancy might have said, "I'd like to see her dead or kill her."

Once more, Miller shifted her area of inquiry and asked how Pfister's "Owner's Closet" key had ended up a few yards from his motel door.

He didn't seem to know and his lack of knowledge had left Miller weary, frustrated, and angry. She was only one piece of the legal machinery that surrounded the murder of Nancy Pfister. If the sheriff's department and the DA's office and the other powers that be in Aspen were willing to accept Trey's confession, even if there were holes in it, there was little else she could do. But she was determined to make him aware of her disdain.

"I don't want you to walk out of here," she told him, "thinking that I have believed you hook, line, and sinker because... I don't buy everything that you're selling me today. Okay?"

"That's your privilege."

She wasn't quite ready to give up.

Before the couple was first interviewed by the police, she asked, had Trey prepared his wife for what to tell them?

"No," he said. "To this moment, she does not know that I did this and quite frankly, I intend to leave it an open question in her mind as to whether I actually did it or whether I just pled to get her loose... The message that I intend to give her is that I was made an offer by the DA's office that would result in her complete and permanent release... My wife had recently said that she hated her [Nancy Pfister]... I'm not sure that my wife really knows the meaning of the word... My wife is not a hateful person...

"*I* did not hate Nancy Pfister... Even when I figured out she was an alcoholic, I still liked her, but felt bad for her..."

Miller had run out of questions or maybe patience. The confession was dwindling to an end, with certain pieces of evidence mysteriously left unexplored.

Why, for example, could cell phone records not have been used to determine where Kathy and Trey were physically throughout Monday, Tuesday, and Wednesday of the last week of February, instead of everyone in law enforcement seemingly trying to guess the answer? Why were some glaring inconsistencies between Trey's account now and information obtained in earlier police interviews with other people not mentioned during his confession? Only time would bring these inconsistencies to the surface, after the case file had been unsealed two months later. By then, it would be too late to make a difference. The DA's office and the sheriff's department were ready to accept the confession and to sign off on the release of Nancy Styler and Kathy Carpenter.

Lisa Miller could do nothing more, and whatever else she felt sitting with Trey for the last time, she kept to herself.

. . .

That wasn't true for Michael Cleverly, after he learned about the confession.

"I don't think anyone," he said, "is completely satisfied with the outcome, but no one is as happy or as miserable as they might be.

"As far as law enforcement goes, I think they had the same displeasure I had over the confession. Bob Braudis wasn't happy about it. Joe DiSalvo wasn't happy, either. This whole thing wasn't quite as bad as the Claudine Longet case, but no crusading DA stepped up here to see that justice was served. If Dr. Styler gets anything less than twenty hard years in prison, I'll be very upset."

Invoking the memory or the spirit of Hunter Thompson, Cleverly made one last statement about the case and about the town he'd recently left behind to relocate to Hotchkiss, Colorado:

"All in all, this was the sleazy, chicken-shit Aspen way of dealing with the murder. If Hunter were here and had watched this, he'd have said it better than I just did. I've been disenchanted for years with how Aspen is now doing things, but only recently did it turn into a homicidal rage. These feelings include Woody Creek now, too. I've felt that way about it ever since Hunter died. Nancy is gone and George Stranahan is putting his ranch up for sale and that's the end. People like me and Hunter and Nancy revered the people who'd made Aspen what it was when I first got here. Art and Betty Pfister were the gold standard, but that world no longer exists.

"Then people like the Stylers came here and wanted to be like the motherfuckers who ruined the place for the rest of us. It's over. You can't turn back. I can't find enough expletives for how I feel about what these people have done."

Epilogue

The Aspen Farmers' Market is held on Sunday and began as a small venue where local growers could bring in their produce and independently sell it to townspeople. Fruits and vegetables originally dominated the action, unfolding approximately two blocks north of the courthouse, and the vendors and their goods occupied about a hundred yards or so of pavement. The market succeeded and crafts began to creep in, until it became overrun "with potholders and wind chimes," as one disgruntled Aspenite put it. The event expanded into a second block, and on summer Sundays people went downtown, picked up food for the coming week, bought knickknacks, and saw their friends or neighbors in the heart of the small community.

Nancy Pfister had often gone to the market in her Australian cowboy hat, as a nod to the memory of her father and to her life as a global traveler. Whenever people saw the hat bobbing at one of the stalls, they knew she was in town and probably making new connections. While shopping, she was always lively, even if hung over, and always ready to talk about her latest or her upcoming adventure. She'd be going abroad again one of these days and might buy a house in another country and you should get a plane ticket and come along with her because it would be a lot of fun and...

She just remembered that she'd been invited to a gathering later today and did you want to join her there at six p.m.? Her friends were coming and you'd enjoy meeting them and some other people there...

And do you know that couple standing over by the corn or those people next to the tomatoes? If you don't, I'll introduce you to them before I leave...

And then she'd grin and walk away, leaving behind her trademark giggle, her cowboy hat disappearing into the crowd.

On Monday, February 24, 2014, Bob Braudis received a message from Nancy Pfister about the kind of festivity she was always asking friends or strangers to join her at, but it wasn't the event that was important.

"I got an e-mail from her on Monday at three-thirty in the afternoon..." Braudis told the police in his interview following the murder. "She was inviting me and my girlfriend to a party on Tuesday... At John Gates's up on Independence Pass... A lady from New York was going to be there... I responded by e-mail and maybe texts, two or three times over the next twenty-four hours with no reply from Nancy... She had mentioned that she was jet-lagged, having trouble sleeping... I thought she was sleeping off her travels."

During the criminal investigation, Braudis not only mentioned the timing of this message to those who were interrogating him, but later showed it to a reporter. It was dated 3:30 p.m. on Monday. That's 15:30 hours in military or official time—and six hours *after* Trey Styler said he killed Nancy Pfister.

Merlin Broughton told the authorities that someone he knew had had contact with Pfister on Tuesday, February 25.

"This girl," Broughton said, "talked to Nancy on Tuesday... She had talked to Joe [DiSalvo] earlier... That could be important because everyone who I knew talked to Nancy on Monday... She had talked to Joe and let him know that Nancy called and left a message on Tuesday."

It was only one of the major inconsistencies in Trey's confession, inconsistencies that for some reason the detectives seemed to ignore. Trey told Miller and Gibson about putting Pfister's prescription pill bottles in a plastic bag on Monday morning at around 9:30 a.m., to make it appear that Pfister had suddenly departed her home and gone to parts unknown. The pills, he said, were in the trunk of his Jaguar until Wednesday evening, when he dropped them off in the Dumpster in Basalt.

In her twenty hours of interviews with the detectives, Kathy Carpenter told them that she'd spoken with Nancy Styler on Monday morning "to see how things were going"—within the same time frame that Trey had claimed that his wife was sleeping and that he was alone and in possession of her phone.

Kathy said that two days later, on Wednesday, she talked with Nancy Styler again and quoted her as saying about Nancy Pfister: "There's no sign of her . . . Maybe she took off with someone. Her pills and everything are here . . ."

When Kathy found the body, according to what she told Miller and John Zamora, "The pills were gone . . . She always had to have her pills. Ambien, etc. . . . I noticed they were gone when I went into the house . . . I said that's not like her . . . That's so bizarre. I'd asked if her pills were there and she [Nancy Styler] said yeah . . ."

Teresa Wyatt and Daniel Treme had always enjoyed going to the farmers' market on Sunday and running into people they knew, including Nancy Pfister. The summer after she was killed, they found that they didn't go as often because something was missing that couldn't be replaced. Or several things were gone: a smile that exploded across a whole face and drew you in; a ratty old straw cowboy hat and a string of pearls; and a constant sense of the unpredictable or a chance for some unexpected fun.

For Teresa, Aspen had a poignancy now that hadn't been in town before. And she was bitter about it.

"I don't ever want to see or talk with Kathy again. I don't think she could ever live in Aspen in the future. I think her life could be in danger and the same goes for Nancy Styler.

"Nancy Pfister wasn't perfect. I'm the first to admit that. She was bossy. She'd say 'Go do this' and under my breath I'd say, 'Yes, master,' but I saw it all as entertainment. Nancy was a magnet, a force, the life of the party. Aspen doesn't feel the same. The farmers' market is different now. When you met her, you never knew what game she was going to play. The game is over. You don't go downtown and see her anymore. The magic is gone.

"What happened in this case isn't justice. It isn't justice for Nancy. It isn't justice for my friend. Absolutely no one in town wants to talk about this. They just want it to go away. Did someone put pressure on the legal system to shut this down? I don't know, but they could have. That's how things work in Aspen."

After some time had passed following Trey's confession and the release of the other two suspects from jail, David Olmsted was approached by a few people whom he described as "friends of Art and Betty Pfister." They asked him to launch a new investigation into the murder because they were worried that the truth hadn't come out, and they wanted him to keep digging. Money was available for this work and he thought about taking up their offer, but there were complications. He'd been employed by Nancy Styler's defense team and didn't want to do something like this, unless Nancy herself approved of it. When she gave no indication of supporting the reopening of the case, Olmsted declined.

In mid-September 2014, Nancy Styler began making appearances on national television programs. The first was ABC's *20/20* and she came off as mystifyingly distant, if not downright cold, when it came to certain subjects. Showing no concern for what had happened to anyone, including her husband, she told the TV audience the same thing that she'd told the Aspen detectives—she'd wanted to wring Nancy Pfister's neck. While offering no support for Trey and no insight into why he'd admitted to the crime, she acted as if she now believed that he'd told the truth in his confession and was guilty of murder. She didn't speculate about the kind of pressure he may have been under right before the homicide—pressure that he'd repeatedly told the police had come from attempting to relieve his wife's suffering and her suicidal levels of stress.

When Deborah Roberts, the *20/20* host, tried to get Nancy to talk about any possible involvement she may have had in the murder, or any knowledge of it before or after the fact, Styler brushed her off, creating the impression that she was smarter and more calculating than anyone else in this situation. If one wanted to unearth any feelings she had about the tragedy, any feelings at all, one came up empty-handed.

Her next appearance was on NBC's *Dateline*, where she told the audience about the letter Trey had written her, following his confession, denying his involvement in the murder. According to her *Dateline* interview, he then called her and changed his story again, admitting his guilt. She must have believed him the second time because she now decided to take action. After thirty-two years of marriage, she filed for a divorce from Trey, whom she now called "a monster," reverted to her maiden name, moved to the East Coast, and asked Judge Nichols to seal her portion of the Nancy Pfister case file forever. The judge complied.

Kathy Carpenter was also interviewed by *Dateline* and told the same story she'd been telling from the beginning, while interrupting herself from time to time because she was crying. At the close of the two-hour episode, she proclaimed that she wanted to ask Juliana Pfister for forgiveness, but when asked what she needed to be forgiven for, she couldn't quite say.

In March 2015, CBS's *48 Hours* aired the last of the three major networks' episodes on the case. During the program, Lisa Miller was more outspoken than ever before, declaring that she believed that Nancy Styler and Kathy had had some involvement in the murder or at least some knowledge of it. Once again, both women adamantly denied this and Styler's lawyer, Garth McCarty, labeled the probe into Nancy Pfister's death "one of the worst investigations I've ever seen. Someone should lose their job over this."

Occasionally, David Olmsted went to the farmers' market for fresh produce. Like many others, he was drawn to the center of town, to its homey feeling and its pristine beauty at the foot of a great mountain. He always met other shoppers there who came together to talk about the one thing they all had in common: Aspen. Those who knew what Olmsted did for a living asked him what he felt about the Pfister case, now that it was over and fading into the history and lore of the community. What did David *really* think happened up on West Buttermilk Road in the last week of February 2014?

After hearing this question often enough, he gradually developed a workable answer and gave it to everyone who inquired:

"I believe that Trey Styler didn't do what he said he did on that day that he said he did it. He may have killed Nancy Pfister, but he didn't do it *then*."

Chuckling to himself, he said, "It reminds me of that lyric by Don Henley in one of his songs after he left the Eagles: 'The more I know, the less I understand.'"

He sighed and shook his head and said, "If you ever find a case stranger than this one, call me."

The murder was resolved, if not solved, but even the brilliant Aspen sunlight that spread over the Roaring Fork Valley in the summer of 2014 couldn't remove all the darkness or questions that lingered on Buttermilk Mountain. As with the Claudine Longet case of the mid-1970s, no one was certain that justice had been served in the murder of Nancy Pfister. Her demise was still surrounded by a series of maddening "what-ifs" involving all of the principals:

What if Kathy Carpenter had called the police when her AA sponsor Megan Mulligan told her to—after Megan heard Kathy say that Nancy Styler wanted to kill Nancy Pfister? What if Pfister hadn't taunted her impoverished tenants, demanding $14,000 more from them, but had given them back their possessions without another round of humiliation? What if the storage locker business in Basalt had opened at 8:30 a.m. on Monday morning, February 24, instead of two hours later? What if Trey had taken the settlement from his former employer, CAC, rather than hiring a lawyer? (In the winter of 2015, Trey lost his final battle to collect the money he was awarded from attorney John G. Powell.) What if Basalt municipal worker Robert Larson hadn't looked in the Dumpster holding the trash bag full of damning evidence? What if DA investigator Lisa Miller hadn't taken a vacation in the second week of June and the preliminary hearing had gone forward on schedule on the ninth? Would Trey still have confessed to a crime that many believed he did not commit alone?

The only certainty was that official Aspen had gotten what it wanted. On the one-year anniversary of the discovery of Pfister's body, Sheriff DiSalvo reiterated to the *Aspen Times* his satisfaction with the legal outcome.

"I think there's a blessing because there wasn't a trial," he said. "That's probably the thing I'm the most grateful for. I think it would have been hard on friends and family of Nancy to see and hear that evidence that, frankly, I don't think anybody should have to see."

So they wouldn't see it, but suspicion would continue to hover over Nancy Styler and Kathy Carpenter, no matter where they went or what they did in the future. The women had learned one of the harshest lessons of crime: you don't have to intend harm to help cause it. You just have to ignore your own behavior or participation long enough until it can't be ignored anymore. They'd wriggled away and were now free to start their lives over, but as with the Claudine Longet case, the damage they'd left behind in the Roaring Fork Valley would be talked about for decades—especially after Trey committed suicide, hanging himself with a bedsheet in his cell on the morning of August 6, 2015, in Canon City, Colorado. A few months later, Nancy Pfister collected on the one-million-dollar life insurance policy Trey had taken out on himself years before. The shadow covering Buttermilk Mountain had only grown darker.